AT HOME
with the WORD®
2020

LARGE PRINT EDITION

Sunday Scriptures and Scripture Insights

YEAR A

Tat-siong Benny Liew, PHD

Rev. Patrick Hartin

Susan Gleason Anderson, MA

Teresa Marshall-Patterson, MA

LTP

RGY
NING
ATIONS

Acknowledgments

Nihil Obstat
Rev. Mr. Daniel G. Welter, JD
Chancellor
Archdiocese of Chicago
April 1, 2019

Imprimatur
Most Rev. Ronald A. Hicks
Vicar General
Archdiocese of Chicago
April 1, 2019

The Nihil Obstat and Imprimatur are declarations that the material is free from doctrinal or moral error, and thus is granted permission to publish in accordance with c. 827. No legal responsibility is assumed by the grant of this permission. No implication is contained herein that those who have granted the Nihil Obstat and Imprimatur agree with the content, opinions, or statements expressed.

AT HOME WITH THE WORD® 2020
© 2019 Archdiocese of Chicago:
Liturgy Training Publications,
3949 South Racine Avenue,
Chicago, IL 60609; 800-933-1800;
fax: 800-933-7094; email:
orders@ltp.org; website: www.LTP.
org. All rights reserved.

This book was edited by Mary G.
Fox. Lauren L. Murphy was the
production editor, Anna Manhart
was the cover designer, Maggie
Urgo was the interior designer,
and Kari Nicholls was the
production artist.

The cover for this year's At Home
with the Word® is by William
Hernandez. The interior art is by
Kathy Ann Sullivan.

Printed in the United States of
America

ISBN 978-1-61671-455-0

AHW20L

This large print edition of At Home with the Word® is designed to accommodate the needs of our readers. In comparison with our regular print At Home with the Word®, this design uses a different type font and size, eliminates italics, adds space and a line between columns, increases contrast on the cover and interior, and uses different paper stock for better readability. In addition, Old Testament references (typically italicized) are set off with European quotation marks (« »).

WELCOME TO
At Home with the Word® 2020

THE AUTHORS OF THE INTRODUCTIONS

Marielle Frigge, OSB, taught Scripture and theology for thirty-three years at Mount Marty College in Yankton, South Dakota, and is now formation director for Sacred Heart Monastery. Michael Cameron teaches Scripture and history of Christianity in the theology department at the University of Portland in Oregon.

SCRIPTURE READINGS

For each Sunday, you will find the three readings and Responsorial Psalm from the Lectionary for Mass, from which readings are proclaimed in Roman Catholic churches in the United States.

SCRIPTURE INSIGHTS

Two authors have written Scripture Insights for 2020. Father Patrick Hartin, a priest of the Diocese of Spokane, Washington, taught New Testament studies and Christian spirituality at Gonzaga University from 1995 to 2016. His doctorate in New Testament is from the University of South Africa (Pretoria). His books include James, in the Sacra Pagina Series (2003), Exploring the Spirituality of the Gospels (2010), and A Window into the Spirituality of Paul (2015), all from Liturgical Press. Father Hartin wrote the Scripture Insights from the First Sunday of Advent through the Solemnity of the Ascension of the Lord.

Tat-siong Benny Liew is Class of 1956 Professor in New Testament Studies at the College of the Holy Cross, Worcester, Massachusetts. He is the author of Politics of Parousia (Brill, 1999) and What Is Asian American Biblical Hermeneutics? (University of Hawaii Press, 2008). In addition, he is the editor of the Semeia volume on "The Bible in Asian America" (with Gale Yee; SBL, 2002), Present and Future of Biblical Studies (Brill, 2018), and Colonialism and the Bible: Contemporary Reflections from the Global South (with Fernando Segovia; Lexington, 2018). Liew is also the executive editor of an academic journal, Biblical Interpretation (Brill), and the series editor of T&T Clark's Study Guides to the New Testament

(Bloomsbury). He wrote Scripture Insights for the Seventh Sunday of Easter through the end of the liturgical year.

PRACTICE OF FAITH, HOPE, CHARITY

Two authors wrote the Practice of Faith, Hope, or Charity. Susan Gleason Anderson is a parish director of religious education and has served in catechetical ministry for nearly twenty years. She holds a master of arts degree from the University of Chicago Divinity School, where she studied theology. She wrote the practices for the Seventh Sunday of Easter through the Solemnity of Our Lord Jesus Christ, King of the Universe.

Teresa Marshall-Patterson facilitates the Christian initiation process and liturgical ministries at St. Vincent de Paul Catholic Church in Andover, Kansas. She is the author of We Learn About Our Parish Church (LTP, 2010). Her master of arts in pastoral ministries is from St. Mary's University, Winona. She wrote the practices from the First Sunday of Advent through the Solemnity of the Ascension of the Lord.

ADDITIONAL DOWNLOADABLE QUESTIONS AND ACTIVITIES

Download additional questions and activities for three audiences: families, Christian initiation groups, and other adult groups. The link http://www.ltp.org/ahw will take you to the At Home with the Word® Extra Content page. Click on the desired audience, Adult Faith-Sharing Groups, Christian Initiation Groups, or Families.

WEEKDAY READINGS

See the opening of each liturgical time for a list of Scripture texts read at Mass on weekdays and on feasts falling on weekdays.

ART FOR 2020

On the cover, William Hernandez, Portland, Oregon, has illustrated Ezekiel's vision in the valley of dry bones. This is the fourth of several scenes from salvation history to appear on the covers of At Home with the Word®. The reading is from Ezekiel 37:1–14. In the interior art, Kathy Ann Sullivan uses a scratchboard technique to evoke the seasons, from our ancestors on the Jesse tree to the oil lamps for Ordinary Time in the fall.

Table of Contents

The Lectionary

by Marielle Frigge, OSB

WHAT IS A LECTIONARY?

The word lectionary comes from the Latin word legere, "to read," and names a collection of Scripture readings from both the Old and New Testaments that are proclaimed throughout the liturgical year in a particular order. Christian lectionaries were in use already in the fourth century, but before the invention of the printing press in the mid-fifteenth century, readings differed from place to place. Printing allowed for a more standardized lectionary, so that Catholics around the world could hear the same Bible readings at Mass on any given day.

However, in the four centuries before the Second Vatican Council (1963–65), the lectionary had a somewhat limited ability to touch the faith lives of Catholics. Most could not understand what was read because Scripture readings as well as the prayers of the Mass were proclaimed in Latin. Further, because the lectionary of that time used only particular selections from the Bible repeated year after year, Catholics received a restricted exposure to the riches of Scripture.

GIFTS OF THE SECOND VATICAN COUNCIL

After the Second Vatican Council, not only were the biblical readings made available in the language of the people, but the structure of the lectionary was expanded as well. These changes resulted from a fresh understanding of the role of Scripture in the liturgy. Returning to the ancient understanding that Christ is present in the Scriptures, the Council Fathers further emphasized that the Eucharist nourishes God's people at two tables: the proclaimed Word of God and the Eucharistic banquet. For this reason, the revised Lectionary includes much more Scripture. Rather than repeating a yearly pattern, it includes a three-year cycle for Sundays and a two-year cycle for weekdays. Through this expanded array of selections, it aims to present the broad sweep of the salvation story, arranged purposefully around the liturgical year with the four major liturgical seasons of Advent, Christmas Time,

Lent, and Easter Time punctuating the many weeks of Ordinary Time.

These great liturgical seasons instruct the faithful in the most significant aspects of salvation history. The liturgical year begins with Advent, expressing the ancient longing and hope of God's covenant people for redemption. Christmas Time celebrates the Incarnation of the Lord, God's Word of salvation fully present and active in the world, made flesh in Jesus the Christ. During Lent, the Scripture readings call Christians to deeper conversion: to amend their ways of failing to respond to God's saving Word, to cultivate greater intimacy with God, and to rejoice that he never ceases to offer life-changing mercy. These Scriptures about conversion speak powerfully to those preparing for initiation. Easter Time proclaims the Paschal Mystery, the redeeming Death and Resurrection of Jesus Christ. That mystery leads us into life in divine Spirit, poured out upon all the faithful at Pentecost, sending us out to serve. In addition to highlighting the liturgical seasons, the Lectionary illuminates other key mysteries of Catholic faith in solemnities such as the Most Holy Trinity, the Most Holy Body and Blood of Christ, the Assumption of the Blessed Virgin Mary, and in feasts such as the Presentation of the Lord and the Exaltation of the Holy Cross.

FOUR SUNDAY SCRIPTURE SELECTIONS

At Home with the Word® provides all four Scripture passages of each Sunday: a selection from the Old Testament (except during Easter Time when we hear from Acts of the Apostles); a Responsorial Psalm or canticle; a New Testament reading from one of the letters, Acts of the Apostles, or Revelation; and, most important, a Gospel passage. Each year of the three-year cycle draws from a particular Gospel account: Matthew in Year A, Mark in Year B, and Luke in Year C. The Gospel of John, so highly symbolic and profound, is heard in the liturgical seasons. The Lectionary includes readings from John on several Sundays of Lent, during the sacred Triduum, and most Sundays of Easter Time. Because Mark is the shortest Gospel account, some Sundays of Ordinary Time in Year B use passages from John.

The pattern of today's Catholic Lectionary has served as a model for lectionaries of several other Christian churches. As a result, Catholics and many Protestants hear the same Scripture passages proclaimed on Sundays. The biblical Word of God thus draws them closer.

Understanding how the four Scripture passages of each Sunday are related can help us appreciate how the Lectionary invites Christians to understand, ponder, and integrate the message of God's Word. The First Reading from the Old Testament usually bears some connection to the Gospel passage, often by means of a significant person, event, or image. Rooted in the ancient practice of the Jewish synagogue, the Responsorial, which follows the First Reading, is usually from a psalm and represents the people's response to God's Word in the First Reading. In this way the first two Scripture passages mirror a theme woven throughout the Bible: God always takes the initiative to address humankind, speaking a Word that invites a response from God's people. The Responsorial may also illustrate or clarify what the First Reading proclaims, or may be related to the liturgical season, and thus is intended to foster meditation on the Word of God.

Frequently the Second Reading, always from the New Testament, follows the ancient practice of lectio continua (Latin for "continuous reading"), so that on each Sunday we hear important selections in order from a particular book. For example, the Second Reading is often an excerpt from one of the letters of St. Paul, and by continuous reading over several Sundays, the Lectionary presents some of his major theological insights in a particular letter.

During Ordinary Time the Lectionary presents continuous reading in the Gospels also, allowing us to see each evangelist's distinctive way of unfolding the Gospel story. For example, in Year A, from the Fourteenth Sunday of Ordinary Time to the end of the liturgical year in November, we hear the Gospel of Matthew from chapter 11 through chapter 25. Not every verse of Matthew is included, and occasionally a Sunday solemnity or feast requires a reading from a different Gospel, but continuous reading relates major aspects of Matthew's narrative, just as it does for Mark's in Year B and Luke's in Year C. Over time, through continuous reading, we can become familiar with the particular content and qualities of each Gospel account.

THE LECTIONARY AS A VISUAL SIGN

The Lectionary nourishes us with its words proclaimed in the liturgy—the Lord's own voice speaking to his people. It also nourishes us as a visual sign of the Lord's presence among us. The United States Conference of Catholic Bishops reminds Catholics that gestures and physical objects used in liturgy are "signs by which Christians express and deepen their relationship to God" (Built of Living Stones: Art, Architecture, and Worship, 23). Although the Lectionary's proper place during the liturgy is on the ambo (the special podium from which readings are proclaimed), a part of the Lectionary—the Gospel readings—has been made into a separate Book of the Gospels. That book, often richly decorated, may be carried in the entrance procession on Sundays and holy days. It is placed on the altar at the beginning of Mass and then, when the assembly rises to sing the Alleluia, the Gospel reader may processes with the book to the ambo, accompanied by servers holding candles. In response to the deacon or priest's introduction to the Gospel Reading, the people respond, signing their forehead, lips, and heart with a small cross. Observing such signs and ceremonies, one could not miss the special reverence we give to the Word of God—especially in the Gospel.

In the bishops' teaching about the ambo, from which the Scriptures are proclaimed, we find an apt crystallization of the Church's conviction about the role of Scripture in the Mass. Urging that the ambo should be of a size and placement that draws attention to the sacred Word, the document says, "Here the Christian community encounters the living Lord in the word of God and prepares itself for the 'breaking of the bread' and the mission to live the word that will be proclaimed" (Built of Living Stones, 61).

Introduction to the Gospel according to Matthew

by Michael Cameron

The first Gospel is anonymous, but early tradition ascribed it to Matthew, the tax collector who became an Apostle (Matthew 9:9). Most scholars today read it as an expanded "second edition" of the Gospel according to Mark. Readers quickly notice great blocks of Jesus' spoken teaching. It might be that this Gospel account was placed first in the New Testament because it stood out as the "teaching Gospel."

Scholars' best estimates date Matthew's composition to the 80s of the first century and place it possibly at Antioch in Syria (Acts 11:26). That multicultural city would have nurtured this Gospel account's passionate devotion to Jesus as well as its profound knowledge of ancient Jewish traditions, ethical concerns, and cultural coloring.

The Gospel according to Matthew came out of a circle of converted scribes (teachers of Jewish tradition) who had been "instructed in the kingdom of heaven" (13:52). It shows a teacher's touch. Between the stories of the Messiah's birth (chapters 1–2) and Death (chapters 26–28), the account is organized into "five books" (perhaps imitating the five books of Moses). Each features a narrative section leading into one of Jesus' five great teaching discourses (chapters 5–7, including the Sermon on the Mount, and 10, 13, 18, 24–25). Most outstanding are the Sermon's Beatitudes (5:3–10), the Lord's Prayer (6:9–13), and the golden rule (7:12).

Matthew's view of Jesus is exalted. Genealogically descended from Abraham and David (1:1–17), Jesus carries a prophetic name, Emmanuel, "God with us" (1:23; Isaiah 7:14). He is a king from birth (2:2), who effortlessly conquers disease and evil "by a word" (8:16). That word rings with majestic authority ("You have heard it said . . . but I say to you . . ." six times in 5:21–48), and will never pass away (24:35). Because Jesus has received "all power in heaven and on earth" (28:18), he decides to whom he will reveal the Father (11:27), who will "inherit the kingdom" (25:34), or who will hear "I never knew you" (7:23). Yet he is "humble of heart" (11:29), saying, "I am with you always, until the end of the age" (28:20).

Jesus' first concern to restore "the lost sheep of the house of Israel" (10:6; 15:24) widens into this Gospel's universal outlook that embraces "all nations" (24:14; 28:19). Matthew links Jewish and Christian perspectives by the theme of "fulfillment," wherein Old Testament events, characters, laws, and prophetic visions are renewed in Jesus. Fulfillment of the prophets is a constant refrain in the stories of Jesus' birth (1:23; 2:6, 15, 18, 23), ministry (4:14–16; 8:17; 12:16–21; 13:35; 21:4–5), and Passion (27:9–10). His version of the Sermon on the Mount presumes a new Law written on the heart (Jeremiah 31:31–34), but it neither destroys nor weakens the old: "I have come not to abolish but to fulfill," he says (5:17). Far from repealing the Law, Jesus' Gospel intensifies its demands to include inner motivations and attitudes (5:20–48). His disciples are to reflect in kind, if not in degree, God's own indiscriminate love for others (5:43–48). This love and its corresponding just relationships epitomize the Law and Prophets (7:12; 22:36–40). The first covenant thus remains the deep root from which the new covenant continually flowers.

At first, Matthew's strong Jewishness seems at odds with its vehemence against Jewish leaders and their practices (15:1–14; 23:1–36), but Matthew expresses the characteristic Jewish concern for final accountability before God, who renders rewards according to one's works. The prophets similarly denounced those who fail to practice God's commands (Isaiah 29:14).

Jesus' demands on his community are just as exacting. Half-hearted Christians are sternly warned: those who do good only for show will be excluded from the Kingdom (6:1–18; 7:21). Only serious disciples can expect to enter (22:1–14; 25:1–31).

Yet Matthew mixes severity and sweetness. A childlike attitude is

extolled (18:3–4). Latecomers to the Kingdom are welcomed if they are earnest (20:1–16; 21:28–32). Sinners can be forgiven if they forgive others (6:14–15; 18:21–35). Despite its rigors, Jesus' way is so appealing that disciples find his yoke "easy," and his burden "light" (11:28–29).

Unique among the Gospel accounts, Matthew pays attention to the community of Jesus' followers; only Matthew uses the word church (ekklesia; 16:18; 18:17). The Apostles and especially Peter serve as models, yet often they seem to slouch toward glory. Several times Jesus chides them for their lack of faith. "O you of little faith" (6:30; 8:26; 14:31; 16:8) sounds solemn in English, but actually translates Jesus' needling one-word nickname for the disciples, oligopistoi ("little-faiths"). Peter embodies the paradox of the beloved stumbling disciple (perfectly captured in Matthew's unique story about Peter walking on water only to sink and be rescued; 14:28–31). Peter spoke before he thought, slept at his post, and denied the Lord. But because he was the first to confess Jesus' true identity as Son of God, Jesus poetically renamed him (Peter means "rock") when he spoke of building his Church (16:18). Warts and all, the Twelve are foundation stones of the Kingdom community (19:28). Faltering yet faithful, they were appropriate first hearers of the Savior-King's call, "Come to me, all you who labor and are burdened, and I will give you rest" (11:28).

Finally, Matthew contains many treasures found nowhere else. His Christmas stories uniquely tell of Joseph's dreams, the adoring Magi, the star, Herod's murderous fury, and the Holy Family's flight into Egypt (chapters 1–2). Matthew's pithy phrases, "salt of the earth" (5:13), "pearls before swine" (7:6), "wolves in sheep's clothing" (7:15), "wise as serpents" (10:16), "strain at a gnat and swallow a camel" (23:24), are part of our language. Certain parables are found only in Matthew: the wheat and the weeds (13:24–30), the good and bad fish (13:47–48), the unforgiving servant (18:21–35), the workers in the vineyard (20:1–16), the two sons (21:28–32), and the ten virgins (25:1–13). Matthew alone tells of Peter finding the coin to pay his temple tax in a fish's mouth (17:24–27), and recounts Judas' final remorse (27:3–10), the dream of Pilate's wife (27:19), and the earthquakes (27:51; 28:2). All of these make Matthew's account of the Gospel a powerful teaching resource.

Introduction to the Gospel according to John

by Michael Cameron

This Gospel has no year of its own in the Lectionary's three-year cycle, but it is strongly represented <u>every</u> year during Christmas, Lent, and Easter Time; it also appears in Ordinary Time in Mark for Year B, Sundays 17–21. John shares some features of the first three Gospels (called "synoptic" for "seeing together"). Some stories overlap, characters seen in the Synoptics reappear, and John clearly voices the evangelistic, instructional purpose of all the Gospels: that you may believe and receive life in Jesus' name (20:31).

But its vision stands majestically apart, like the eagle that became this Gospel's symbol. It is rooted in the teaching of a mysterious unnamed figure, the "disciple whom Jesus loved" (13:23; 19:26; 20:2; 21:7, 20), who authenticates this Gospel's "testimony" (19:35; 21:24). It uniquely portrays the divine Word acting with God and as God to create all things (1:1–5), taking human flesh to reveal the Father's glory (1:1, 14–18).

John communicates in distinctive ways. The Synoptics tell Jesus' story in compact vignettes; John constructs chapter-long dramas (see especially chapters 4, 9, and 11). The first three Gospels contain pithy, memorable sayings about God's Kingdom; John's Jesus speaks hypnotically repetitive discourses focused on eternal life (for example, 6:22–59; 10:1–18; chapters 14–17). The Synoptics' homespun parables pique curiosity about Jesus' message; the Johannine Jesus poetically develops elements like water (4:7–15), bread (6:25–35), and light (3:19–21; 9:4–5; 12:35–36) into metaphors for contemplating divine truth.

John tells unique stories about Jesus: He changes water into wine (2:1–11), disputes with Nicodemus (3:1–21), engages the Samaritan woman at the well (4:4–26), heals a man born blind (9:1–41), raises dead Lazarus (11:1–45), chides the doubting Thomas (20:24–29), and cooks post-Easter breakfast for the disciples (21:1–14). John also varies details from some familiar synoptic stories, among which Jesus "cleanses the Temple" early in his ministry rather than late (2:13–22); the Synoptics' Passover meal ("the Last Supper") is a meal before Passover where Jesus washes the disciples' feet (13:4–15); the synoptic Jesus anguishes before death, but in John goes to the Cross with serenity (12:27; 18:11); and unlike the Synoptics, John has Jesus die on the day of preparation for Passover when the Passover lambs are sacrificed. These repeated references to Passover heighten the sacrificial symbolism of Jesus' death. Likewise, a strong liturgical symbolism makes Jesus' death the true Passover lamb sacrifice (1:29), his risen body the true Temple (2:21), and his sacramental Body and Blood the true food and drink of Israel's wilderness journey (6:53–58).

John's hallmark strategies of indirectness and double meanings entice characters to move from surface earthly meanings to encoded heavenly meanings. Some catch on, like the woman at the well (4:4–26), but others miss the point, like Nicodemus, (3:3–10), the crowds (7:32–36), and Pilate

(18:33–38). This indirectness separates truly committed disciples from the half-hearted window shoppers (2:23–25). Jesus performs "signs" (not "miracles") that lure people up the new ladder of Jacob arching from earth's pictures to heaven's glory (1:51; Genesis 28:12). This imagery of signs ends in a plain revelation about Jesus' divinity not found in the Synoptic Gospels. His seven solemn "I AM" statements (6:35; 8:12; 10:7; 10:11; 11:25; 14:6; 15:1) recall God's revelation to Moses as "I AM" (Exodus 3:14) and testify to Jesus as the only source of life. So the inner truth of the blind man seeing is, "I am the light of the world" (9:5), and of the dead man rising, "I am the resurrection and the life" (11:25).

Jesus' signs hint at his divine glory (2:11) to be fully revealed at his "hour" (2:4; 7:30; 8:20; 13:1). Like the disciples, readers put things together only after the Resurrection (2:22); then we realize that as Jesus was "lifted up" for crucifixion by the Romans, he was lifted up to glory by his Father (3:14; 8:28; 12:32). He mounted his Cross like a king ascending his throne, as

Pilate's placard unwittingly proclaimed (19:19–22). The Son's mission was to reunite the world to its source of eternal life in God (3:16; 4:34; 17:4). He died with satisfaction that this work was accomplished, and announced, "It is finished!" (19:30).

In the Gospel according to John, God the Father is unseen and mostly silent, but pervasively present. The Father sent the Son, loves him (5:20; 15:9), bears him witness (5:37; 8:18), glorifies him (8:54), and dwells with him (14:11). The Father grants the Son to have life in himself, to judge the world, and to raise the dead (5:19–30). Father and Son together gave life to the world at creation (1:1–2), and continue to do so (5:17). God the Son in human flesh has "explained" the Father, literally "brought God into the open" (1:18). The Son does this so completely that Jesus says, "Whoever has seen me has seen the Father" (14:9; 12:45).

But divine life emanates from a third mysterious presence, "the Spirit of truth" (14:17). The Father and the Son together send the Spirit (15:26), who teaches the disciples about what Jesus said and who he was (14:26; 16:13). By the Spirit's indwelling, divine life flows through them like a river (7:38–39; 14:17).

John depicts the disciples as fruitful vine branches that the Father lovingly tends (15:1–5). Omitting all other ethical instruction, this Gospel says that the only measure of the disciples' fruitfulness is their love for one another (13:34–35; 15:12–17).

True to character, this Gospel is sometimes one-sided. John's sense of Jesus' real humanity is relatively weak; and though teaching that "salvation is from the Jews" (4:22), it can be hostile toward Judaism (8:21–26, 37–59). John must be balanced by the rest of the New Testament and the Church's later teaching. But its profound spiritual theology of the Word made flesh (1:14) has decisively shaped Christian theology, spirituality, and art, ever since it was written in the late first century.

Introduction to St. Paul and His Letters

by Michael Cameron

PAUL'S CONVERSION

Saul of Tarsus was born about the same time as Jesus, to a pious Jewish family in Tarsus, in the Roman province of Cilicia (modern eastern Turkey). Well-educated and extremely religious, this son of Roman citizens was a member of the strict Pharisees (Philippians 3:5–6). In Christianity's earliest days, he says, "I persecuted the church of God beyond measure and even tried to destroy it" (Galatians 1:14–15). But then came the sudden turning point of his life: just outside Damascus, a brilliant flash of light blinded his eyes, buckled his legs, and altered his mind about God's design for human salvation (Acts 9:1–19). Christ's last known post-Resurrection appearance suddenly brought the Pharisee to birth as an Apostle, as "one born abnormally" (1 Corinthians 15:8).

Since Moses had said that anyone hanged on a tree was cursed by God, the crucified Christ had been a stumbling block to Saul, the Jew. But God revealed to Paul (Saul's Greek name) the awesome truth that this crucified man was God's power and wisdom (1 Corinthians 1:24). Christ's Death and Resurrection had turned the page of world history and unleashed the powers and blessings of the Age to Come. In that knowledge, Paul discounted everything that went before in his life as "rubbish" in comparison to knowing Christ, even his prized Jewish pedigree. Paul's blockbuster insight was that, for Jews and Gentiles alike, saving faith in Jesus Christ alone, not the works of Moses' Law, made one a part of God's people (Philippians 3:5–10).

PAUL'S MISSION AND TEACHINGS

That insight released a mighty energy in Paul to announce Christ to the whole world. So began Paul's thirty-plus-year missionary ministry. He suffered beatings, imprisonments, and repeated brushes with death, but by the mid-60s of the first century, he had planted a network of vibrant Christian communities throughout the eastern Mediterranean basin.

Concerned to stay in touch with his churches, to feed them with sound teaching, and to protect them from poachers, he wrote letters that eventually became part of our New Testament. Their profound theology, breathless style, and stirring imagery have kindled and rekindled Christian faith ever since.

Paul never knew the earthly Jesus, and he speaks little of stories familiar to us from the Gospels (though he knew Peter and the Apostles personally, used their traditions, and quotes Jesus' words at the first Eucharist). Paul's thinking flows almost exclusively from the reality of the Lord's Death and Resurrection—the moment when God's power decisively defeated sin and inaugurated the Age to Come.

Paul explains that event with an outpouring of vivid metaphors. His imagery of "justification" imagines a scene at the Judgment Day when Christ's Death acquits us of breaking the Law of Mount Sinai (Romans 3:21–31). His liturgical concept of "sanctification" pictures Christ giving believers the holiness needed to approach God in purity (1 Corinthians 6:11). Paul connects to economic imagery when he speaks of "redemption," portraying Christ's costly Death buying us back from slavery to sin (Romans 3:24; 1 Corinthians 6:20). His political-military picture envisions humanity's ancient and chronic warfare with God brought to an end in "reconciliation" (Romans 5:10–11). He evokes the family with his "adoption" image, conveying our change of status when Christ made us over from slaves to children of God (Romans 8:14–15; Galatians 4:4–7).

Christians behave not according to external laws, Paul teaches, but by the force of the Holy Spirit, who produces in believers the many fruits of the new life (Galatians 5:22–23), the greatest of which is love (1 Corinthians 13:13). The same love of God displayed in Christ's Death pours forth into our hearts through the Holy Spirit (Romans 5:5–8). The Spirit remakes us in the image of Christ: "all of us, gazing with unveiled face on the glory of the Lord, are being transformed into the same image from glory to glory, as from the Lord who is the Spirit" (2 Corinthians 3:18).

Christ somehow joined us to himself at his Cross so that when he died, we died (2 Corinthians 5:14). Christians "baptized into Christ's death" die to their old selves and rise to newness of life (Romans 6:3–4). In this new humanity, which leaves behind old identities, the oneness of Christ knows "neither Jew nor Greek, slave nor free, male nor female" (Galatians 3:28). All drink of the same Spirit who makes them the mystical "Body of Christ" (1 Corinthians 12:12–27), the Church, whose members offer worship to God while humbly serving one another. In Christ we are "the new creation: the old things have passed away; behold, the new things have come" (2 Corinthians 5:17).

But the new life emerging in Christians conflicts with the world as it is. Paul leaves social change to God while urging Christians to live patiently within the structures of society as they stand until the new age takes over. So slaves do not seek freedom, the unmarried do not seek marriage, and Gentiles do not seek circumcision, because "the world in its present form is passing away" (1 Corinthians 7:17–31).

For the time being we see God, the world, and ourselves in a blur, but one day we will understand everything (1 Corinthians 13:12). Bodily death is pure gain: we depart to "be with Christ" (Philippians 1:23)—Paul does not say more—and await the resurrection of the body, when Christ "will change our lowly body to conform with his glorious body" (Philippians 3:21). We will be radically different, but somehow still ourselves, just as wheat stalks are both different from, and the same as, the tiny seeds they come from (1 Corinthians 15:36–49). When that moment comes, Christ's work will be done, and God will be "all in all" (1 Corinthians 15:28).

But for Paul and his readers, including us, the present remains the time for work. With the hope of the Resurrection constantly drawing us on, Paul says, we must "be firm, steadfast, always fully devoted to the work of the Lord, knowing that in the Lord your labor is not in vain" (1 Corinthians 15:58).

Studying and Praying Scripture

by Michael Cameron

A recent study claimed that only 22 percent of American Catholics read the Bible regularly, and just 8 percent are involved in Scripture groups. Not many know how profoundly biblical the Roman Catholic Church has been from her very roots, having "always venerated the divine scriptures as she venerates the Body of the Lord" (Dei Verbum [Dogmatic Constitution on Divine Revelation], 21). How may Catholics learn to read Scripture? This essay sketches a path for seekers.

PREPARING TO READ

Become an apprentice to the Bible. Ordinary people can reach a good level of understanding, but at a cost: the Bible yields its riches to those who give themselves to the search for understanding. Start by reading daily, even if only for a few minutes. Join a group that reads and discusses Scripture together.

You will need tools. Think of yourself as a prospector for the

Bible's gold. Nuggets on the ground are easily picked up, but the really rich veins lie beneath the surface. Digging requires study, commitment, and skills.

Invest in tools that reap the harvest of others' labors. Buy a study Bible with introductions, explanatory notes, and maps. Use another translation for devotional reading and comparison. Get access to a Bible dictionary with detailed information on biblical books, concepts, geography, out-lines, customs, and so forth. Bible concordances will help you find all occurrences of particular words. A dictionary of biblical theology will give guidance on major theological ideas. A Bible atlas will give a sense of the locations and movements in the biblical stories. Recent Church documents on the Bible offer rich instruction to seekers.

Reading for Knowledge

Get to know historical contexts suggested by a passage. Learn all you can about the Bible's basic story line, its "salvation history," beginning with Israel and continuing in the Church.

Salvation by God's grace, obedience to God's will, and judgment on sin are basic to both Old and New Testaments. Learn about the covenants with Abraham and David that emphasize God's grace. The covenant with Moses presumes God's grace and emphasizes obedience. Both covenant traditions reemerge and are fulfilled in the New Covenant in Jesus, who pours out his life to save all people (grace) but is extremely demanding of his disciples (obedience).

Read entire books of the Bible in order to gain a sense of the "whole cloth" from which the snippets of the Sunday Lectionary are cut. Try to imagine what the books meant for their original authors and audiences. Ask how and why a book was put together: What is its structure, outline, main themes, literary forms, overall purpose?

Get to know the Old Testament narratives and psalms, but learn the Gospel accounts especially. The Lectionary's yearly focus on Matthew, Mark, or Luke offers an opportunity to learn each one.

John is the focus during the Church's special seasons.

READING FOR WISDOM

Read as one who seeks God, like the writer of Psalm 119. Ask what the text is asking you to believe, do, or hope for. Jesus' powerful proclamation in Mark 1:15 gives a strong framework: "This is the time of fulfillment" (now is the time to be attentive and ready to act); "the kingdom of God is at hand" (God is about to speak and act); "repent" (be willing to change your mind and move with fresh direction); "believe in the gospel" (embrace the grace that has already embraced you).

Read books straight through, a self-contained section at a time, carefully, slowly, and meditatively. Stop where natural breaks occur at the end of stories or sequences of thought.

Beware the sense that you already know what a text is going to say. Read attentively, asking what God is teaching you through this text at this minute about your life or about your communities—family, church, work, neighborhood, nation. Trust the Holy Spirit to guide you to what you need.

READING FOR WORSHIP

The goal of reading the Bible is not learning new facts or getting merely private inspiration for living, but entering into deeper communion with God. Allow the Bible to teach you to pray by giving you the words to use in prayer. The psalms are especially apt for this, but any part of the Bible may be prayed. This practice, dating back more than fifteen hundred years, is called lectio divina, Latin for "sacred reading."

Read Scripture in relation to the Eucharist. The Bible both prepares for Jesus' real presence and helps us understand it. The same Jesus who healed the lepers, stilled the storm, and embraced the children is present to us in the Word and in the Sacrament.

The Bible is a library of spiritual treasures waiting to be discovered. The Church intends that this treasury be "wide open to the Christian faithful" (Dei Verbum [Dogmatic Constitution on Divine Revelation], 22).

RESOURCES

Brown, Raymond E., ss. <u>101 Questions and Answers on the Bible</u>. Mahwah, NJ: Paulist Press, 2003.

Casey, Michael. <u>Sacred Reading: The Ancient Art of Lectio Divina</u>. Liguori, MS: Liguori, 1997.

Frigge, Marielle, OSB. <u>Beginning Biblical Studies</u>. Winona, MN: Anselm Academic, 2013.

Hahn, Scott. <u>Catholic Bible Dictionary</u>. New York: Doubleday, 2009.

Magrassi, Mariano. <u>Praying the Bible</u>. Collegeville, MN: Liturgical Press, 1998.

New Collegeville Bible Commentary Series. Collegeville, MN: Liturgical Press. (Short books on individual books of the Bible, various dates.)

Paprocki, Joe. <u>The Bible Blueprint, A Catholic's Guide to Understanding and Embracing God's Word</u>. Chicago: Loyola Press, 2009.

<u>The Bible Documents: A Parish Resource</u>. Chicago: Liturgy Training Publications, 2001.

<u>The Catholic Study Bible, 3rd Edition</u>. General editor, Donald Senior, CP. New York: Oxford, 2016.

Advent

Prayer before Reading the Word

Sustain us, O God,
on our Advent journey
as we go forth to welcome
the One who is to come.

Plant within our hearts
your living Word of promise,
and make haste to help us
as we seek to understand
what we went out to see in the
        Advent wilderness:
your patience nurturing your
        saving purpose
        to fulfillment,
your power in Jesus making all
        things new.

We ask this through our Lord
        Jesus Christ, your Son,
who lives and reigns with you
in the unity of the Holy Spirit,
one God for ever and ever. Amen.

Prayer after Reading the Word

Joy and gladness, O God,
attend the advent of your reign
        in Jesus,
for whenever the Good News is
        proclaimed to the poor,
feeble limbs are made steady,
and fearful hearts grow strong.

Give us strength for witnessing,
that we may go and tell others
        what we see and hear.
Give us patience for waiting,
until the precious harvest of
        your Kingdom,
when the return of your Son
will make your saving
        work complete.

Grant this through our Lord
        Jesus Christ,
who was, who is, and who is
        to come,
your Son, who lives and reigns
        with you
in the unity of the Holy Spirit,
one God for ever and ever. Amen.

Weekday Readings

December 2: Isaiah 4:2–6;
Matthew 8:5–11

December 3: Isaiah 11:1–10;
Luke 10:21–24

December 4: Isaiah 25:6–10a;
Matthew 15:29–37

December 5: Isaiah 26:1–6;
Matthew 7:21, 24–27

December 6: Isaiah 29:17–24;
Matthew 9:27–31

December 7:
Isaiah 30:19–21, 23–26;
Matthew 9:35—10:1, 5a, 6–8

December 9: Solemnity of the Immaculate Conception of the Blessed Virgin Mary Genesis 3:9–15, 20; Ephesians 1:3–6, 11–12; Luke 1:26–38

December 10: Isaiah 40:1–11;
Matthew 18:12–14

December 11: Isaiah 40:25–31;
Matthew 11:28–30

December 12: Feast of Our Lady of Guadalupe Zechariah 2:14–17 or Revelation 11:19a; 12:1–6a, 10ab; Luke 1:26–38 or Luke 1:39–47

December 13: Isaiah 48:17–19;
Matthew 11:16–19

December 14: Sirach 48:1–4, 9–11;
Matthew 17:9a, 10–13

December 16: Numbers 24:2–7,
15–17a; Matthew 21:23–27

December 17: Genesis 49:2, 8–10;
Matthew 1:1–17

December 18: Jeremiah 23:5–8;
Matthew 1:18–25

December 19: Judges 13:2–7,
24–25a; Luke 1:5–25

December 20: Isaiah 7:10–14;
Luke 1:26–38

December 21: Song of Songs
2:8–14 or Zephaniah
3:14–18a; Luke 1:39–45

December 23: Malachi 3:1–4,
23–24; Luke 1:57–66

December 24: 2 Samuel 7:1–5,
8b–12, 14a, 16; Luke 1:67–79

December 1, 2019

FIRST SUNDAY OF ADVENT

READING I Isaiah 2:1–5

This is what Isaiah, son of Amoz,
saw concerning Judah
 and Jerusalem.
 In days to come,
the mountain of the LORD's house
 shall be established as
  the highest mountain
 and raised above the hills.
All nations shall stream toward it;
 many peoples shall come
  and say:
"Come, let us climb
  the LORD's mountain,
 to the house of the God of Jacob,
that he may instruct us in his ways,
 and we may walk in his paths."
For from Zion shall go
  forth instruction,
 and the word of the LORD
  from Jerusalem.
He shall judge between
  the nations,
 and impose terms on
  many peoples.
They shall beat their swords
  into plowshares
 and their spears into
  pruning hooks;
one nation shall not raise
  the sword against another,
 nor shall they train for
  war again.
O house of Jacob, come,
 let us walk in the light of
  the LORD!

RESPONSORIAL PSALM
Psalm 122:1–2, 3–4, 4–5, 6–7, 8–9

R. Let us go rejoicing to
  the house of the Lord.
I rejoiced because they said to me,
 "We will go up to the house
  of the LORD."
And now we have set foot
 within your gates,
  O Jerusalem. R.

Jerusalem, built as a city
 with compact unity.
To it the tribes go up,
 the tribes of the LORD. R.

According to the decree for Israel,
 to give thanks to the name
  of the LORD.
In it are set up judgment seats,
 seats for the house of David. R.

Pray for the peace of Jerusalem!
　May those who love you prosper!
May peace be within your walls,
　prosperity in your buildings.　R.

Because of my brothers and friends
　I will say, "Peace be within you!"
Because of the house of the LORD,
　　our God,
　I will pray for your good.　R.

READING II
Romans 13:11–14

Brothers and sisters: You know the time; it is the hour now for you to awake from sleep. For our salvation is nearer now than when we first believed; the night is advanced, the day is at hand. Let us then throw off the works of darkness and put on the armor of light; let us conduct ourselves properly as in the day, not in orgies and drunkenness, not in promiscuity and lust, not in rivalry and jealousy. But put on the Lord Jesus Christ, and make no provision for the desires of the flesh.

GOSPEL　Matthew 24:37–44

Jesus said to his disciples: "As it was in the days of Noah, so it will be at the coming of the Son of Man. In those days before the flood, they were eating and drinking, marrying and giving in marriage, up to the day that Noah entered the ark. They did not know until the flood came and carried them all away. So will it be also at the coming of the Son of Man. Two men will be out in the field; one will be taken, and one will be left. Two women will be grinding at the mill; one will be taken, and one will be left. Therefore, stay awake! For you do not know on which day your Lord will come. Be sure of this: if the master of the house had known the hour of night when the thief was coming, he would have stayed awake and not let his house be broken into. So too, you also must be prepared, for at an hour you do not expect, the Son of Man will come."

Practice of Faith

Many of us work feverishly during this time of year to meet job or school deadlines and buy presents. Today's Second Reading and Gospel challenge us to prepare ourselves for something truly great. By nurturing our faith through service done in love, we can begin to appreciate what Pope Francis exhorts in The Light of Faith: "faith is also a light coming from the future and opening before us vast horizons which guide us beyond our isolated selves towards the breadth of communion. We come to see that faith does not dwell in shadow and gloom; it is a light for our darkness" (4) (w2 .vatican.va/content/francesco/en /encyclicals/documents/papa -francesco_20130629_enciclica -lumen-fidei.html). ◆ Put aside time during Advent to read sections of this encyclical on faith and consider how it can become a star to brighten our journey. ◆ Allow yourself a little more time for prayer in this busy season to prepare for the coming of our Savior. ◆ Consider declining a seasonal demand or frivolous commitment in order to say yes to preparing more for Jesus.

Download more questions and activities for families, Christian initiation groups, and other adult groups at http://www.ltp.org/ahw.

Scripture Insights

As we enter a new liturgical year, we prepare ourselves for the coming of Christ. We learn again how God comes into our world and into our individual lives to set us free.

Our readings call us to embrace God's transforming presence in our lives. The First Reading from Isaiah comes from a popular song the Israelites sang in captivity. It lifted their spirits as they reflected on God's promises to lead them back to their homeland. This song tells of a new age when God will reveal himself so that not only the Israelites but "all nations shall stream toward" the house of the Lord, the Temple in Jerusalem where God will bring peace among all humanity: "They shall beat their swords into plowshares."

St. Paul continues this theme of transformation by reminding us that our salvation is closer now than when we first believed! Our minds and actions need to embrace the necessary changes. True transformation can occur only through the power of Christ's grace: "Put on the Lord Jesus Christ." Like a new set of clothes, Christ embraces us totally and transforms the essence of our being.

The Gospel reiterates the urgency to stay awake and prepare for the Lord's coming at the end of our lives or at the end of the world. We do not approach this encounter in fear and trepidation but, in the spirit of our first two readings, with a joyous expectation of God's fulfillment of the longings in our hearts for true happiness, peace, and rest, as St. Augustine addressed God, "For you have made us for yourself, and our heart is restless until it rests in you."

◆ What does Paul mean when he says: "Put on the Lord Jesus Christ"?

◆ In what way does Isaiah's song proclaim that God's salvation is intended for all humanity?

◆ How do you live out daily Jesus' call to "Stay awake! For you do not know on which day your Lord will come"?

December 8, 2019

SECOND SUNDAY OF ADVENT

READING I Isaiah 11:1–10

On that day, a shoot shall sprout
      from the stump of Jesse,
   and from his roots
      a bud shall blossom.
The spirit of the LORD shall rest
      upon him:
   a spirit of wisdom and
      of understanding,
a spirit of counsel and of strength,
   a spirit of knowledge and
      of fear of the LORD,
   and his delight shall be
      the fear of the LORD.
Not by appearance shall he judge,
   nor by hearsay shall he decide,
but he shall judge the poor
      with justice,
   and decide aright for
      the land's afflicted.
He shall strike the ruthless
      with the rod of his mouth,
   and with the breath of his lips
      he shall slay the wicked.
Justice shall be the band
      around his waist,
   and faithfulness a belt
      upon his hips.

Then the wolf shall be
      a guest of the lamb,
   and the leopard shall lie down
      with the kid;
the calf and the young lion shall
      browse together,
   with a little child to guide them.
The cow and the bear shall
      be neighbors,
   together their young shall rest;
   the lion shall eat hay like the ox.
The baby shall play by the
      cobra's den,
   and the child lay his hand
      on the adder's lair.
There shall be no harm or ruin
      on all my holy mountain;
   for the earth shall be filled
      with knowledge of the LORD,
   as water covers the sea.
On that day, the root of Jesse,
   set up as a signal for the nations,
the Gentiles shall seek out,
   for his dwelling shall
      be glorious.

RESPONSORIAL PSALM Psalm 72:1–2, 7–8, 12–13, 17 (see 7)

R. Justice shall flourish in his time,
      and fullness of peace
      for ever.

O God, with your judgment
      endow the king,
  and with your justice,
      the king's son;
he shall govern your people
      with justice
and your afflicted ones
      with judgment.   R.

Justice shall flower in his days,
  and profound peace,
      till the moon be no more.
May he rule from sea to sea,
  and from the River to
      the ends of the earth.   R.

For he shall rescue the poor
      when he cries out,
  and the afflicted when
      he has no one to help him.
He shall have pity for the lowly
      and the poor;
the lives of the poor
      he shall save.   R.

May his name be blessed forever;
  as long as the sun his name
      shall remain.
In him shall all the tribes of
      the earth be blessed;
  all the nations shall proclaim
      his happiness.   R.

READING II Romans 15:4–9

Brothers and sisters: Whatever was written previously was written for our instruction, that by endurance and by the encouragement of the Scriptures we might have hope. May the God of endurance and encouragement grant you to think in harmony with one another, in keeping with Christ Jesus, that with one accord you may with one voice glorify the God and Father of our Lord Jesus Christ.

Welcome one another, then, as Christ welcomed you, for the glory of God. For I say that Christ became a minister of the circumcised to show God's truthfulness, to confirm the promises to the patriarchs, but so that the Gentiles might glorify God for his mercy. As it is written:

«Therefore, I will praise you
      among the Gentiles
  and sing praises to your name.»

GOSPEL Matthew 3:1–12

John the Baptist appeared, preaching in the desert of Judea and saying, "Repent, for the kingdom of heaven is at hand!" It was of him that the prophet Isaiah had spoken when he said:

«A voice of one crying out
  in the desert,
Prepare the way of the Lord,
  make straight his paths.»

John wore clothing made of camel's hair and had a leather belt around his waist. His food was locusts and wild honey. At that time Jerusalem, all Judea, and the whole region around the Jordan were going out to him and were being baptized by him in the Jordan River as they acknowledged their sins.

When he saw many of the Pharisees and Sadducees coming to his baptism, he said to them, "You brood of vipers! Who warned you to flee from the coming wrath? Produce good fruit as evidence of your repentance. And do not presume to say to yourselves, 'We have Abraham as our father.' For I tell you, God can raise up children to Abraham from these stones. Even now the ax lies at the root of the trees. Therefore every tree that does not bear good fruit will be cut down and thrown into the fire. I am baptizing you with water, for repentance, but the one who is coming after me is mightier than I. I am not worthy to carry his sandals. He will baptize you with the Holy Spirit and fire. His winnowing fan is in his hand. He will clear his threshing floor and gather his wheat into his barn, but the chaff he will burn with unquenchable fire."

Practice of Charity

In Paul's reading, he urges the Romans to "welcome one another, then, as Christ welcomed you, for the glory of God." To learn more about how the US Catholic bishops advocate for immigrants, read the bishops' pastoral statement Welcoming the Stranger Among Us: Unity in Diversity and Catholic Social Teaching on immigration at usccb.org. ◆ Invite to your home a neighbor or colleague who feels isolated from others. ◆ Challenge yourself to find common ground with someone with whom you have different beliefs. ◆ Support political candidates who work on solutions to social justice issues.

Download more questions and activities for families, Christian initiation groups, and other adult groups at http://www.ltp.org/ahw.

Scripture Insights

Today's First Reading from Isaiah looks forward to the coming of the long-awaited Messiah, who will be filled with the fullness of God's Spirit. He will bring peace to the world, a peace he describes in a vision where "the calf and the young lion shall browse together." The coming of Jesus inaugurates this fulfillment.

The reading from the Letter to the Romans connects back to the hopes of the Old Testament. Jesus' coming fulfills the promises made to the patriarchs and extends them to the Gentiles "so that they might glorify God for his mercy." Jesus' coming brings all peoples together in their praise and glory of God.

In the Gospel reading, God's Word comes to the people in the desert through the person of John the Baptist. The desert is the place where the Israelites had wandered for forty years and where God formed them into a people. The prophets foresaw that God would lead the people back to the desert to form them again into God's people. John the Baptist, who resembles the prophets with his clothing and diet, calls for a change of heart: "Repent, for the kingdom of heaven is at hand!" John speaks of one who is to come, one who is far greater than he. While John baptized with water, the one to come, Jesus, will baptize "with the Holy Spirit and with fire." As John the Baptist called on his people to set things right, so we are called this Advent to set things right with God as we await the coming of Jesus at Christmas and welcome his presence into our lives.

◆ How do the first two readings show the connection between the Old and New Testaments?

◆ What does John the Baptist mean when he says that Jesus will "baptize with the Holy Spirit and with fire"?

◆ How does Advent help you to experience Christ's coming into your life?

December 15, 2019

THIRD SUNDAY OF ADVENT

READING I Isaiah 35:1–6a, 10

The desert and the parched land
will exult;
the steppe will rejoice
and bloom.
They will bloom with
abundant flowers,
and rejoice with joyful song.
The glory of Lebanon will be
given to them,
the splendor of Carmel
and Sharon;
they will see the glory of the LORD,
the splendor of our God.
Strengthen the hands that
are feeble,
make firm the knees that
are weak,
say to those whose hearts
are frightened:
Be strong, fear not!
Here is your God,
he comes with vindication;
with divine recompense
he comes to save you.
Then will the eyes of the blind
be opened,
the ears of the deaf be cleared;
then will the lame leap like a stag,
then the tongue of the mute
will sing.

Those whom the LORD has
ransomed will return
and enter Zion singing,
crowned with everlasting joy;
they will meet with joy
and gladness,
sorrow and mourning will flee.

RESPONSORIAL PSALM
Psalm 146:6–7, 8–9, 9–10
(see Isaiah 35:4)

R. Lord, come and save us.
or: Alleluia.

The LORD God keeps faith forever,
secures justice for the oppressed,
gives food to the hungry.
The LORD sets captives free.   R.

The LORD gives sight to the blind;
the LORD raises up
those who were bowed down.
The LORD loves the just;
the LORD protects strangers.   R.

The fatherless and the widow
he sustains,
but the way of the wicked
he thwarts.
The LORD shall reign forever;
your God, O Zion,
through all generations.   R.

Reading II James 5:7–10

Be patient, brothers and sisters, until the coming of the Lord. See how the farmer waits for the precious fruit of the earth, being patient with it until it receives the early and the late rains. You too must be patient. Make your hearts firm, because the coming of the Lord is at hand. Do not complain, brothers and sisters, about one another, that you may not be judged. Behold, the Judge is standing before the gates. Take as an example of hardship and patience, brothers and sisters, the prophets who spoke in the name of the Lord.

Gospel Matthew 11:2–11

When John the Baptist heard in prison of the works of the Christ, he sent his disciples to Jesus with this question, "Are you the one who is to come, or should we look for another?" Jesus said to them in reply, "Go and tell John what you hear and see: the blind regain their sight, the lame walk, lepers are cleansed, the deaf hear, the dead are raised, and the poor have the good news proclaimed to them. And blessed is the one who takes no offense at me."

As they were going off, Jesus began to speak to the crowds about John, "What did you go out to the desert to see? A reed swayed by the wind? Then what did you go out to see? Someone dressed in fine clothing? Those who wear fine clothing are in royal palaces. Then why did you go out? To see a prophet? Yes, I tell you, and more than a prophet. This is the one about whom it is written:

«Behold, I am sending my
    messenger ahead of you;
he will prepare your way
    before you.»

Amen, I say to you, among those born of women there has been none greater than John the Baptist; yet the least in the kingdom of heaven is greater than he."

Practice of Faith

The Second Reading from James and the Gospel from Matthew illustrate the importance of patience and faith. In Matthew, Jesus sends reassurance to the imprisoned John the Baptist, who hears of healing and the Good News being proclaimed. ◆ The Second Vatican Council document the Dogmatic Constitution on Divine Revelation describes God's desire to be united with humankind through his Word. The second paragraph of the document states: "By this revelation, then, the invisible God (see Colossians 1:15, 1 Timothy 1:17) from the fullness of his love addresses men and women as friends (see Exodus 33:11; John 15:14-15) and lives among them (see Baruch 3:38), in order to invite and receive them into his own company." Read the complete paragraph to learn more about how God is revealed through Scripture (vatican.va/archive/hist _councils/ii_vatican_council /documents/vat-ii_const _19651118 _dei-verbum_en.html). ◆ Think about people in your life whom you trust and how their words and actions of love reflect those of our Savior. Send them an email or thank-you card for the influence they have made in your life.

Download more questions and activities for families, Christian initiation groups, and other adult groups at http://www.ltp.org/ahw.

Scripture Insights

As we approach Christmas, today's readings speak about an active, joyful waiting. With this type of waiting, total trust is placed in God while we do everything to accomplish our task. St. James, in the Second Reading, offers an example of patient waiting. Farmers sow seeds in the ground, then let nature take its course.

The Gospel offers the perfect example of waiting in John the Baptist, whose whole life was spent in active waiting for the coming of the promised Messiah. As he languishes in Herod's prison, he hears of a different Jesus than he expected. Following the Jewish tradition, John believed the Messiah would be a powerful figure who would overthrow the Romans and establish the Kingdom of God.

John sends his disciples to inquire of Jesus: "Are you the one who is to come, or should we look for another?" Jesus quotes from the prophet Isaiah: "The blind regain their sight, the lame walk, lepers are cleansed, the deaf hear, the dead are raised, and the poor have the good news proclaimed to them." These words challenge John's idea of the Messiah. Jesus says that the true reading of Scripture looks forward to a messiah who would touch the lives of people where they are. He would heal them spiritually and physically and restore them to a relationship with God. Jesus is saying that his actions show who he is.

As Christians, we lead our lives like John the Baptist, waiting patiently while actively striving to prepare a way for Christ into our lives and into the lives of others.

♦ Describe Isaiah's joyful vision of the transformation that God's coming accomplishes.

♦ What does Jesus mean when he says, "Among those born of women, there has been none greater than John the Baptist; yet the least in the kingdom of heaven is greater than he"?

♦ How do you prepare daily for Christ's coming into your life?

43

December 22, 2019

FOURTH SUNDAY OF ADVENT

READING I Isaiah 7:10–14

The LORD spoke to Ahaz, saying: Ask for a sign from the LORD, your God; let it be deep as the netherworld, or high as the sky! But Ahaz answered, "I will not ask! I will not tempt the LORD!" Then Isaiah said: Listen, O house of David! Is it not enough for you to weary people, must you also weary my God? Therefore the Lord himself will give you this sign: the virgin shall conceive, and bear a son, and shall name him Emmanuel.

RESPONSORIAL PSALM
Psalm 24:1–2, 3–4 5–6 (7c, 10b)

R. Let the Lord enter;
	he is king of glory.

The LORD's are the earth and
		its fullness;
	the world and those who
		dwell in it.
For he founded it upon the seas
	and established it upon
		the rivers. R.

Who can ascend the mountain
		of the LORD?
	or who may stand
		in his holy place?
One whose hands are sinless,
		whose heart is clean,
	who desires not what is vain. R.

He shall receive a blessing from
		the LORD,
	a reward from God his savior.
Such is the race that seeks for him,
	that seeks the face of
		the God of Jacob. R.

READING II Romans 1:1–7

Paul, a slave of Christ Jesus, called to be an apostle and set apart for the gospel of God, which he promised previously through his prophets in the holy Scriptures, the gospel about his Son, descended from David according to the flesh, but established as Son of God in power according to the Spirit of holiness through resurrection from the dead, Jesus Christ our Lord. Through him we have received the grace of apostleship, to bring about the obedience of faith, for the sake of his name, among all the Gentiles, among whom are you also, who are called to belong to Jesus Christ; to all the beloved of God in Rome, called to be holy. Grace to you and peace from God our Father and the Lord Jesus Christ.

GOSPEL Matthew 1:18–24

This is how the birth of Jesus Christ came about. When his mother Mary was betrothed to Joseph, but before they lived together, she was found with child through the Holy Spirit. Joseph her husband, since he was a righteous man, yet unwilling to expose her to shame, decided to divorce her quietly. Such was his intention when, behold, the angel of the Lord appeared to him in a dream and said, "Joseph, son of David, do not be afraid to take Mary your wife into your home. For it is through the Holy Spirit that this child has been conceived in her. She will bear a son and you are to name him Jesus, because he will save his people from their sins." All this took place to fulfill what the Lord had said through the prophet:

« Behold, the virgin shall
        conceive and bear a son,
and they shall name him
        Emmanuel, »

which means "God is with us." When Joseph awoke, he did as the angel of the Lord had commanded him and took his wife into his home.

Practice of Charity

One of the ways to extend our giving is through buying alternative gifts that assist people in developing countries to advance their earning potential. Giving your loved one a gift of a donation that purchases a goat for a family or provides for a child's tuition raises awareness of world poverty among family members and peer groups, and it helps people around the world to make a living and advance educational opportunities. ◆ Check out websites for Heifer International®, Compassion International®, Unbound, Catholic Relief Services, Samaritan's Purse®, and other groups that instill hope and practical help in regions of poverty. ◆ Consider sponsoring a child in a developing country with a monthly donation and letters of encouragement. ◆ Volunteer to help at a center that supports unwed mothers or befriend single parents in your parish or community who are struggling to get by.

Download more questions and activities for families, Christian initiation groups, and other adult groups at http://www.ltp.org/ahw.

Scripture Insights

On this final Sunday before Christmas, the readings highlight the foundation of our faith in Jesus' identity and, by extension, our identity as his followers. Matthew opened his Gospel, in imitation of the Old Testament, with a genealogy of Jesus Christ that identifies him as a descendant of Abraham though the lineage of David. Today's reading gives Matthew's account of Jesus' birth presented from Joseph's perspective.

Joseph's dilemma regarding Mary's pregnancy is resolved when in a dream an angel reveals that the child is conceived "though the Holy Spirit." The child to be born is the Son of God and the son of Mary. This is Jesus' identity: fully divine and fully human. Matthew supports this by quoting from Isaiah's prophecy: "Behold the virgin shall conceive and bear a son, and they shall name him Emmanuel."

This is the same Gospel message that St. Paul hands on so clearly in the beginning of his Letter to the Romans (today's Second Reading). The message of the Good News of our salvation centers on the person of Jesus: fully human, as a descendant of David and foretold by the prophets, and fully divine, as the Son of God and demonstrated by the Resurrection.

Jesus' identity has significant implications for us. We are called to "belong to Jesus Christ" by being transformed in holiness through the grace and peace that comes through Jesus' Resurrection. This is our faith. This is our inheritance: "We belong to Jesus Christ" as God's beloved children called to be saints. As such, like St. Paul, we are called to witness to this message by our lives.

◆ What is the significance of the name "Emmanuel"?

◆ How do Matthew and Paul, respectively, illustrate that Jesus is both Son of God and Son of Man?

◆ How do you live out your identity of being "called to belong to Jesus Christ," as God's beloved child, called to be a saint?

Christmas Time

Prayer before Reading the Word

Almighty God, Creator of all,
whose Word was present with you
          in the beginning
and whose wisdom was placed
at the service of your plan,
enlighten us to know the
          glorious hope
to which you have called us;
fill us with faith in Jesus and
with love toward all your people,
that we who have seen in Christ
the glory of your Word made flesh
may bear into the world you
          so love,
the Light no darkness can
          extinguish:
your Son, our Lord Jesus Christ,
who lives and reigns with you
in the unity of the Holy Spirit,
one God for ever and ever. Amen.

Prayer after Reading the Word

Your Word, O God of
          ageless glory,
dwelling with you from
          before time,
has become flesh and lived
          among us,
and we have seen the glory of
          your Christ.

Place on our lips the word
          of salvation,
in our hearts a love that
          welcomes all,
and, in the depths of our being,
the light of faith and hope,
which the darkness can
          never overcome.

We ask this through our Lord
          Jesus Christ, your Son,
who lives and reigns with you
in the unity of the Holy Spirit,
one God for ever and ever. Amen.

Weekday Readings

December 25: Solemnity of the Nativity of the Lord
Day: Isaiah 52:7–10;
Hebrews 1:1–6; John 1:1–18

December 26: Feast of St. Stephen
Acts 6:8–10; 7:54–59;
Matthew 10:17–22

December 27: Feast of St. John, Apostle and Evangelist
1 John 1:1–4; John 20:1a, 2–8

December 28: Feast of the Holy Innocents, Martyrs
Sirach 3:2–6, 12–14;
Colossians 3:12–21 or 3:12–17; Matthew 2:13–15, 19–23

December 30: Sixth Day within the Octave of the Lord
1 John 2:12–17;
Luke 2:36–40

December 31: Seventh Day within the Octave of the Lord
1 John 2:18–21; / John 1:1–18

January 1: Solemnity of Mary, the Holy Mother of God
Numbers 6:22–27; Galatians 4:4–7; Luke 2:16–21

January 2: 1 John 2:22–28;
John 1:19–28

January 3: 1 John 2:29—3:6;
John 1:29–34

January 4: 1 John 3:7–10;
John 1:35–42

January 6: 1 John 3:22—4:6;
    Matthew 4:12–17, 23–25
January 7: 1 John 4:7–10;
    Mark 6:34–44
January 8: 1 John 4:11–18;
    Mark 6:45–52
January 9: 1 John 4:19—5:4;
    Luke 4:14–22a
January 10: 1 John 5:5–13;
    Luke 5:12–16
January 11: 1 John 5:14–21;
    John 3:22–30

December 25, 2019

THE NATIVITY OF THE LORD, NIGHT

READING I Isaiah 9:1-6

The people who walked
    in darkness
    have seen a great light;
upon those who dwelt in the land
    of gloom
    a light has shone.
You have brought them
    abundant joy
    and great rejoicing,
as they rejoice before you as at
    the harvest,
    as people make merry when
    dividing spoils.
For the yoke that burdened them,
    the pole on their shoulder,
and the rod of their taskmaster
    you have smashed, as on the
    day of Midian.
For every boot that tramped
    in battle,
    every cloak rolled in blood,
    will be burned as fuel
    for flames.
For a child is born to us, a son is
    given us;
    upon his shoulder
    dominion rests.
They name him Wonder-
    Counselor, God-Hero,
    Father-Forever, Prince of Peace.
His dominion is vast
    and forever peaceful,
from David's throne, and over
    his kingdom,
    which he confirms and sustains
by judgment and justice,
    both now and forever.
The zeal of the LORD of hosts will
    do this!

RESPONSORIAL PSALM
Psalm 96:1–2, 2–3, 11–12, 13 (Luke 2:11)

R. Today is born our Savior, Christ
    the Lord.

Sing to the LORD a new song;
    sing to the LORD, all you lands.
Sing to the LORD; bless
    his name. R.

Announce his salvation, day
    after day.
    Tell his glory among the nations;
    among all peoples, his wondrous
    deeds. R.

Let the heavens be glad and the
　　earth rejoice;
　let the sea and what fills
　　　it resound;
　let the plains be joyful and all
　　　that is in them!
Then shall all the trees of the
　　forest exult.　R.

They shall exult before the LORD,
　　for he comes;
　for he comes to rule the earth.
He shall rule the world with justice
　and the peoples with his
　　　constancy.　R.

READING II　Titus 2:11–14

Beloved: The grace of God has
appeared, saving all and training
us to reject godless ways and
worldly desires and to live
temperately, justly, and devoutly in
this age, as we await the blessed
hope, the appearance of the glory
of our great God and savior Jesus
Christ, who gave himself for us to
deliver us from all lawlessness and
to cleanse for himself a people as
his own, eager to do what is good.

GOSPEL　Luke 2:1–14

In those days a decree went out
from Caesar Augustus that the
whole world should be enrolled.
This was the first enrollment,
when Quirinius was governor
of Syria. So all went to be enrolled,
each to his own town. And Joseph
too went up from Galilee from
the town of Nazareth to Judea,
to the city of David that is called
Bethlehem, because he was of the
house and family of David, to be
enrolled with Mary, his betrothed,
who was with child. While they
were there, the time came for her
to have her child, and she gave
birth to her firstborn son. She
wrapped him in swaddling clothes
and laid him in a manger, because
there was no room for them in
the inn.

Now there were shepherds in
that region living in the fields
and keeping the night watch over
their flock. The angel of the Lord
appeared to them and the glory of
the Lord shone around them, and
they were struck with great fear.
The angel said to them, "Do not
be afraid; for behold, I proclaim to
you good news of great joy that will
be for all the people. For today in
the city of David a savior has been
born for you who is Christ and
Lord. And this will be a sign for

you: you will find an infant wrapped in swaddling clothes and lying in a manger." And suddenly there was a multitude of the heavenly host with the angel, praising God and saying:

"Glory to God in the highest
and on earth peace to those
on whom his favor rests."

Practice of Charity

The enrollment described in Luke's Gospel had to be a tremendous hardship for families who lived far from their hometown. Today, with people dispersed around the globe, we may not be able to fathom returning to the family's town of origin. More than two thousand years ago, the shepherds were summoned, as are we today, to give glory to the Savior: God's gift for humanity. ◆ What presence will you provide others rather than "presents" this Christmas? ◆ Consider being with someone whose family is away during the holiday season. ◆ Spend time getting to know someone who may be struggling with an issue. Being present with those who are lonely or distressed could be our prayer to the One who is always present with us.

Download more questions and activities for families, Christian initiation groups, and other adult groups at http://www.ltp.org/ahw.

54

Scripture Insights

Luke's narrative of Jesus' birth is rich in symbolism. The evangelist begins his account by situating it against the background of the Roman Empire. Jesus is born during the reign of Augustus, who had brought a peace to the world that it had not known for centuries. Notice how the angels proclaim Jesus' birth to the shepherds: "Glory to God in the highest / and on earth peace to those on whom his favor rests." Contrasted to the peace that Augustus brought through military power, the birth of Jesus will bring a far deeper and more lasting spiritual peace through God's grace that strengthens the bonds between God and humanity as well as among people.

Jesus' birth fulfills the prophecy of peace that we hear from Isaiah in the First Reading: "For a child is born to us, a son is given us. . . . [He is] Prince of Peace."

Luke's description also sets the stage for Jesus' ministry. His birth has universal significance. The first to learn of Jesus' birth were not kings in palaces but ordinary shepherds in the fields—people society looked down on. Jesus is born in a stable, lying in a manger, a feeding trough for animals, since there was no other place for him. Born like an outcast, Jesus identifies with all those whom society marginalizes and rejects.

St. Paul's letter to Titus captures the implications of Jesus' birth for us. God's grace has been revealed in Jesus as God's salvation for all people. We are called to respond to this gift by leading lives that conform to the hope we have in our "savior Jesus Christ."

◆ How does the peace offered by Jesus' birth differ from the peace established by Emperor Augustus?

◆ What major themes do you draw from Luke's account of Jesus' birth?

◆ What is the Good News about Jesus' birth that you would like to share with others this Christmas Day?

December 29, 2019

READING I
Sirach 3:2–6, 12–14

God sets a father in honor over
    his children;
  a mother's authority he
    confirms over her sons.
Whoever honors his father atones
    for sins,
  and preserves himself from them.
When he prays, he is heard;
  he stores up riches who reveres
    his mother.
Whoever honors his father
    is gladdened by children,
  and, when he prays, is heard.
Whoever reveres his father will
    live a long life;
  he who obeys his father brings
    comfort to his mother.

My son, take care of your father
    when he is old;
  grieve him not as long as he lives.
Even if his mind fail, be
    considerate of him;
  revile him not all the days of
    his life;
kindness to a father will not be
    forgotten,
  firmly planted against
    the debt of your sins
—a house raised in justice
    to you.

RESPONSORIAL PSALM
Psalm 128:1–2, 3, 4–5 (see 1)

R. Blessed are those who fear the
    Lord and walk in his ways.

Blessed is everyone who fears
    the LORD,
  who walks in his ways!
For you shall eat the fruit of
    your handiwork;
  blessed shall you be,
    and favored.   R.

Your wife shall be like
    a fruitful vine
  in the recesses of your home;
your children like olive plants
    around your table.   R.

Behold, thus is the man blessed
    who fears the LORD.
The LORD bless you from Zion:
    may you see the prosperity
      of Jerusalem
  all the days of your life.   R.

READING II
Colossians 3:12–21

Shorter: Colossians 3:12–17

Brothers and sisters: Put on, as God's chosen ones, holy and beloved, heartfelt compassion, kindness, humility, gentleness, and patience, bearing with one another and forgiving one another, if one has a grievance against another; as the Lord has forgiven you, so must you also do. And over all these put on love, that is, the bond of perfection. And let the peace ofChrist control your hearts, the peace into which you were also called in one body. And be thankful. Let the word of Christ dwell in you richly, as in all wisdom you teach and admonish one another, singing psalms, hymns, and spiritual songs with gratitude in your hearts to God. And whatever you do, in word or in deed, do everything in the name of the Lord Jesus, giving thanks to God the Father through him.

Wives, be subordinate to your husbands, as is proper in the Lord. Husbands, love your wives, and avoid any bitterness toward them. Children, obey your parents in everything, for this is pleasing to the Lord. Fathers, do not provoke your children, so they may not become discouraged.

GOSPEL
Matthew 2:13–15, 19–23

When the magi had departed, behold, the angel of the Lord appeared to Joseph in a dream and said, "Rise, take the child and his mother, flee to Egypt, and stay there until I tell you. Herod is going to search for the child to destroy him." Joseph rose and took the child and his mother by night and departed for Egypt. He stayed there until the death of Herod, that what the Lord had said through the prophet might be fulfilled,

«Out of Egypt I called my son.»

When Herod had died, behold, the angel of the Lord appeared in a dream to Joseph in Egypt and said, "Rise, take the child and his mother and go to the land of Israel, for those who sought the child's life are dead." He rose, took the child and his mother, and went to the land of Israel. But when he heard that Archelaus was ruling over Judea in place of his father Herod, he was afraid to go back there. And because he had been warned

57

in a dream, he departed for the region of Galilee. He went and dwelt in a town called Nazareth, so that what had been spoken through the prophets might be fulfilled,

> «He shall be called
> a Nazorean.»

Practice of Hope

Church teaching tells us that the family is the context through which we learn about God and become aware of God's will. Vatican II's Dogmatic Constitution on the Church emphasizes the importance of the domestic church and that families should do all that they can to nurture and support it. Although Joseph, Mary, and Jesus and their extended family suffered many hardships, their bond of support and prayer was vital for spiritual survival. The bishops offer suggestions for building the domestic church on their website: reading from Scripture during family prayer, placing crucifixes prominently in the home, and traditions based on the liturgical calendar. Find more suggestions at www.usccb.org /beliefs-and-teachings/vocations /parents/tools-for-building-a -domestic-church.cfm. ◆ Develop the practice of carefully listening to family members to fully understand their daily happenings, desires, and feelings. ◆ Plan some activities that all family members can do together, such as a trip to the zoo, park, science museum, or library. ◆ Volunteer as a family for a parish ministry, such as ushering, simple landscaping, or helping the elderly with yard work or light home repairs.

Download more questions and activities for families, Christian initiation groups, and other adult groups at http://www.ltp.org/ahw.

Scripture Insights

Our reading from the Book of Sirach sets the tone for the Feast of the Holy Family by drawing attention to the loving relationships that should permeate every family. The commandment "Honor your father and your mother" is the foundation for this reflection. Love for parents continues throughout life and brings with it the reward of many blessings.

Paul's letter to the Colossians focuses on family life. Paul reminds us of our identity as "God's chosen ones, holy and beloved." We are called to live out our identity in all relationships especially within the family. Paul uses a beautiful analogy: just as we consciously select our clothes every day, so we should consciously clothe ourselves daily with the virtues inspired by Jesus: "compassion, kindness, humility."

On this first Sunday of Christmas Time, our minds turn to the heart of the message of the Incarnation. The Gospel offers a beautiful narrative that reflects the life of the Holy Family. The Son of God entered the human family as a helpless child, cared for by a loving family. Joseph and Mary immediately exercise their role as protectors of their child amid dire circumstances. They become refugees, escaping the tyranny of King Herod, who had ordered the death of their child. Just as the Joseph in the Old Testament went to Egypt to save his family from starvation, so Joseph in the New Testament takes his family to Egypt under God's inspiration to save them. Once King Herod had died, God brings the Holy Family back from Egypt to safety in Nazareth. Joseph and Mary illustrate the primary role of every parent: to trust in God's guidance as they care for and protect their child.

◆ How does Joseph in the Old Testament foreshadow Joseph in the New Testament?

◆ How should adult children continue to fulfill the commandment "Honor your father and your mother"?

◆ What good news does this Feast of the Holy Family convey to your family?

January 5, 2020

THE EPIPHANY OF THE LORD

READING I Isaiah 60:1-6

Rise up in splendor, Jerusalem!
　　Your light has come,
　the glory of the Lord shines
　　upon you.
See, darkness covers the earth,
　and thick clouds cover
　　the peoples;
but upon you the LORD shines,
　and over you appears his glory.
Nations shall walk by your light,
　and kings by your
　　shining radiance.
Raise your eyes and look about;
　they all gather and come to you:
your sons come from afar,
　and your daughters in the arms
　　of their nurses.

Then you shall be radiant at what
　　you see,
　your heart shall throb
　　and overflow,
for the riches of the sea shall be
　　emptied out before you,
　the wealth of nations shall be
　　brought to you.
Caravans of camels shall fill you,
　dromedaries from Midian
　　and Ephah;

all from Sheba shall come
　bearing gold and frankincense,
　and proclaiming the praises
　　of the LORD.

RESPONSORIAL PSALM
Psalm 72:1-2, 7-8, 10-11, 12-13 (see 11)

R. Lord, every nation on earth
　　will adore you.

O God, with your judgment
　　endow the king,
　and with your justice
　　the king's son;
he shall govern your people
　　with justice
　and your afflicted ones
　　with judgment.   R.

Justice shall flower in his days,
　and profound peace, till
　　the moon be no more.
May he rule from sea to sea,
　and from the River to the ends
　　of the earth.   R.

The kings of Tarshish and the Isles
　　shall offer gifts;
　the kings of Arabia and Seba
　　shall bring tribute.

All kings shall pay him homage,
   all nations shall serve him.   R.

For he shall rescue the poor when
      he cries out,
   and the afflicted when he has
      no one to help him.
He shall have pity for the lowly
      and the poor;
   the lives of the poor he
      shall save.   R.

READING II
Ephesians 3:2–3a, 5–6

Brothers and sisters: You have
heard of the stewardship of God's
grace that was given to me for
your benefit, namely, that the
mystery was made known to me
by revelation. It was not made
known to people in other
generations as it has now been
revealed to his holy apostles and
prophets by the Spirit: that the
Gentiles are coheirs, members
of the same body, and copartners
in the promise in Christ Jesus
through the gospel.

GOSPEL Matthew 2:1–12

When Jesus was born in
Bethlehem of Judea, in the days of
King Herod, behold, magi from

the east arrived in Jerusalem,
saying, "Where is the newborn
king of the Jews? We saw his star
at its rising and have come to
do him homage." When King
Herod heard this, he was greatly
troubled, and all Jerusalem with
him. Assembling all the chief
priests and the scribes of the
people, he inquired of them where
the Christ was to be born. They
said to him, "In Bethlehem of
Judea, for thus it has been written
through the prophet:

« And you, Bethlehem,
      land of Judah,
   are by no means least among
      the rulers of Judah;
since from you shall come a ruler,
   who is to shepherd my
      people Israel. »

Then Herod called the magi
secretly and ascertained from
them the time of the star's
appearance. He sent them to
Bethlehem and said, "Go and
search diligently for the child.
When you have found him, bring
me word, that I too may go and do
him homage." After their audience
with the king they set out. And
behold, the star that they had seen

at its rising preceded them, until it came and stopped over the place where the child was. They were overjoyed at seeing the star, and on entering the house they saw the child with Mary his mother. They prostrated themselves and did him homage. Then they opened their treasures and offered him gifts of gold, frankincense, and myrrh. And having been warned in a dream not to return to Herod, they departed for their country by another way.

Practice of Hope

The readings for Epiphany give hope as they show that God's gift of Jesus is for everyone. Pope Francis emphasizes ecumenism in his exhortation The Joy of the Gospel: "We must never forget that we are pilgrims journeying alongside one another. This means that we must have sincere trust in our fellow pilgrims, putting aside all suspicion or mistrust, and turn our gaze to what we are all seeking: the radiant peace of God's face. Trusting others is an art and peace is an art" (244). ◆ Just as the Magi followed the star, seek out and be inspired by the spiritual work of writers, artists, or musicians, regardless of denomination.
◆ Invite to Mass family members or friends who may not be Catholic and then attend a service in that family's faith community. Discuss the similarities of expression of faith.

Download more questions and activities for families, Christian initiation groups, and other adult groups at http://www.ltp.org/ahw.

Scripture Insights

The prophet Isaiah contrasts a picture of the world living in darkness with "the glory of the Lord" shining on Jerusalem. The nations of the world are drawn toward this light. Isaiah proclaims a profound truth: God's love and salvation, first offered to Israel, is meant to be shared with all nations. This message calls for joy: "your heart shall throb and overflow."

Paul stresses the theme that God's salvation is intended for all people. This mystery, hidden beforehand, has now been revealed to Paul through the inspiration of the Spirit: all human beings are called to become "coheirs, members of the same body, and copartners in the promise in Christ Jesus through the gospel."

Our Gospel narrative expresses this same mystery. On the day of Christ's birth, the first to receive the Good News were Jewish shepherds in the fields. Now, at the Epiphany, pagan astrologers, wise men from the East, the Magi, come searching for the "newborn King of the Jews" by following the light of a star. This event fulfills Isaiah's prophecy announced in the First Reading. The contrast of King Herod to the Magi is remarkable: the leader of the Jewish people refuses to accept the news of the Jewish king's birth and plans to kill him, while these pagan Magi have traveled far searching for this king and prostrate themselves in worship before him. Their gifts symbolize their belief: gold, the most precious of metals, is a suitable gift for a king.

Frankincense, used in worship, symbolizes the child's divinity. Myrrh, used in preparing a body for burial, symbolizes Jesus' humanity. We recall how after Jesus' death his body was anointed with "myrrh and aloes" (John 19:38–42).

Our readings remind us of the powerful truth that God's love is for everyone. Like the Magi, we are called to open our hearts to accept that love.

◆ Why does the prophet Isaiah call on his readers to rejoice?

◆ How would you explain the "mystery" that St. Paul speaks about in the Second Reading?

◆ Was there an "epiphany" in your life that brought you closer to the Lord?

January 12, 2020

FEAST OF THE BAPTISM OF THE LORD

Reading I
Isaiah 42:1–4, 6–7

Thus says the LORD:
Here is my servant whom
    I uphold,
  my chosen one with whom
    I am pleased,
upon whom I have put my spirit;
  he shall bring forth justice to
    the nations,
not crying out, not shouting,
  not making his voice heard
    in the street.
A bruised reed he shall not break,
  and a smoldering wick he shall
    not quench,
until he establishes justice on
    the earth;
  the coastlands will wait for
    his teaching.

I, the LORD, have called you
    for the victory of justice,
  I have grasped you by the hand;
I formed you, and set you
  as a covenant of the people,
  a light for the nations,
to open the eyes of the blind,
  to bring out prisoners from
    confinement,
  and from the dungeon,
    those who live in darkness.

Responsorial Psalm Psalm 29:1–2, 3–4, 3, 9–10 (11b)

R. The Lord will bless his people
    with peace.

Give to the LORD, you sons of God,
  give to the LORD glory
    and praise,
Give to the LORD the glory due
    his name;
  adore the LORD in holy
    attire. R.

The voice of the LORD is over
    the waters,
  the LORD, over vast waters.
The voice of the LORD is mighty;
  the voice of the LORD
    is majestic. R.

The God of glory thunders,
  and in his temple all say, "Glory!"
The LORD is enthroned above
    the flood;
  the LORD is enthroned as king
    forever. R.

READING II Acts 10:34–38

Peter proceeded to speak to those gathered in the house of Cornelius, saying: "In truth, I see that God shows no partiality. Rather, in every nation whoever fears him and acts uprightly is acceptable to him. You know the word that he sent to the Israelites as he proclaimed peace through Jesus Christ, who is Lord of all, what has happened all over Judea, beginning in Galilee after the baptism that John preached, how God anointed Jesus of Nazareth with the Holy Spirit and power. He went about doing good and healing all those oppressed by the devil, for God was with him."

GOSPEL Matthew 3:13–17

Jesus came from Galilee to John at the Jordan to be baptized by him. John tried to prevent him, saying, "I need to be baptized by you, and yet you are coming to me?" Jesus said to him in reply, "Allow it now, for thus it is fitting for us to fulfill all righteousness." Then he allowed him. After Jesus was baptized, he came up from the water and behold, the heavens were opened for him, and he saw the Spirit of God descending like a dove and coming upon him. And a voice came from the heavens, saying, "This is my beloved Son, with whom I am well pleased."

Practice of Faith

Jesus begins his ministry of servant leadership as he rises from the waters and is affirmed by "the Spirit of God descending like a dove and coming upon him." We are called to mission, by virtue of our Baptism, by our actions and attitudes to "consecrate the world itself to God" (Dogmatic Constitution on the Church, 34).

◆ If you haven't talked with or written your godparent in a while, take this opportunity to reconnect with your sacramental sponsor.

◆ Talk with your family members about how each of us is called to be Jesus—hope in a world filled with anxiety and doubt. Discuss how we can inspire others as we recognize the myriad ways that God affirms us on life's journey.

Download more questions and activities for families, Christian initiation groups, and other adult groups at http://www.ltp.org/ahw.

Scripture Insights

Today marks the end of the Christmas season. Matthew describes the baptism and anointing by the Holy Spirt of the adult Jesus in a richly symbolic way that expresses Jesus' acceptance of the mission that the Father has given him as God's suffering servant. Jesus' baptism unfolds in the form of a drama in two parts. The first part focuses on Jesus' acceptance of his mission. Jesus comes to John to be baptized, but John objects: "I need to be baptized by you." Although Jesus is the Lamb of God who is without sin, by this action, Jesus, as the Lamb, identifies himself with humanity in order to take away the sins of the world (John 1:29). Jesus' baptism looks forward to his death. When saying that by accepting baptism he "fulfills all righteousness," Jesus submits himself to his Father's will, consenting to a path leading to suffering, death, and Resurrection for the forgiveness of humanity's sins.

The second part of Matthew's drama focuses on the Father's

response to Jesus' acceptance. God identifies Jesus unambiguously as "my beloved Son, with whom I am well pleased."

Finally, "the heavens were opened" at Jesus' baptism, reversing what happened through Adam's sin. Adam's rejection of God destroyed the intimate relationship between humankind and God. Now Jesus' baptism restores God's relationship with humankind intended at the beginning of creation.

By accepting Baptism, we embrace what Jesus accomplished for us. Through the waters of Baptism, we become a new creation, our sins are forgiven, and we enter an intimate relationship as a beloved child of God, Father, Son, and Spirit, together with all who, like us, have become a new creation through the waters of Baptism.

◆ What is meant when Jesus says: "Allow it now, for thus it is fitting for us to fulfill all righteousness"?

◆ How do you understand the term "a beloved child of God"?

◆ How do you see the grace of Baptism transforming your life?

Ordinary Time, Winter

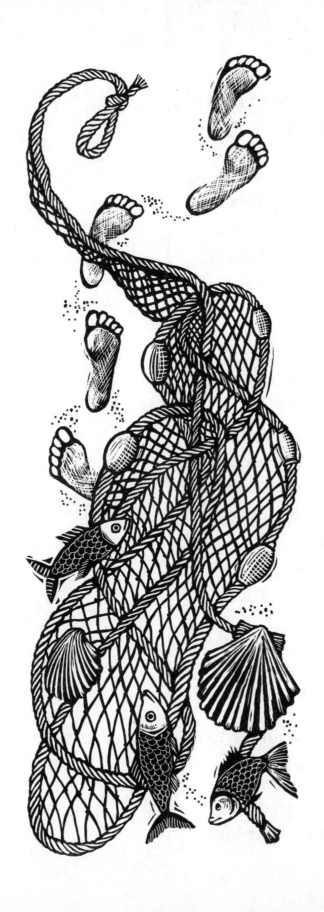

Prayer before Reading the Word

Not to the wise and powerful of
    this world,
O God of all blessedness,
but to those who are poor in spirit
do you reveal in Jesus
the righteousness of your Kingdom.

Gathered here,
like the disciples on the mountain,
we long to listen as Jesus, the
    teacher, speaks.
By the power of his word
refashion our lives
in the pattern of the Beatitudes.

We ask this through our Lord
    Jesus Christ, your Son,
who lives and reigns with you
in the unity of the Holy Spirit,
one God, for ever and ever. Amen.

Prayer after Reading the Word

God of all the nations,
we proclaim your wisdom and
    your power
in the mystery of Christ's Cross.

We have heard Christ's call
and it compels us to follow.
Let the truth of the Gospel
break the yoke of our selfishness.
Let the Cross draw us and
    all people
to the joy of salvation.

We ask this through our Lord
    Jesus Christ, your Son,
who lives and reigns with you
in the unity of the Holy Spirit,
one God for ever and ever. Amen.

Weekday Readings

January 13: 1 Samuel 1:1–8;
　　Mark 1:14–20

January 14: 1 Samuel 1:9–20;
　　Mark 1:21–28

January 15: 1 Samuel 3:1–10,
　　19–20; Mark 1:29–39

January 16: 1 Samuel 4:1–11;
　　Mark 1:40–45

January 17: 1 Samuel 8:4–7,
　　10–22a; Mark 2:1–12

January 18: 1 Samuel 9:1–4, 17–19;
　　10:1a; Mark 2:13–17

January 20: 1 Samuel 15:16–23;
　　Mark 2:18–22

January 21: 1 Samuel 16:1–13;
　　Mark 2:23–28

January 22: 1 Samuel 17:32–33, 37,
　　40–51; Mark 3:1–6

January 23: 1 Samuel 18:6–9;
　　19:1–7; Mark 3:7–12

January 24: 1 Samuel 24:3–21;
　　Mark 3:13–19

**January 25: Feast of the
　　Conversion of St. Paul
　　the Apostle
　　Acts 22:3–16 or Acts 9:1–22;
　　Mark 16:15–18**

January 27: 2 Samuel 5:1–7, 10;
　　Mark 3:22–30

January 28: 2 Samuel 6:12b–15,
　　17–19; Mark 3:31–35

January 29: 2 Samuel 7:4–17;
　　Mark 4:1–20

January 30: 2 Samuel 7:18–19,
　　24–29; Mark 4:21–25

January 31: 2 Samuel 11:1–4a,
　　5–10a, 13–17; Mark 4:26–34

February 1: 2 Samuel 12:1–7a,
　　10–17; Mark 4:35–41

February 3: 2 Samuel 15:13–14, 30;
　　16:5–13; Mark 5:1–20

February 4: 2 Samuel 18:9–10, 14b,
　　24–25a, 30—19:3;
　　Mark 5:21–43

February 5: 2 Samuel 24:2, 9–17;
　　Mark 6:1–6

February 6: 1 Kings 2:1–4, 10–12;
　　Mark 6:7–13

February 7: Sirach 47:2–11;
　　Mark 6:14–29

February 8: 1 Kings 3:4–13;
　　Mark 6:30–34

February 10: 1 Kings 8:1–7, 9–13;
Mark 6:53–56

February 11: 1 Kings 8:22–23,
27–30; Mark 7:1–13

February 12: 1 Kings 10:1–10;
Mark 7:14–23

February 13: 1 Kings 11:4–13;
Mark 7:24–30

February 14: 1 Kings 11:29–32;
12:19; Mark 7:31–37

February 15: 1 Kings 12:26–32;
13:33–34; Mark 8:1–10

February 17: James 1:1–11;
Mark 8:11–13

February 18: James 1:12–18;
Mark 8:14–21

February 19: James 1:19–27;
Mark 8:22–26

February 20: James 2:1–9;
Mark 8:27–33

February 21: James 2:14–24, 26;
Mark 8:34—9:1

**February 22: Feast of the Chair
of St. Peter the Apostle
1 Peter 5:1–4; Matthew
16:13–19**

February 24: James 3:13–18;
Mark 9:14–29

February 25: James 4:1–10;
Mark 9:30–37

January 19, 2020

SECOND SUNDAY IN ORDINARY TIME

READING I Isaiah 49:3, 5–6

The LORD said to me:
>   You are my servant,
>   Israel, through whom
>   I show my glory.
Now the LORD has spoken
>   who formed me as his servant
>   from the womb,
that Jacob may be brought
>   back to him
>   and Israel gathered to him;
and I am made glorious in
>   the sight of the LORD,
>   and my God is now my strength!
It is too little, the LORD says,
>   for you to be my servant,
>   to raise up the tribes of Jacob,
>   and restore the survivors
>   of Israel;
I will make you a light to
>   the nations,
>   that my salvation may reach
>   to the ends of the earth.

RESPONSORIAL PSALM
Psalm 40:2, 4, 7–8, 8–9, 10 (8a, 9a)

R. Here am I, Lord;
>   I come to do your will.

I have waited, waited for the LORD,
>   and he stooped toward me
>   and heard my cry.
And he put a new song into
>   my mouth,
>   a hymn to our God.   R.

Sacrifice or offering you wished not,
>   but ears open to obedience you
>   gave me.
Holocausts or sin-offerings you
>   sought not;
>   then said I, "Behold I come."   R.

"In the written scroll
>   it is prescribed for me,
to do your will, O my God,
>   is my delight,
>   and your law is within my
>   heart!"   R.

I announced your justice
>   in the vast assembly;
I did not restrain my lips,
>   as you, O LORD, know.   R.

READING II
1 Corinthians 1:1–3

Paul, called to be an apostle of Christ Jesus by the will of God, and Sosthenes our brother, to the church of God that is in Corinth, to you who have been sanctified in Christ Jesus, called to be holy, with all those everywhere who call upon the name of our Lord Jesus Christ, their Lord and ours. Grace to you and peace from God our Father and the Lord Jesus Christ.

GOSPEL John 1:29–34

John the Baptist saw Jesus coming toward him and said, "Behold, the Lamb of God, who takes away the sin of the world. He is the one of whom I said, 'A man is coming after me who ranks ahead of me because he existed before me.' I did not know him, but the reason why I came baptizing with water was that he might be made known to Israel." John testified further, saying, "I saw the Spirit come down like a dove from heaven and remain upon him. I did not know him, but the one who sent me to baptize with water told me, 'On whomever you see the Spirit come down and remain, he is the one who will baptize with the Holy Spirit.' Now I have seen and testified that he is the Son of God."

Practice of Hope

How do you ensure that the information you read and hear is from a trusted authority? To whom do you turn when you feel anxiety? In today's Gospel, John the Baptist declares the supreme identity of Jesus as the "Lamb of God, who takes away the sin of the world," and how God's Spirit came upon him. ◆ In this new year, consider studying Matthew's Gospel account to understand more about the divinity and humanity of Jesus. ◆ Purchase a spiritual reader with the Church's daily readings and commentary to guide your thoughts in the months ahead. ◆ As you listen or watch the world's news throughout the week, try praying through it, asking for God's help, but remembering that God is in control of the chaos. Search for a news source that also delivers positive news so that you can see solace and hope in people who do God's will.

Download more questions and activities for families, Christian initiation groups, and other adult groups at http://www.ltp.org/ahw.

Scripture Insights

As we begin this new season, our readings remind us of a significant outcome of our Christian faith: we are called to be witnesses. John's Gospel presents the Baptist differently from the other Gospel accounts: the prophet does not dress in an austere manner or challenge people with a rhetoric of fire and doom. Instead, the Baptist is portrayed as a witness, one of many throughout John's Gospel, to testify to the person of Jesus. The Baptist identifies Jesus as superior to him: "A man is coming after me who ranks ahead of me because he existed before me." The Baptist testifies to Jesus' baptism and the Spirit descending upon Jesus and concludes by saying: "I have seen and testified that he is the Son of God."

The prophet Isaiah testifies to another figure, the servant, whose task is to lead the Israelites back to God. He reminds them that they are to be witnesses to all the nations of the world: "I will make you a light to the nations / that my salvation may reach to the ends of the earth." This servant foreshadows Jesus' mission of witnessing to all people God's plan of salvation.

In greeting his community in Corinth, Paul identifies himself as an Apostle, sent to testify to the message of Jesus Christ throughout the world. Paul reminds the Corinthians that they are "called to be holy" and that their lives are transformed by the person and message of Jesus Christ.

We also are called to be holy and, through our Baptism, our lives are to witness to the person of Jesus Christ.

◆ How does the servant in the First Reading foreshadow the person of Jesus?

◆ How does each reading alert you to your call to be a witness to Christ?

◆ When has it been difficult for you to be a witness to Jesus and his message?

January 26, 2020

THIRD SUNDAY IN ORDINARY TIME

READING I Isaiah 8:23—9:3

First the LORD degraded the
land of Zebulun and the land
of Naphtali; but in the end he has
glorified the seaward road, the land
west of the Jordan, the District of
the Gentiles.

Anguish has taken wing,
dispelled is darkness:
for there is no gloom where
but now there was distress.
The people who walked
in darkness
have seen a great light;
upon those who dwelt in the land
of gloom
a light has shone.
You have brought them
abundant joy
and great rejoicing,
as they rejoice before you
as at the harvest,
as people make merry when
dividing spoils.
For the yoke that burdened them,
the pole on their shoulder,
and the rod of their taskmaster
you have smashed,
as on the day of Midian.

RESPONSORIAL PSALM
Psalm 27:1, 4, 13–14 (1a)

R. The Lord is my light
and my salvation.

The LORD is my light
and my salvation;
whom should I fear?
The LORD is my life's refuge;
of whom should I be afraid?   R.

One thing I ask of the LORD;
this I seek:
to dwell in the house of the LORD
all the days of my life,
that I may gaze on the loveliness
of the LORD,
and contemplate his temple.   R.

I believe that I shall see
the bounty of the LORD
in the land of the living.
Wait for the LORD with courage;
be stouthearted,
and wait for the Lord.   R.

READING II
1 Corinthians 1:10–13, 17

I urge you, brothers and sisters, in
the name of our Lord Jesus Christ,
that all of you agree in what you

say, and that there be no divisions among you, but that you be united in the same mind and in the same purpose. For it has been reported to me about you, my brothers and sisters, by Chloe's people, that there are rivalries among you. I mean that each of you is saying, "I belong to Paul," or "I belong to Apollos," or "I belong to Cephas," or "I belong to Christ." Is Christ divided? Was Paul crucified for you? Or were you baptized in the name of Paul? For Christ did not send me to baptize but to preach the gospel, and not with the wisdom of human eloquence, so that the cross of Christ might not be emptied of its meaning.

GOSPEL Matthew 4:12–23

<u>Shorter: Matthew 4:12–17</u>

When Jesus heard that John had been arrested, he withdrew to Galilee. He left Nazareth and went to live in Capernaum by the sea, in the region of Zebulun and Naphtali, that what had been said through Isaiah the prophet might be fulfilled:

«Land of Zebulun and
        land of Naphtali,
    the way to the sea,
        beyond the Jordan,
    Galilee of the Gentiles,
    the people who sit in darkness
        have seen a great light,
    on those dwelling in a land
        overshadowed by death
    light has arisen.»

From that time on, Jesus began to preach and say, "Repent, for the kingdom of heaven is at hand."

As he was walking by the Sea of Galilee, he saw two brothers, Simon who is called Peter, and his brother Andrew, casting a net into the sea; they were fishermen. He said to them, "Come after me, and I will make you fishers of men." At once they left their nets and followed him. He walked along from there and saw two other brothers, James, the son of Zebedee, and his brother John. They were in a boat, with their father Zebedee, mending their nets. He called them, and immediately they left their boat and their father and followed him.

He went around all of Galilee, teaching in their synagogues, proclaiming the gospel of the kingdom, and curing every disease and illness among the people.

Practice of Hope

Today's Gospel portrays a transition of roles and circumstances that are life changing. Jesus begins preaching in a new region and urges listeners to follow him, leaving their way of life. How do you listen to the urgings of the Spirit? Do you pray throughout the day for guidance, especially regarding significant decisions? Prayerful discernment is needed to determine how best to use the talents and gifts that God has given us. ◆ The US bishops provide resources on prayer and discernment at www.usccb.org /beliefs-and-teachings/vocations /discerning-women/prayer-and -discernment-resources.cfm. ◆ Learn more about Ignatian spirituality to discover how the Spiritual Exercises, the Examen, and other tools can lead you to make Christ-oriented decisions.

Information can be found at jesuits.org/spirituality. ◆ Consider how you can become more prayerful and deliberate about being led by Christ rather than the trappings of a profit-driven society.

Download more questions and activities for families, Christian initiation groups, and other adult groups at http://www.ltp.org/ahw.

Scripture Insights

The geographical references in today's readings from Isaiah and Matthew are highly significant. The lands of Zebulun and Naphtali were the territories of the northern-most tribes of Israel. In 721 BC, the Assyrians invaded these regions and destroyed the northern kingdom of Israel. Later, in 587 BC, the Babylonians destroyed the southern kingdom of Judah, sending the population into exile. Matthew uses these geographical allusions deliberately to teach that Jesus' public ministry inaugurates the restoration of God's Kingdom where it was first extinguished. Jesus brings God's light and salvation into these areas of desolation, fulfilling the prophet Isaiah's hope: "The people who walked in darkness / have seen a great light; / upon those who dwelt in the land of gloom / a light has shone."

Jesus enters Galilee with the challenge: "Repent, for the kingdom of heaven is at hand." Unambiguously, Jesus proclaims his intention of inaugurating God's Kingdom. He issues a call to enter a new relationship with God by undergoing a change of heart.

Jesus invites two sets of brothers, Peter and Andrew and James and John, to follow him. His call comes amid their daily occupations. They respond promptly by abandoning their ordinary activities and redirecting their lives to a new way of service to the Lord and the establishment of his Kingdom.

Jesus' call comes to each of us in our everyday activities. In Baptism, we are called to recognize that "the kingdom of heaven is at hand." In our daily lives, we experience Jesus' presence and witness that we are his followers.

◆ Why does Matthew refer to the "land of Zebulun and land of Naphtali"?

◆ When Jesus calls the four fishermen to follow him, they respond immediately. What is your impression of these disciples?

◆ Everyone has been called to follow the Lord. How do you experience Jesus' calling in your daily activities?

February 2, 2020

THE PRESENTATION OF THE LORD

READING I Malachi 3:1–4

Thus says the Lord GOD:
Lo, I am sending my messenger
    to prepare the way before me;
And suddenly there will come to
        the temple
    the LORD whom you seek,
And the messenger of the covenant
        whom you desire.
    Yes, he is coming, says the LORD
        of hosts.
But who will endure the day of
        his coming?
    And who can stand when
        he appears?
For he is like the refiner's fire,
    or like the fuller's lye.
He will sit refining and
        purifying silver,
    and he will purify the sons
        of Levi,
Refining them like gold or
        like silver
    that they may offer due sacrifice
        to the LORD.
Then the sacrifice of Judah
        and Jerusalem
    will please the LORD,
    as in the days of old, as in years
        gone by.

RESPONSORIAL PSALM
Psalm 24:7, 8, 9, 10 (8)

R. Who is this king of glory? It is
        the Lord!

Lift up, O gates, your lintels;
    reach up, you ancient portals,
    that the king of glory may
        come in! R.

Who is this king of glory?
    The LORD, strong and mighty,
    the LORD, mighty in battle. R.

Lift up, O gates, your lintels;
    reach up, you ancient portals,
    that the king of glory may
        come in! R.

Who is this king of glory?
    The LORD of hosts; he is the king
        of glory. R.

READING II
Hebrews 2:14–18

Since the children share in blood
and flesh, Jesus likewise shared in
them, that through death he might
destroy the one who has the power
of death, that is, the Devil, and
free those who through fear of
death had been subject to slavery

all their life. Surely he did not help angels but rather the descendants of Abraham; therefore, he had to become like his brothers and sisters in every way, that he might be a merciful and faithful high priest before God to expiate the sins of the people. Because he himself was tested through what he suffered, he is able to help those who are being tested.

GOSPEL Luke 2:22–32

<u>Longer: Luke 2:22–40</u>

When the days were completed for their purification according to the law of Moses, Mary and Joseph took Jesus up to Jerusalem to present him to the Lord, just as it is written in the law of the Lord, «Every male that opens the womb shall be consecrated to the Lord», and to offer the sacrifice of a «pair of turtledoves or two young pigeons», in accordance with the dictate in the law of the Lord.

Now there was a man in Jerusalem whose name was Simeon. This man was righteous and devout, awaiting the consolation of Israel, and the Holy Spirit was upon him.

It had been revealed to him by the Holy Spirit that he should not see death before he had seen the Christ of the Lord. He came in the Spirit into the temple; and when the parents brought in the child Jesus to perform the custom of the law in regard to him, he took him into his arms and blessed God, saying:

"Now, Master, you may let your
          servant go
     in peace, according to your word,
for my eyes have seen
          your salvation,
     which you prepared in the sight
          of all the peoples
a light for revelation to
          the Gentiles,
     and glory for your people Israel."

Practice of Faith

People come into our lives who may have prophetic purposes, but we may not realize it at the time. This happened to Mary and Joseph as they presented Jesus in the Temple in Jerusalem. There they found Simeon, a "righteous and devout" man, who proclaimed the significance of Jesus' birth and mission. God also placed there the prophetess Anna, who declared the same to all who would listen. ◆ As you contemplate the happenings of each day in prayer, consider how God has placed your loved ones, friends, and coworkers in your life as testimony of God's love for you. Remember the internal and external messages that you heard throughout the day that were filled with goodness, truth, and beauty, for these are from God. ◆ Just as Jesus was presented and recognized for his sacred mission even as an infant, think about your roles today and how you are blessed to fulfill them with grace. Pray to live with dignity, humility, and courage.

Scripture Insights

The Eastern Churches celebrate this feast as "The Meeting," a reference to the long-awaited meeting of the Messiah with his people, represented by Simeon and Anna in the Temple.

The Feast of the Presentation of the Lord is rooted within Old Testament traditions. The Book of Exodus stipulates that every firstborn Israelite male, human or animal, belongs to God. When Pharaoh would not allow the Israelites to leave Egypt and slavery, God saved the people. Consequently, the firstborn now belongs to God: "Consecrate to me every firstborn; whatever opens the womb among the Israelites, whether of human being or beast, belongs to me" (Exodus 13:2). The Israelites carried out this instruction by presenting their firstborn to God in the Temple: the firstborn of their animals was sacrificed to God while their firstborn sons were bought back by substituting animal sacrifices in their place to God.

Mary and Joseph fulfill this law by presenting Jesus in the Temple and making an offering. Through the power of the Holy Spirit, Simeon recognizes Jesus as the Messiah, prophesying that "my eyes have seen your salvation / which you prepared in the sight of all the peoples." He stresses that this revelation is for everyone: pagans and Jews alike. Jesus' life will involve rejection and suffering, while his mother will experience tremendous sorrow: "And you yourself a sword will pierce" (Luke 2:35). Simeon is ready to die, while Anna (who is in the account in the longer version of the Gospel reading) will live to spread the good news of the Messiah.

◆ Why do Jesus' parents offer in sacrifice "a pair of turtledoves or two young pigeons" in the Temple when Jesus is born?

◆ What is significant about the presence of Simeon and Anna in the Temple when Jesus is presented there?

◆ Today's Gospel reflects our experience of meeting Christ in Baptism and in the Eucharist. How is this meeting a key to your life?

February 9, 2020

FIFTH SUNDAY IN ORDINARY TIME

READING I Isaiah 58:7–10

Thus says the LORD:
Share your bread with the hungry,
shelter the oppressed and
the homeless;
clothe the naked when you
see them,
and do not turn your back on
your own.
Then your light shall break forth
like the dawn,
and your wound shall quickly
be healed;
your vindication shall go
before you,
and the glory of the LORD
shall be your rear guard.
Then you shall call, and the LORD
will answer;
you shall cry for help, and he
will say: Here I am!
If you remove from your midst
oppression, false accusation
and malicious speech;
if you bestow your bread on
the hungry
and satisfy the afflicted;
then light shall rise for you in
the darkness,
and the gloom shall become
for you like midday.

RESPONSORIAL PSALM
Psalm 112:4–5, 6–7, 8–9 (4a)

R. The just man is a light in
darkness to the upright.
or: Alleluia.

Light shines through the darkness
for the upright;
he is gracious and merciful
and just.
Well for the man who is gracious
and lends,
who conducts his affairs
with justice. R.

He shall never be moved;
the just one shall be in
everlasting remembrance.
An evil report he shall not fear;
his heart is firm, trusting in
the Lord. R.

His heart is steadfast; he shall
not fear.
Lavishly he gives to the poor;
his justice shall endure forever;
his horn shall be exalted
in glory. R.

READING II
1 Corinthians 2:1–5

When I came to you, brothers and sisters, proclaiming the mystery of God, I did not come with sublimity of words or of wisdom. For I resolved to know nothing while I was with you except Jesus Christ, and him crucified. I came to you in weakness and fear and much trembling, and my message and my proclamation were not with persuasive words of wisdom, but with a demonstration of Spirit and power, so that your faith might rest not on human wisdom but on the power of God.

GOSPEL Matthew 5:13–16

Jesus said to his disciples: "You are the salt of the earth. But if salt loses its taste, with what can it be seasoned? It is no longer good for anything but to be thrown out and trampled underfoot. You are the light of the world. A city set on a mountain cannot be hidden. Nor do they light a lamp and then put it under a bushel basket; it is set on a lampstand, where it gives light to all in the house. Just so, your light must shine before others, that they may see your good deeds and glorify your heavenly Father."

Practice of Charity

Jesus urges us to be salt and light for the world; we are to be flavorful and useful to lead others to salvation. Pope Francis describes our evangelizing call in <u>The Joy of the Gospel</u> to a hurting world that needs encouragement and hope: "The Church must be a place of mercy freely given, where everyone can feel welcomed, loved, forgiven and encouraged to live the good life of the Gospel" (114). ◆ Reflect on the pope's encouragement as we live and work amid people in need of the Good News. Journal about ways that you can be salt and light at home and in the workplace. ◆ Consider helping in a parish ministry such as the Christian initiation process or children's sacramental preparation. Talk with your parish coordinators of faith formation about specific roles in which you can assist. ◆ Light a candle during your prayer time this week to remind yourself of the role that Jesus asks us to fulfill.

<u>Download more questions and activities for families, Christian initiation groups, and other adult groups at http://www.ltp.org/ahw.</u>

Scripture Insights

In the verses preceding today's Gospel, Jesus begins the Sermon on the Mount with the Beatitudes. As Moses formed God's people by giving them the old law on Mount Sinai, so Jesus, the new Moses, forms a new people by giving them his new law.

"You are the salt of the earth," says Jesus. As salt permeates food and brings out its flavor, so as Christians we are called to permeate the world and transform its values. "You are the light of the world," continues Jesus. In the Gospel of John, Jesus proclaims: "I am the light of the world" (8:12). As Jesus' followers, we are called to let his light shine through our lives, drawing others to this light.

In the letter to the followers in Corinth, Paul shows how his life witnessed to the light of Christ. He tells the Corinthians that when he came to them, he did not preach using great rhetorical gifts. Instead, he allowed the Spirit to speak through him. Physically, Paul came "in weakness and fear and much trembling." The power of the Spirit, however, transformed his human inadequacies to communicate the message of the crucified and Risen Christ.

Paul argues that God's power, God's grace, works through the lives of believers by attracting many to follow and accept the Good News. The prophet Isaiah offered the same idea. The witness of an authentic life attracts people to the message. The prophet affirms this vision: "If you bestow your bread on the hungry / and satisfy the afflicted; / then your light shall rise for you in the darkness."

◆ How does Matthew's Gospel account present Jesus in the Sermon on the Mount as a new Moses?

◆ What does the Second Reading tell you about Paul? Do these words surprise you?

◆ How can you become a more effective light in the darkness?

February 16, 2020

SIXTH SUNDAY IN ORDINARY TIME

READING I Sirach 15:15–20

If you choose you can keep the
    commandments, they will
    save you;
  if you trust in God, you too
    shall live;
he has set before you fire
    and water;
  to whichever you choose,
    stretch forth your hand.
Before man are life and death,
    good and evil,
  whichever he chooses shall be
    given him.
Immense is the wisdom of
    the LORD;
  he is mighty in power, and
    all-seeing.
The eyes of God are on those who
    fear him;
  he understands man's
    every deed.
No one does he command to
    act unjustly,
  to none does he give license
    to sin.

RESPONSORIAL PSALM
Psalm 119:1–2, 4–5, 17–18, 33–34 (1b)

R. Blessed are they who follow the
    law of the Lord!

Blessed are they whose way
    is blameless,
  who walk in the law of the Lord.
Blessed are they who observe
    his decrees,
  who seek him with all their
    heart. R.

You have commanded that
    your precepts
  be diligently kept.
Oh, that I might be firm in the ways
  of keeping your statutes! R.

Be good to your servant,
    that I may live
  and keep your words.
Open my eyes, that I may consider
  the wonders of your law. R.

Instruct me, O Lord, in the way of
    your statutes,
  that I may exactly observe them.
Give me discernment, that I may
    observe your law
  and keep it with all my heart. R.

Reading II
1 Corinthians 2:6–10

Brothers and sisters:

We speak a wisdom to those who are mature, not a wisdom of this age, nor of the rulers of this age who are passing away. Rather, we speak God's wisdom, mysterious, hidden, which God predetermined before the ages for our glory, and which none of the rulers of this age knew; for, if they had known it, they would not have crucified the Lord of glory. But as it is written:

《What eye has not seen, and ear
    has not heard,
  and what has not entered the
    human heart,
  what God has prepared for
    those who love him,》
this God has revealed to us through the Spirit.

For the Spirit scrutinizes everything, even the depths of God.

Gospel Matthew 5:17–37
Shorter: Matthew 5:20–22a,
27–28, 33–34a, 37

Jesus said to his disciples:

"Do not think that I have come to abolish the law or the prophets. I have come not to abolish but to fulfill. Amen, I say to you, until heaven and earth pass away, not the smallest letter or the smallest part of a letter will pass from the law, until all things have taken place. Therefore, whoever breaks one of the least of these commandments and teaches others to do so will be called least in the kingdom of heaven. But whoever obeys and teaches these commandments will be called greatest in the kingdom of heaven. I tell you, unless your righteousness surpasses that of the scribes and Pharisees, you will not enter the kingdom of heaven.

"You have heard that it was said to your ancestors, 《You shall not kill; and whoever kills will be liable to judgment.》 But I say to you, whoever is angry with his brother will be liable to judgment; and whoever says to his brother, 'Raqa,' will be answerable to the Sanhedrin; and whoever says, 'You fool,' will be liable to fiery Gehenna. Therefore, if you bring your gift to the altar, and there recall that your brother has anything against you, leave your gift there at the altar, go first and be reconciled with your brother, and then come and offer your gift. Settle with your opponent quickly while on the way to court. Otherwise your opponent will hand you over to the judge, and the judge will hand you over to the guard, and you will be thrown into prison. Amen, I say to you, you will not be released until you have paid the last penny.

"You have heard that it was said, «You shall not commit adultery.» But I say to you, everyone who looks at a woman with lust has already committed adultery with her in his heart. If your right eye causes you to sin, tear it out and throw it away. It is better for you to lose one of your members than to have your whole body thrown into Gehenna. And if your right hand causes you to sin, cut it off and throw it away. It is better for you to lose one of your members than to have your whole body go into Gehenna.

"It was also said, «Whoever divorces his wife must give her a bill of divorce.» But I say to you, whoever divorces his wife—unless the marriage is unlawful—causes her to commit adultery, and whoever marries a divorced woman commits adultery.

"Again you have heard that it was said to your ancestors, «Do not take a false oath, but make good to the Lord all that you vow.» But I say to you, do not swear at all; not by heaven, for it is God's throne; nor by the earth, for it is his footstool; nor by Jerusalem, for it is the city of the great King. Do not swear by your head, for you cannot make a single hair white or black. Let your 'Yes' mean 'Yes,' and your 'No' mean 'No.' Anything more is from the evil one."

Practice of Hope

The wisdom of following God's laws can bring us peace. ◆ Reflect on the meaning of the following statement that the Constitution on the Church draws on from the Letter to Diognetus: "what the soul is in the body, let Christians be in the world" (38). ◆ Consider journaling about how you are called to offer your skills, talents, and fruits of the Spirit for the common good. ◆ Talk with a neighbor or friend who is struggling.

Scripture Insights

The reading from the Book of Sirach sets the scene for all of today's readings. Sirach offers practical wisdom on how to live according to God's instructions. The writer reminds us that God has gifted us with the power to choose freely: "Before man are life and death, good and evil, whichever he chooses shall be given him."

Paul's letter to the Corinthians shows what the call to choose life means. Embrace God's love by living according to God's wisdom, a plan hidden until now, a plan of love for the salvation of all humanity. Jesus Christ, the crucified "Lord of glory," accomplished the Father's plan through his death and Resurrection.

During the Gospel reading, Jesus continues the Sermon on the Mount as he illustrates how his message "fulfills the law and the prophets." He selects the fifth, sixth, and eighth commandments to indicate the heart of his new way of life: "You have heard how it was said, You shall not kill. . . . But I say to you, whoever is angry with his brother will be liable to judgment." Jesus demonstrates that murder stems from within the human heart. The out-of-control emotion of anger within us, if left unchecked, leads to murder. To choose life in Christ means to pay attention not only to one's actions but, more important, to their roots within our inner being, to the emotions within us. While this is true of the fifth commandment, it also applies to all other commandments. Life in Christ implies that our whole being needs transformation, starting within our very depths.

◆ How does Jesus advise us to avoid murder, adultery, and making false statements?

◆ What is Jesus' main concern when he says, "do not swear at all"?

◆ How do you try to live according to the challenge to choose life?

February 23, 2020

SEVENTH SUNDAY IN ORDINARY TIME

READING I
Leviticus 19:1–2, 17–18

The LORD said to Moses,
  "Speak to the whole Israelite
        community and tell them:
  Be holy, for I, the Lord, your
        God, am holy.

"You shall not bear hatred for
        your brother or sister in
        your heart.
Though you may have to reprove
        your fellow citizen,
  do not incur sin because of him.
Take no revenge and cherish no
        grudge against any of
        your people.
You shall love your neighbor
        as yourself.
I am the LORD."

RESPONSORIAL PSALM
Psalm 103:1–2, 3–4, 8, 10, 12–13 (8a)

R. The Lord is kind and merciful.

Bless the LORD, O my soul;
  and all my being, bless his
        holy name.

Bless the LORD, O my soul,
  and forget not all his
        benefits. R.

He pardons all your iniquities,
  heals all your ills.
He redeems your life
        from destruction,
  crowns you with kindness
        and compassion. R.

Merciful and gracious is the LORD,
  slow to anger and abounding
        in kindness.
Not according to our sins does he
        deal with us,
  nor does he requite us according
        to our crimes. R.

As far as the east is from the west,
  so far has he put our
        transgressions from us.
As a father has compassion on
        his children,
  so the Lord has compassion on
        those who fear him. R.

READING II
1 Corinthians 3:16–23

Brothers and sisters:

Do you not know that you are the temple of God, and that the Spirit of God dwells in you? If anyone destroys God's temple, God will destroy that person; for the temple of God, which you are, is holy.

Let no one deceive himself. If any one among you considers himself wise in this age, let him become a fool, so as to become wise. For the wisdom of this world is foolishness in the eyes of God, for it is written:

«God catches the wise in their
       own ruses,»
and again:

«The Lord knows the thoughts
       of the wise,
    that they are vain.»
So let no one boast about human beings, for everything belongs to you, Paul or Apollos or Cephas, or the world or life or death, or the present or the future: all belong to you, and you to Christ, and Christ to God.

GOSPEL Matthew 5:38–48

Jesus said to his disciples:

"You have heard that it was said, «An eye for an eye and a tooth for a tooth.» But I say to you, offer no resistance to one who is evil. When someone strikes you on your right cheek, turn the other one as well. If anyone wants to go to law with you over your tunic, hand over your cloak as well. Should anyone press you into service for one mile, go for two miles. Give to the one who asks of you, and do not turn your back on one who wants to borrow.

"You have heard that it was said, «You shall love your neighbor and hate your enemy.» But I say to you, love your enemies and pray for those who persecute you, that you may be children of your heavenly Father, for he makes his sun rise on the bad and the good, and causes rain to fall on the just and the unjust. For if you love those who love you, what recompense will you have? Do not the tax collectors do the same? And if you greet your brothers only, what is unusual about that? Do not the pagans do the same? So be perfect, just as your heavenly Father is perfect."

Practice of Faith

Dealing with difficult people at home or work is one of life's biggest challenges. Scores of books and websites are devoted to this issue; however, the simple commandments found in the First Reading and Gospel are the basis for healthy living; we are asked to love our enemies and pray for those who bother us. ◆ During your next prayer time, consider praying specifically for those in your life who are troubling to you or whose demeanor or activities cause you anxiety. Ask for patience and guidance when you are with them next. ◆ The Golden Rule, based on Matthew 7:12, has been translated and relayed in many languages and faith traditions for centuries. Consider posting one of these versions at home or your work location to encourage discussion about this foundational belief of how people should treat one another. To find a poster, simply search on the Internet for several versions worth posting.

Download more questions and activities for families, Christian initiation groups, and other adult groups at http://www.ltp.org/ahw.

Scripture Insights

"Be holy, for I, the LORD, your God, am holy." These words challenge us to imitate God in our actions. The word "holy" embraces the concept of wholeness, as opposed to being divided. Leviticus illustrates this meaning: "You shall not bear hatred for your brother in your heart." Instead, follow the command: "Love your neighbor as yourself."

In Matthew's account of the Gospel, Jesus clearly builds on this passage from Leviticus. "Be perfect, just as your heavenly Father is perfect." To "be perfect" is the same as to "be holy." Such holiness would mean that the individual is undivided in their interior and exterior lives. Jesus offers three succinct scenarios of humiliation that reflect Mediterranean culture: being struck on the right cheek by a backhanded slap is an insult; being sued in court where one is humiliated by losing property or dignity; and being forced to carry something by Roman soldiers (see Simon of Cyrene carrying Jesus' Cross [Matthew 27:32]). All of these cultural situations required action to defend one's honor. Instead, Jesus advises a different approach: Find another way to respond that avoids violence. Rise above these insults. Jesus is abrogating a basic law of the Middle East, enduring to the present, known as the Law of Talion, the law of retaliation: "An eye for an eye and a tooth for a tooth." Jesus invites his followers to find a third way that rises above humiliation and avoids retaliating in the same way. Use your imagination to discover how best to overcome the insult in ways that rise above it and beyond violence.

◆ How is the word "holy" explained by the concept of "wholeness" in each of today's readings?

◆ Explain how the three scenarios described in today's Gospel are a rejection of the Law of Talion.

◆ In what way do you live Paul's teaching that "you are the temple of God"?

Lent

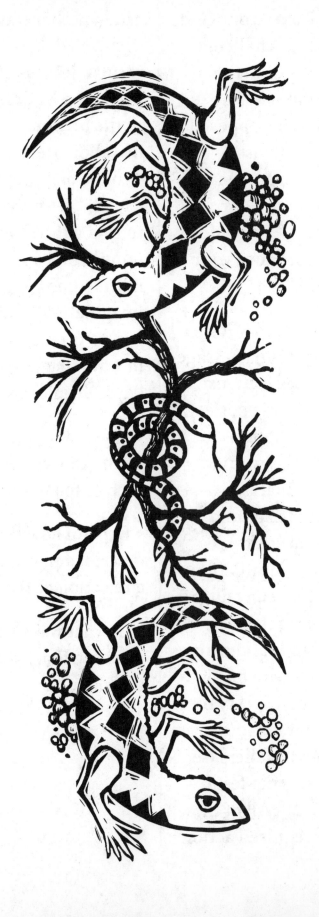

Prayer before Reading the Word

To Abraham and Sarah you
        called out,
O God of mystery,
inviting them to journey to a land
        of promise.
To us also you call out,
inviting us to pass through Lent to
        Easter's glory.
Open our ears, therefore, to listen
        to Jesus,
the Beloved Son in whom you are
        well pleased,
so that, embracing the mystery of
        the Cross,
we may come to the holy
        mountain, to immortal life,
and a share in Christ's
        transfigured glory.

We ask this through our Lord
        Jesus Christ, your Son,
who lives and reigns with you
in the unity of the Holy Spirit,
one God for ever and ever. Amen.

Prayer after Reading the Word

O God, the living fountain of
        new life,
to the human race, parched
        with thirst,
you offer the living water of grace
that springs up from the rock,
our Savior Jesus Christ.
Grant your people the gift of
        the Spirit,
that we may learn to profess
        our faith
with courage and conviction
and announce with joy
the wonders of your saving love.

We ask this through our Lord
        Jesus Christ, your Son,
who lives and reigns with you
in the unity of the Holy Spirit,
one God for ever and ever. Amen.

Weekday Readings

February 26: Ash Wednesday
Joel 2:12–18;
2 Corinthians 5:20—6:2;
Matthew 6:1–6, 16–18
February 27: Deuteronomy
30:15–20; Luke 9:22–25
February 28: Isaiah 58:1–9a;
Matthew 9:14–15
February 29: Isaiah 58:9b–14;
Luke 5:27–32

March 2: Leviticus 19:1–2, 11–18;
Matthew 25:31–46
March 3: Isaiah 55:10–11;
Matthew 6:7–15
March 4: Jonah 3:1–10;
Luke 11:29–32
March 5: Esther C:12, 14–16,
23–25; Matthew 7:7–12
March 6: Ezekiel 18:21–28;
Matthew 5:20–26
March 7: Deuteronomy 26:16–19;
Matthew 5:43–48

March 9: Daniel 9:4b–10;
Luke 6:36–38
March 10: Isaiah 1:10, 16–20;
Matthew 23:1–12
March 11: Jeremiah 18:18–20;
Matthew 20:17–28
March 12: Jeremiah 17:5–10;
Luke 16:19–31
March 13: Genesis 37:3–4, 12–13a,
17b–28a;
Matthew 21:33–43, 45–46
March 14: Micah 7:14–15, 18–20;
Luke 15:1–3, 11–32

March 16: 2 Kings 5:1–15b;
Luke 4:24–30
March 17: Daniel 3:25, 34–43;
Matthew 18:21–35
March 18: Deuteronomy 4:1, 5–9;
Matthew 5:17–19
March 19: Solemnity of St. Joseph,
Spouse of the Blessed
Virgin Mary
2 Samuel 7:4–5a, 12–14a, 16;
Romans 4:13, 16–18, 22;
Matthew 1:16, 18–21, 24a or
Luke 2:41–51a
March 20: Hosea 14:2–10;
Mark 12:28–34
March 21: Hosea 6:1–6;
Luke 18:9–14

March 23: Isaiah 65:17–21;
    John 4:43–54
March 24: Ezekiel 47:1–9, 12;
    John 5:1–16
March 25: Solemnity of the
    Annunciation of the Lord
    Isaiah 7:10–14; 8:10;
    Hebrews 10:4–10;
    Luke 1:26–38
March 26: Exodus 32:7–14;
    John 5:31–47
March 27: Wisdom 2:1a, 12–22;
    John 7:1–2, 10, 25–30
March 28: Jeremiah 11:18–20;
    John 7:40–53

March 30: Daniel 13:1–9, 15–17,
    19–30, 33–62
    or 13:41c–62; John 8:1–11
March 31: Numbers 21:4–9;
    John 8:21–30
April 1: Daniel 3:14–20, 91–92, 95;
    John 8:31–42
April 2: Genesis 17:3–9;
    John 8:51–59
April 3: Jeremiah 20:10–13;
    John 10:31–42
April 4: Ezekiel 37:21–28;
    John 11:45–56

April 6: Isaiah 42:1–7;
    John 12:1–11
April 7: Isaiah 49:1–6;
    John 13:21–33, 36–38
April 8: Isaiah 50:4–9a;
    Matthew 26:14–25

March 1, 2020

FIRST SUNDAY OF LENT

READING I
Genesis 2:7–9; 3:1–7

The LORD God formed man out of the clay of the ground and blew into his nostrils the breath of life, and so man became a living being.

Then the LORD God planted a garden in Eden, in the east, and placed there the man whom he had formed. Out of the ground the LORD God made various trees grow that were delightful to look at and good for food, with the tree of life in the middle of the garden and the tree of the knowledge of good and evil.

Now the serpent was the most cunning of all the animals that the LORD God had made. The serpent asked the woman, "Did God really tell you not to eat from any of the trees in the garden?" The woman answered the serpent: "We may eat of the fruit of the trees in the garden; it is only about the fruit of the tree in the middle of the garden that God said, 'You shall not eat it or even touch it, lest you die.'"

But the serpent said to the woman: "You certainly will not die! No, God knows well that the moment you eat of it your eyes will be opened and you will be like gods who know what is good and what is evil." The woman saw that the tree was good for food, pleasing to the eyes, and desirable for gaining wisdom. So she took some of its fruit and ate it; and she also gave some to her husband, who was with her, and he ate it. Then the eyes of both of them were opened, and they realized that they were naked; so they sewed fig leaves together and made loincloths for themselves.

RESPONSORIAL PSALM
Psalm 51:3–4, 5–6, 12–13, 17 (see 3a)

R. Be merciful, O Lord,
　　　　for we have sinned.

Have mercy on me, O God,
　　　　in your goodness;
　in the greatness of
　　　　your compassion
　　　　wipe out my offense.
Thoroughly wash me from my guilt
　and of my sin cleanse me.　R.

For I acknowledge my offense,
 and my sin is before me always:
"Against you only have I sinned,
 and done what is evil
  in your sight." R.

A clean heart create for me, O God,
 and a steadfast spirit renew
  within me.
Cast me not out from
  your presence,
and your Holy Spirit take not
  from me. R.

Give me back the joy of
  your salvation,
 and a willing spirit sustain
  in me.
O Lord, open my lips,
 and my mouth shall proclaim
  your praise. R.

READING II
Romans 5:12, 17–19

Longer: Romans 5:12–19

Brothers and sisters: Through one man sin entered the world, and through sin, death, and thus death came to all men, inasmuch as all sinned.

For if, by the transgression of the one, death came to reign through that one, how much more will those who receive the abundance of grace and of the gift of justification come to reign in life through the one Jesus Christ. In conclusion, just as through one transgression condemnation came upon all, so, through one righteous act, acquittal and life came to all. For just as through the disobedience of the one man the many were made sinners, so, through the obedience of the one, the many will be made righteous.

GOSPEL Matthew 4:1–11

At that time Jesus was led by the Spirit into the desert to be tempted by the devil. He fasted for forty days and forty nights, and afterwards he was hungry. The tempter approached and said to him, "If you are the Son of God, command that these stones become loaves of bread." He said in reply, "It is written:

«One does not live on
  bread alone,
 but on every word that
  comes forth
 from the mouth of God.»

Then the devil took him to the holy city, and made him stand on the parapet of the temple, and said to him, "If you are the Son of God, throw yourself down. For it is written:

≪He will command his angels
    concerning you
  and with their hands
    they will support you,
lest you dash your foot against
    a stone."≫

Jesus answered him, "Again it is written,

≪You shall not put the Lord,
    your God, to the test."≫

Then the devil took him up to a very high mountain, and showed him all the kingdoms of the world in their magnificence, and he said to him, "All these I shall give to you, if you will prostrate yourself and worship me." At this, Jesus said to him, "Get away, Satan! It is written:

≪The Lord, your God,
    shall you worship
  and him alone shall
    you serve."≫

Then the devil left him and, behold, angels came and ministered to him.

Practice of Faith

For centuries, men and women have retreated to places of isolation to experience deeper communication with God. We are called to practice self-discipline, to fast, and to give to those in need to become more enlightened about our failings and to heighten our sensitivities to those who hunger, need shelter, or are oppressed by violence or unjust political systems. While it's true that we are always tempted to sin, it is during Lent that we journey with Jesus to the desert spiritually to prepare for our ultimate mission and purpose. ◆ Find the Catechism of the Catholic Church online and read about the different expressions of prayer: vocal, meditation, and contemplative (2700–2724). ◆ During this Lenten season, choose a type of prayer that you haven't yet experienced fruitfully to learn more about it. Perhaps you will want to consider lectio divina or meditation. The bishops' website offers resources and ideas: www.usccb .org/prayer -and-worship/prayers-and-devotions /index.cfm.

Scripture Insights

The season of Lent offers a time to grow in the life of Christ. The reading from the Book of Genesis reminds us of our solidarity with all humanity: we are born into a situation of alienation from God. In the beginning, God created humanity as good. God's will was not forced upon us. Instead, God gave us the gift of free will. In this narrative of our first parents, the gift of freedom was used to reject God's will. Within our being, we too experience the same desire to do things our way, relying on ourselves and turning away from God's grace and guidance.

In our reading from the Letter to the Romans, Paul celebrates Jesus Christ's victory over sin and death through his Resurrection. Christ's grace empowers us to overcome this alienation from God and restores us to the relationship God intended from the beginning: "For just as through the disobedience of the one man [Adam], the many were made sinners, so, through the obedience of the one [Jesus Christ], the many will be made righteous" (Romans 5:19).

Today's Gospel contains an account of Jesus' temptations in the desert. Like the people of Israel who spent forty years in the desert, Jesus, the new Israel, spends forty days in the desert where he is also tempted. Unlike the people of Israel, Jesus remains faithful to his Father's will and mission: "For we do not have a high priest who is unable to sympathize with our weaknesses, but one who has similarly been tested in every way, yet without sin" (Hebrews 4:15).

◆ How does the story of Adam and Eve capture the human tendency to use the gift of freedom to turn away from God?

◆ Examine each of the three temptations and reflect on how Jesus' scriptural quotations explain their meaning.

◆ Have you experienced times in your life when God's grace enabled you to overcome temptation?

103

March 8, 2020

SECOND SUNDAY OF LENT

READING I Genesis 12:1–4a

The LORD said to Abram: "Go forth from the land of your kinsfolk and from your father's house to a land that I will show you.

"I will make of you
a great nation,
and I will bless you;
I will make your name great,
so that you will be a blessing.
I will bless those who bless you
and curse those who
curse you.
All the communities of
the earth
shall find blessing in you."

Abram went as the LORD directed him.

RESPONSORIAL PSALM
Psalm 33:4–5, 18–19, 20, 22 (22)

R. Lord, let your mercy be on us,
as we place our trust in you.

Upright is the word of the LORD,
and all his works are
trustworthy.
He loves justice and right;
of the kindness of the LORD
the earth is full.   R.

See, the eyes of the LORD are upon
those who fear him,
upon those who hope for
his kindness,
to deliver them from death
and preserve them in spite
of famine.   R.

Our soul waits for the LORD,
who is our help and our shield.
May your kindness, O LORD,
be upon us
who have put our hope
in you.   R.

READING II
2 Timothy 1:8b–10

Beloved: Bear your share of hardship for the gospel with the strength that comes from God.

He saved us and called us to a holy life, not according to our works but according to his own design and the grace bestowed on us in Christ Jesus before time began, but now made manifest through the appearance of our savior Christ Jesus, who destroyed death and brought life and immortality to light through the gospel.

GOSPEL Matthew 17:1–9

Jesus took Peter, James, and John his brother, and led them up a high mountain by themselves. And he was transfigured before them; his face shone like the sun and his clothes became white as light. And behold, Moses and Elijah appeared to them, conversing with him. Then Peter said to Jesus in reply, "Lord, it is good that we are here. If you wish, I will make three tents here, one for you, one for Moses, and one for Elijah." While he was still speaking, behold, a bright cloud cast a shadow over them, then from the cloud came a voice that said, "This is my beloved Son, with whom I am well pleased; listen to him." When the disciples heard this, they fell prostrate and were very much afraid. But Jesus came and touched them, saying, "Rise, and do not be afraid." And when the disciples raised their eyes, they saw no one else but Jesus alone.

As they were coming down from the mountain, Jesus charged them, "Do not tell the vision to anyone until the Son of Man has been raised from the dead."

Practice of Faith

When was the last time that you felt awestruck? This feeling may occur with the realization of something after the fact (perhaps years later) and we thank God for the outcome. Some people refer to such events as a "God moment." Still, these events pale in comparison to the witness of Peter, James, and John to the Transfiguration of Jesus. In today's world, Jesus touches us, just as he touched them. The awesome presence of God is everywhere.

◆ In your prayer time, remember the occasions in your life when you felt God was with you, possibly saving or consoling you through the actions of others. Acknowledge God's daily divine presence in your life. ◆ If you don't already have this in your home, make a special place for prayer. Perhaps you have an area where you can place a candle, crucifix, pictures, reading material, or anything that invites you to spend more quality time with our Creator.

Download more questions and activities for families, Christian initiation groups, and other adult groups at http://www.ltp.org/ahw.

Scripture Insights

Our readings today fortify our Lenten journey with the accounts of two journeys. In the First Reading, God commands Abram to set out on a journey to a "land that I will show you." Trusting in God, Abram leaves behind his family, friends, and homeland.

The Gospel account of Jesus' Transfiguration occurs in the context of Jesus' journey to Jerusalem, the place of his suffering and death. Jesus had revealed to his disciples that he was the Messiah who would bring spiritual liberation through suffering, death, and resurrection. Now Jesus takes his three closest disciples, Peter, James, and John, up a mountain where he appears in his risen glory, conversing with Moses and Elijah, who signify the Law and the prophets. This vision points symbolically to Jesus as the fulfilment of the entire Old Testament.

A further symbol emerges when "a bright cloud casts a shadow over them." The cloud symbolizes God's presence, and the Father identifies Jesus as he did at Jesus' baptism: "This is my beloved Son, with whom I am well pleased; listen to him." These disciples are privileged witnesses to Jesus' glory as God's Son who fulfills the plan as foretold in the Old Testament. This vision fortifies the Apostles for what lies ahead. As they descend the mountain, Jesus tells Peter, James, and John a second time that he is destined to suffer, die, and be raised from the dead. This vision of the transfigured Jesus offers them strength.

This experience of the disciples offers us courage as well: "Listen to him." The message is clear: the Risen Christ accompanies us through life's journey, where our sufferings and death will culminate in sharing in the resurrected life.

◆ How does Jesus' Transfiguration reveal his identity to his disciples?

◆ Give some examples from the Old Testament where God's presence is symbolized by means of a cloud.

◆ "Listen to him." How does God speak to you today on your Lenten journey?

March 15, 2020

THIRD SUNDAY OF LENT

READING I Exodus 17:3-7

In those days, in their thirst for water, the people grumbled against Moses, saying, "Why did you ever make us leave Egypt? Was it just to have us die here of thirst with our children and our livestock?" So Moses cried out to the LORD, "What shall I do with this people? A little more and they will stone me!" The LORD answered Moses, "Go over there in front of the people, along with some of the elders of Israel, holding in your hand, as you go, the staff with which you struck the river. I will be standing there in front of you on the rock in Horeb. Strike the rock, and the water will flow from it for the people to drink." This Moses did, in the presence of the elders of Israel. The place was called Massah and Meribah, because the Israelites quarreled there and tested the LORD, saying, "Is the LORD in our midst or not?"

RESPONSORIAL PSALM
Psalm 95:1-2, 6-7, 8-9 (8)

R. If today you hear his voice,
        harden not your hearts.

Come, let us sing joyfully to
        the LORD;
    let us acclaim the Rock of
        our salvation.
Let us come into his presence
        with thanksgiving;
    let us joyfully sing psalms
        to him.   R.

Come, let us bow down in worship;
    let us kneel before the LORD
        who made us.
For he is our God,
    and we are the people
        he shepherds,
        the flock he guides.   R.

Oh, that today you would hear
        his voice:
    "Harden not your hearts
        as at Meribah,
    as in the day of Massah
        in the desert,
Where your fathers tempted me;
    they tested me though they had
        seen my works."   R.

READING II
Romans 5:1–2, 5–8

Brothers and sisters: Since we have been justified by faith, we have peace with God through our Lord Jesus Christ, through whom we have gained access by faith to this grace in which we stand, and we boast in hope of the glory of God.

And hope does not disappoint, because the love of God has been poured out into our hearts through the Holy Spirit who has been given to us. For Christ, while we were still helpless, died at the appointed time for the ungodly. Indeed, only with difficulty does one die for a just person, though perhaps for a good person one might even find courage to die. But God proves his love for us in that while we were still sinners Christ died for us.

GOSPEL John 4:5–15, 19b–26, 39a, 40–42

Longer: John 4:5–42

Jesus came to a town of Samaria called Sychar, near the plot of land that Jacob had given to his son Joseph. Jacob's well was there. Jesus, tired from his journey, sat down there at the well. It was about noon.

A woman of Samaria came to draw water. Jesus said to her, "Give me a drink." His disciples had gone into the town to buy food. The Samaritan woman said to him, "How can you, a Jew, ask me, a Samaritan woman, for a drink?"— For Jews use nothing in common with Samaritans. — Jesus answered and said to her, "If you knew the gift of God and who is saying to you, 'Give me a drink,' you would have asked him and he would have given you living water." The woman said to him, "Sir, you do not even have a bucket and the cistern is deep; where then can you get this living water? Are you greater than our father Jacob, who gave us this cistern and drank from it himself with his children and his flocks?" Jesus answered and said to her, "Everyone who drinks this water will be thirsty again; but whoever drinks the water I shall give will never thirst; the water I shall give will become in him a spring of water welling up to eternal life." The woman said to him, "Sir, give me this water, so that I may not be thirsty or have to keep coming here to draw water.

"I can see that you are a prophet. Our ancestors worshiped on this mountain; but you people say that the place to worship is in Jerusalem." Jesus said to her, "Believe me, woman, the hour is coming when you will worship the Father neither on this mountain nor in Jerusalem. You people worship what you do not understand; we worship what we understand, because salvation is from the Jews. But the hour is coming, and is now here, when true worshipers will worship the Father in Spirit and truth; and indeed the Father seeks such people to worship him. God is Spirit, and those who worship him must worship in Spirit and truth." The woman said to him, "I know that the Messiah is coming, the one called the Christ; when he comes, he will tell us everything." Jesus said to her, "I am he, the one who is speaking with you."

Many of the Samaritans of that town began to believe in him. When the Samaritans came to him, they invited him to stay with them; and he stayed there two days. Many more began to believe in him because of his word, and they said to the woman, "We no longer believe because of your word; for we have heard for ourselves, and we know that this is truly the savior of the world."

Practice of Charity

More than 844 million people do not have access to safe water, according to the World Health Organization. Limited access to safe water causes disease, lack of sanitation, and political turmoil. Many women and children are forced to abandon their daily activities and education to transport water to their homes. Several groups, such as Catholic Relief Services, have developed innovative procedures and incentives to assist communities as they drill for water and install piping and sanitation systems.
◆ Explore Catholic Relief Services' work for clean water (www.crs.org /our-work-overseas/program-areas /water-and-sanitation) and search for other sites that seek to provide safe drinking water. ◆ Become more aware of the amount of water that your family uses daily.

Scripture Insights

Today's readings illustrate God's transforming power at work. Jesus breaks numerous cultural taboos by interacting with a woman, a Samaritan, and a person who has had five husbands and now lives with someone not her husband. Despite all of this, Jesus requests a drink of water.

The conversation between Jesus and the woman is revealing. Reaching out, Jesus asks for something ordinary. Given the religious boundaries separating them, the woman tries to draw Jesus into dialogue. Jesus simply replies by revealing himself as the one who has power to grant living water that will become a spring inside of her "welling up to eternal life."

Refusing to be drawn into another dispute about the place of worship (Jerusalem or Mount Gerizim), Jesus reveals that true worship of God is "in Spirit and truth." He makes himself known to her as the Messiah. She becomes a missionary to her people, and many come to Jesus.

John describes a drama of faith. Jesus takes the initiative. He speaks and gradually draws the woman closer to himself. He does not condemn her irregular way of life. He accepts her as she is. He overcomes her objections indirectly by deepening his engagement with her. At the same time, he leads her deeper into the truth. Faith is a personal encounter with Christ, and John shows how powerful this encounter is and what happens when one is receptive to Jesus.

◆ From this Gospel reading, what major differences do you discover about the relationships between Jews and Samaritans?

◆ The First Reading and the Gospel reading both speak about the gift of water. How does this gift transform the lives of the Israelites and the Samaritan woman?

◆ What important insights do you take from our readings today that you would like to share with your family or friends?

FOURTH SUNDAY OF LENT

READING I
1 Samuel 16:1b, 6-7, 10-13a

The LORD said to Samuel: "Fill your horn with oil, and be on your way. I am sending you to Jesse of Bethlehem, for I have chosen my king from among his sons."

As Jesse and his sons came to the sacrifice, Samuel looked at Eliab and thought, "Surely the LORD's anointed is here before him." But the LORD said to Samuel: "Do not judge from his appearance or from his lofty stature, because I have rejected him. Not as man sees does God see, because man sees the appearance but the LORD looks into the heart." In the same way Jesse presented seven sons before Samuel, but Samuel said to Jesse, "The LORD has not chosen any one of these." Then Samuel asked Jesse, "Are these all the sons you have?" Jesse replied, "There is still the youngest, who is tending the sheep." Samuel said to Jesse, "Send for him; we will not begin the sacrificial banquet until he arrives here." Jesse sent and had the young man brought to them. He was ruddy, a youth handsome to behold and making a splendid appearance. The LORD said, "There—anoint him, for this is the one!" Then Samuel, with the horn of oil in hand, anointed David in the presence of his brothers; and from that day on, the spirit of the LORD rushed upon David.

RESPONSORIAL PSALM
Psalm 23:1-3a, 3b-4, 5, 6 (1)

R. The Lord is my shepherd; there is nothing I shall want.

The LORD is my shepherd;
    I shall not want.
  In verdant pastures
    he gives me repose;
beside restful waters he leads me;
  he refreshes my soul.   R.

He guides me in right paths
    for his name's sake.
Even though I walk in the
        dark valley
  I fear no evil; for you are at
        my side
with your rod and your staff
    that give me courage.   R.

You spread the table before me
   in the sight of my foes;
you anoint my head with oil;
   my cup overflows.   R.

Only goodness and kindness
         follow me
   all the days of my life;
and I shall dwell in
         the house of the LORD
   for years to come.   R.

READING II
Ephesians 5:8–14

Brothers and sisters: You were
once darkness, but now you are
light in the Lord. Live as children
of light, for light produces every
kind of goodness and righteousness and truth. Try to learn what
is pleasing to the Lord. Take no
part in the fruitless works of
darkness; rather expose them, for
it is shameful even to mention the
things done by them in secret; but
everything exposed by the light
becomes visible, for everything
that becomes visible is light.
Therefore, it says:

   "Awake, O sleeper,
   and arise from the dead,
   and Christ will give you light."

GOSPEL
John 9:1, 6–9, 13–17, 34–38

Longer: John 9:1–41

As Jesus passed by he saw a man
blind from birth. He spat on the
ground and made clay with the
saliva, and smeared the clay on his
eyes, and said to him, "Go wash in
the Pool of Siloam"—which means
Sent—. So he went and washed,
and came back able to see.

His neighbors and those who had
seen him earlier as a beggar said,
"Isn't this the one who used to
sit and beg?" Some said, "It is," but
others said, "No, he just looks like
him." He said, "I am."

They brought the one who was
once blind to the Pharisees. Now
Jesus had made clay and opened
his eyes on a sabbath. So then
the Pharisees also asked him how
he was able to see. He said to them,
"He put clay on my eyes, and
I washed, and now I can see." So
some of the Pharisees said, "This
man is not from God, because he
does not keep the sabbath." But
others said, "How can a sinful
man do such signs?" And there
was a division among them. So

they said to the blind man again, "What do you have to say about him, since he opened your eyes?" He said, "He is a prophet."

They answered and said to him, "You were born totally in sin, and are you trying to teach us?" Then they threw him out.

When Jesus heard that they had thrown him out, he found him and said, "Do you believe in the Son of Man?" He answered and said, "Who is he, sir, that I may believe in him?" Jesus said to him, "You have seen him, and the one speaking with you is he." He said, "I do believe, Lord," and he worshiped him.

Practice of Hope

Today's Gospel speaks about blindness in all its forms—physical, emotional, and spiritual. Jesus healed a man, blind from birth, who went to the Pharisees but they denied the miracle had happened. Many of us wear blinders as we go through our day because we fail to recognize how God works through people and circumstances. We may neglect the goodness that surrounds us because it doesn't fit within parameters of science or reason. ◆ Journal about ways in which you might be blind to your value as God's child. In this season of Lent, say prayers of thanksgiving for the people and opportunities that have made you more spiritually alive and attentive to others. ◆ Treasure your vision and make an appointment with an optometrist if it has been a while since your last visit. Update your prescription to help you fully appreciate all of God's creation.

Download more questions and activities for families, Christian initiation groups, and other adult groups at http://www.ltp.org/ahw.

Scripture Insights

Our God is a God of surprises. This is evident in our First Reading, where God directs the anointing of David. Samuel, the prophet, goes to Jesse of Bethlehem to anoint one of his eight sons as king. Although Samuel is impressed by the stature of the eldest son, God rejects him, saying: "Not as man sees does God see, because man sees the appearance, but the LORD looks into the heart." David, the youngest son, still a shepherd boy, is chosen to be anointed.

Today's Gospel account of Jesus' healing a man born blind is one of seven signs in John's Gospel. It signifies that Jesus' power to heal extends beyond physical blindness to spiritual blindness. The healing initiates a dialogue among the man born blind, Jesus, and the Pharisees. On first encountering the man born blind, Jesus takes the initiative. He rubs clay on the man's eyes and instructs him to wash in the Pool of Siloam. The man follows Jesus' instructions and is healed. The Pharisees refuse to believe. They reject Jesus because he broke their law by healing on the Sabbath. Here is another example of the God of surprises working in ways that human beings refuse to accept.

Later, Jesus meets the man he had healed. When Jesus identifies himself as the Son of Man, the man immediately responds: "I do believe, Lord," and he worships him. This man has moved from the gift of physical sight to the deeper gift of "spiritual sight." This miracle reflects our relationship with Jesus. Before Baptism, we were spiritually blind. After being washed in the waters of Baptism, we entered a deeper personal relationship with Jesus.

◆ How does God surprise people in both the First Reading and the Gospel reading?

◆ What does Paul mean in the Second Reading when he calls us to "live as children of the light"?

◆ How has God surprised you?

March 29, 2020

FIFTH SUNDAY OF LENT

READING I Ezekiel 37:12–14

Thus says the LORD God: O my people, I will open your graves and have you rise from them, and bring you back to the land of Israel. Then you shall know that I am the LORD, when I open your graves and have you rise from them, O my people! I will put my spirit in you that you may live, and I will settle you upon your land; thus you shall know that I am the LORD. I have promised, and I will do it, says the LORD.

RESPONSORIAL PSALM
Psalm 130:1–2, 3–4, 5–6, 7–8 (7)

R. With the Lord there is mercy
      and fullness of redemption.

Out of the depths I cry to you,
    O LORD;
  LORD, hear my voice!
Let your ears be attentive
  to my voice in supplication.   R.

If you, O LORD, mark iniquities,
  LORD, who can stand?
But with you is forgiveness,
  that you may be revered.   R.

I trust in the LORD;
  my soul trusts in his word.
More than sentinels wait
    for the dawn,
  let Israel wait for the LORD.   R.

For with the LORD is kindness
  and with him is
    plenteous redemption;
and he will redeem Israel
  from all their iniquities.   R.

READING II Romans 8:8–11

Brothers and sisters: Those who are in the flesh cannot please God. But you are not in the flesh; on the contrary, you are in the spirit, if only the Spirit of God dwells in you. Whoever does not have the Spirit of Christ does not belong to him. But if Christ is in you, although the body is dead because of sin, the spirit is alive because of righteousness. If the Spirit of the one who raised Jesus from the dead dwells in you, the one who raised Christ from the dead will give life to your mortal bodies also, through his Spirit dwelling in you.

GOSPEL John 11:3–7, 17, 20–27, 33b–45

Longer: John 11:1–45

The sisters of Lazarus sent word to Jesus, saying, "Master, the one you love is ill." When Jesus heard this he said, "This illness is not to end in death, but is for the glory of God, that the Son of God may be glorified through it." Now Jesus loved Martha and her sister and Lazarus. So when he heard that he was ill, he remained for two days in the place where he was. Then after this he said to his disciples, "Let us go back to Judea."

When Jesus arrived, he found that Lazarus had already been in the tomb for four days. When Martha heard that Jesus was coming, she went to meet him; but Mary sat at home. Martha said to Jesus, "Lord, if you had been here, my brother would not have died. But even now I know that whatever you ask of God, God will give you." Jesus said to her, "Your brother will rise." Martha said, "I know he will rise, in the resurrection on the last day." Jesus told her, "I am the resurrection and the life; whoever believes in me, even if he dies, will live, and everyone who lives and believes in me will never die. Do you believe this?" She said to him, "Yes, Lord. I have come to believe that you are the Christ, the Son of God, the one who is coming into the world."

He became perturbed and deeply troubled, and said, "Where have you laid him?" They said to him, "Sir, come and see." And Jesus wept. So the Jews said, "See how he loved him." But some of them said, "Could not the one who opened the eyes of the blind man have done something so that this man would not have died?"

So Jesus, perturbed again, came to the tomb. It was a cave, and a stone lay across it. Jesus said, "Take away the stone." Martha, the dead man's sister, said to him, "Lord, by now there will be a stench; he has been dead for four days." Jesus said to her, "Did I not tell you that if you believe you will see the glory of God?" So they took away the stone. And Jesus raised his eyes and said, "Father, I thank you for hearing me. I know that you always hear me; but because of the crowd here I have said this, that they may believe that you sent me." And when he had said this, he cried out in a loud voice, "Lazarus, come out!" The dead man came out, tied hand and foot with burial bands, and his face was wrapped in a cloth. So Jesus said to them, "Untie him and let him go."

Now many of the Jews who had come to Mary and seen what he had done began to believe in him.

Practice of Hope

In the Gospel about Lazarus' death, John writes about Jesus' grief of losing his friend and seeing his loved ones grieving as well. The feelings of helplessness, anger, and sadness can be overwhelming. How can you become more sensitive and attentive to those suffering from loss? ◆ Many parishes have groups that specialize in bereavement. If you feel called to minister in this way, contact these parishioners who are experienced in helping others through these difficult transitions. ◆ Hospitality groups at parishes assist with dinners after funerals. If such a group is part of your parish, consider contacting it to learn how you can help provide meals for families affected by terminal illness or a recent death. ◆ Explore what you need to do to make a living will. ◆ Be mindful that the US bishops have gathered prayers and Scripture readings for when a family member or friend is in the final stages of life. These passages may provide some comfort. They can be found at www.usccb.org /prayer-and-worship/bereavement -and-funerals/prayers-for-death -and-dying.cfm.

Download more questions and activities for families, Christian initiation groups, and other adult groups at http://www.ltp.org/ahw.

Scripture Insights

All of today's readings focus on the centrality of the Resurrection. The prophet Ezekiel looks forward to a future when God will send his spirit upon those who have died and "open your graves and have you rise from them."

In his Letter to the Romans, Paul teaches that the present life of Christians is led through the indwelling of "the Spirit of God." This same Spirit who raised Jesus from the dead will also raise their mortal bodies to life in the resurrection of the dead.

The reading from the Gospel of John tells the account of the raising of Jesus' friend Lazarus. This event signifies Jesus' power over death and foreshadows his own Resurrection. Martha's dialogue with Jesus is remarkable. She greets Jesus' arrival with frustration, saying: "Lord, if you had been here, my brother would not have died."

When Jesus tells her that her brother will rise, Martha shows her knowledge that the dead will rise on the last day. Jesus deepens Martha's faith by declaring: "I am the resurrection and the life; whoever believes in me, even if he dies, will live, and everyone who lives and believes in me will never die." When Jesus asks Martha if she believes this, she responds, not with a statement of fact, but with the insight of faith: "Yes, Lord, I believe that you are the Christ, the Son of God." No other person in the entire Gospels has made such a deep confession of true faith in the person of Jesus. Martha exemplifies what Jesus wants from each of us: a confession that moves beyond intellectual knowledge to a personal commitment to and relationship with him.

◆ Reflect on how the teaching on the Spirit of God develops in the First and the Second Readings.

◆ We believe that Jesus is fully human and divine. How do these aspects of Jesus' two natures emerge in our Gospel reading?

◆ Does Martha's confession of faith in Jesus deepen your relationship to the Lord Jesus?

April 5, 2020

PALM SUNDAY OF THE LORD'S PASSION

<u>At the Procession with Palms</u>
GOSPEL Matthew 21:1–11

READING I Isaiah 50:4-7

The Lord GOD has given me
a well-trained tongue,
that I might know how to
speak to the weary
a word that will rouse them.
Morning after morning
he opens my ear that
I may hear;
and I have not rebelled,
have not turned back.
I gave my back to those who
beat me,
my cheeks to those who
plucked my beard;
my face I did not shield
from buffets and spitting.

The Lord GOD is my help,
therefore I am not disgraced;
I have set my face like flint,
knowing that I shall not be
put to shame.

RESPONSORIAL PSALM
Psalm 22:8–9, 17–18, 19–20, 23–24 (2a)

R. My God, my God,
why have you abandoned me?

All who see me scoff at me;
they mock me with parted lips,
they wag their heads:
"He relied on the LORD;
let him deliver him,
let him rescue him,
if he loves him." R.

Indeed, many dogs surround me,
a pack of evildoers closes in
upon me;
they have pierced my hands and
my feet;
I can count all my bones. R.

They divide my garments
among them,
and for my vesture they cast lots.
But you, O LORD, be not far
from me;
O my help, hasten to aid me. R.

I will proclaim your name
to my brethren;
in the midst of the assembly
I will praise you:

"You who fear the LORD,
　　praise him;
all you descendants of Jacob,
　　give glory to him;
revere him, all you descendants
　　of Israel!" R.

READING II
Philippians 2:6–11

Christ Jesus, though he was
　　in the form of God,
did not regard equality with God
something to be grasped.
Rather, he emptied himself,
　　taking the form of a slave,
coming in human likeness;
and found human in appearance,
he humbled himself,
becoming obedient to the point
　　of death,
even death on a cross.
Because of this,
　　God greatly exalted him
and bestowed on him the name
which is above every name,
that at the name of Jesus
every knee should bend,
of those in heaven and on earth
　　and under the earth,
and every tongue confess that
Jesus Christ is Lord,
to the glory of God the Father.

GOSPEL
Matthew 26:14—27:66

Shorter: Matthew 27:11–54

One of the Twelve, who was called Judas Iscariot, went to the chief priests and said, "What are you willing to give me if I hand him over to you?" They paid him thirty pieces of silver, and from that time on he looked for an opportunity to hand him over.

On the first day of the Feast of Unleavened Bread, the disciples approached Jesus and said, "Where do you want us to prepare for you to eat the Passover?" He said, "Go into the city to a certain man and tell him, 'The teacher says, "My appointed time draws near; in your house I shall celebrate the Passover with my disciples."'" The disciples then did as Jesus had ordered, and prepared the Passover.

When it was evening, he reclined at table with the Twelve. And while they were eating, he said, "Amen, I say to you, one of you will betray me." Deeply distressed at this, they began to say to him one after another, "Surely it is not I, Lord?" He said in reply, "He who has dipped his hand into the dish with me is the one who will betray me. The Son of Man indeed goes, as it is written of him, but woe to that man by whom the Son of Man is betrayed. It would be better for that man if he had never been born." Then Judas, his betrayer, said in reply, "Surely it is not I, Rabbi?" He answered, "You have said so."

While they were eating, Jesus took bread, said the blessing, broke it, and giving it to his disciples said, "Take and eat; this is my body." Then he took a cup, gave thanks, and gave it to them, saying, "Drink from it, all of you, for this is my blood of the covenant, which will be shed on behalf of many for the forgiveness of sins. I tell you, from now on I shall not drink this fruit of the vine until the day when I drink it with you new in the kingdom of my Father." Then, after singing a hymn, they went out to the Mount of Olives.

Then Jesus said to them, "This night all of you will have your faith in me shaken, for it is written:

«I will strike the shepherd,
  and the sheep of the flock will
    be dispersed;»

but after I have been raised up, I shall go before you to Galilee." Peter said to him in reply, "Though all may have their faith in you shaken, mine will never be." Jesus said to him, "Amen, I say to you, this very night before the cock crows, you will deny me three times." Peter said to him, "Even though I should have to die with you, I will not deny you." And all the disciples spoke likewise.

Then Jesus came with them to a place called Gethsemane, and he said to his disciples, "Sit here while I go over there and pray." He took along Peter and the two sons of Zebedee, and began to feel sorrow and distress. Then he said to them, "My soul is sorrowful even to death. Remain here and keep watch with me." He advanced a little and fell prostrate in prayer, saying, "My Father, if it is possible, let this cup pass from me; yet, not as I will, but as you will." When he returned to his disciples he found them asleep. He said to Peter, "So you could not keep watch with me for one hour? Watch and pray that you may not undergo the test. The spirit is willing, but the flesh is weak." Withdrawing a second time, he prayed again, "My Father, if it is not possible that this cup pass without my drinking it, your will be done!" Then he returned once more and found them asleep, for they could not keep their eyes open. He left them and withdrew again and prayed a third time, saying the same thing again. Then he returned to his disciples and said to them, "Are you still sleeping and taking your rest? Behold, the hour is at hand when the Son of Man is to be handed over to sinners. Get up, let us go. Look, my betrayer is at hand."

While he was still speaking, Judas, one of the Twelve, arrived, accompanied by a large crowd, with swords and clubs, who had come from the chief priests and the elders of the people. His betrayer had arranged a sign with them, saying, "The man I shall kiss is the one; arrest him." Immediately he went over to Jesus and said, "Hail, Rabbi!" and he kissed him. Jesus answered him,

"Friend, do what you have come for." Then stepping forward they laid hands on Jesus and arrested him. And behold, one of those who accompanied Jesus put his hand to his sword, drew it, and struck the high priest's servant, cutting off his ear. Then Jesus said to him, "Put your sword back into its sheath, for all who take the sword will perish by the sword. Do you think that I cannot call upon my Father and he will not provide me at this moment with more than twelve legions of angels? But then how would the Scriptures be fulfilled which say that it must come to pass in this way?" At that hour Jesus said to the crowds, "Have you come out as against a robber, with swords and clubs to seize me? Day after day I sat teaching in the temple area, yet you did not arrest me. But all this has come to pass that the writings of the prophets may be fulfilled." Then all the disciples left him and fled.

Those who had arrested Jesus led him away to Caiaphas the high priest, where the scribes and the elders were assembled. Peter was following him at a distance as far as the high priest's courtyard, and going inside he sat down with the servants to see the outcome. The chief priests and the entire Sanhedrin kept trying to obtain false testimony against Jesus in order to put him to death, but they found none, though many false witnesses came forward. Finally two came forward who stated, "This man said, 'I can destroy the temple of God and within three days rebuild it.'" The high priest rose and addressed him, "Have you no answer? What are these men testifying against you?" But Jesus was silent. Then the high priest said to him, "I order you to tell us under oath before the living God whether you are the Christ, the Son of God." Jesus said to him in reply, "You have said so. But I tell you: / From now on you will see 'the Son of Man / seated at the right hand of the Power' / and 'coming on the clouds of heaven.'" / Then the high priest tore his robes and said, "He has blasphemed! What further need have we of witnesses? You have now heard the blasphemy; what is your opinion?" They said in reply, "He deserves to die!" Then they spat in his face and struck him, while some slapped him, saying, "Prophesy for us, Christ: who is it that struck you?"

Now Peter was sitting outside in the courtyard. One of the maids came over to him and said, "You too were with Jesus the Galilean." But he denied it in front of everyone, saying, "I do not know what you are talking about!" As he went out to the gate, another girl saw him and said to those who were there, "This man was with Jesus the Nazorean." Again he denied it with an oath, "I do not know the man!" A little later the bystanders came over and said to Peter, "Surely you too are one of them; even your speech gives you away." At that he began to curse and to swear, "I do not know the man." And immediately a cock crowed. Then Peter remembered the words that Jesus had spoken: "Before the cock crows you will deny me three times." He went out and began to weep bitterly.

When it was morning, all the chief priests and the elders of the people took counsel against Jesus to put him to death. They bound him, led him away, and handed him over to Pilate, the governor.

Then Judas, his betrayer, seeing that Jesus had been condemned, deeply regretted what he had done. He returned the thirty pieces of silver to the chief priests and elders, saying, "I have sinned in betraying innocent blood." They said, "What is that to us? Look to it yourself." Flinging the money into the temple, he departed and went off and hanged himself. The chief priests gathered up the money, but said, "It is not lawful to deposit this in the temple treasury, for it is the price of blood." After consultation, they used it to buy the potter's field as a burial place for foreigners. That is why that field even today is called the Field of Blood. Then was fulfilled what had been said through Jeremiah the prophet, «And they took the thirty pieces of silver, the value of a man with a price on his head, a price set by some of the Israelites, and they paid it out for the potter's field just as the Lord had commanded me.»

Now Jesus stood before the governor, who questioned him, "Are you the king of the Jews?" Jesus said, "You say so." And when he was accused by the chief priests and elders, he made no answer.

Then Pilate said to him, "Do you not hear how many things they are testifying against you?" But he did not answer him one word, so that the governor was greatly amazed.

Now on the occasion of the feast the governor was accustomed to release to the crowd one prisoner whom they wished. And at that time they had a notorious prisoner called Barabbas. So when they had assembled, Pilate said to them, "Which one do you want me to release to you, Barabbas, or Jesus called Christ?" For he knew that it was out of envy that they had handed him over. While he was still seated on the bench, his wife sent him a message, "Have nothing to do with that righteous man. I suffered much in a dream today because of him." The chief priests and the elders persuaded the crowds to ask for Barabbas but to destroy Jesus. The governor said to them in reply, "Which of the two do you want me to release to you?" They answered, "Barabbas!" Pilate said to them, "Then what shall I do with Jesus called Christ?" They all said, "Let him be crucified!" But he said, "Why? What evil has he done?" They only shouted the louder, "Let him be crucified!" When Pilate saw that he was not succeeding at all, but that a riot was breaking out instead, he took water and washed his hands in the sight of the crowd, saying, "I am innocent of this man's blood. Look to it yourselves." And the whole people said in reply, "His blood be upon us and upon our children." Then he released Barabbas to them, but after he had Jesus scourged, he handed him over to be crucified.

Then the soldiers of the governor took Jesus inside the praetorium and gathered the whole cohort around him. They stripped off his clothes and threw a scarlet military cloak about him. Weaving a crown out of thorns, they placed it on his head, and a reed in his right hand. And kneeling before him, they mocked him, saying, "Hail, King of the Jews!" They spat upon him and took the reed and kept striking him on the head. And when they had mocked him, they stripped him of the cloak, dressed him in his own clothes, and led him off to crucify him.

As they were going out, they met a Cyrenian named Simon; this man they pressed into service to carry his cross.

And when they came to a place called Golgotha—which means Place of the Skull—, they gave Jesus wine to drink mixed with gall. But when he had tasted it, he refused to drink. After they had crucified him, they divided his garments by casting lots; then they sat down and kept watch over him there. And they placed over his head the written charge against him: This is Jesus, the King of the Jews. Two revolutionaries were crucified with him, one on his right and the other on his left. Those passing by reviled him, shaking their heads and saying, "You who would destroy the temple and rebuild it in three days, save yourself, if you are the Son of God, and come down from the cross!" Likewise the chief priests with the scribes and elders mocked him and said, "He saved others; he cannot save himself. So he is the king of Israel! Let him come down from the cross now, and we will believe in him. He trusted in God;

let him deliver him now if he wants him. For he said, 'I am the Son of God.'" The revolutionaries who were crucified with him also kept abusing him in the same way.

From noon onward, darkness came over the whole land until three in the afternoon. And about three o'clock Jesus cried out in a loud voice, «"Eli, Eli, lema sabachthani?"» which means, "My God, my God, why have you forsaken me?" Some of the bystanders who heard it said, "This one is calling for Elijah." Immediately one of them ran to get a sponge; he soaked it in wine, and putting it on a reed, gave it to him to drink. But the rest said, "Wait, let us see if Elijah comes to save him." But Jesus cried out again in a loud voice, and gave up his spirit.

[Here all kneel and pause for a short time.]

And behold, the veil of the sanctuary was torn in two from top to bottom. The earth quaked, rocks were split, tombs were opened, and the bodies of many saints who had fallen asleep were raised. And coming forth from their tombs after his resurrection, they entered the holy city and appeared to many. The centurion and the men with him who were keeping watch over Jesus feared greatly when they saw the earthquake and all that was happening, and they said, "Truly, this was the Son of God!" There were many women there, looking on from a distance, who had followed Jesus from Galilee, ministering to him. Among them were Mary Magdalene and Mary the mother of James and Joseph, and the mother of the sons of Zebedee.

When it was evening, there came a rich man from Arimathea named Joseph, who was himself a disciple of Jesus. He went to Pilate and asked for the body of Jesus; then Pilate ordered it to be handed over. Taking the body, Joseph wrapped it in clean linen and laid it in his new tomb that he had hewn in the rock. Then he rolled a huge stone across the entrance to the tomb and departed. But Mary Magdalene and the other Mary remained sitting there, facing the tomb.

The next day, the one following the day of preparation, the chief priests and the Pharisees gathered before Pilate and said, "Sir, we remember that this impostor while still alive said, 'After three days I will be raised up.' Give orders, then, that the grave be secured until the third day, lest his disciples come and steal him and say to the people, 'He has been raised from the dead.' This last imposture would be worse than the first." Pilate said to them, "The guard is yours; go, secure it as best you can." So they went and secured the tomb by fixing a seal to the stone and setting the guard.

Practice of Hope

Each of us experiences hard times in our lives that are unavoidable. It might be a difficult pregnancy, failing to get into the desired graduate program, or the death of a loved one. Jesus certainly suffered through a painful, humiliating death. The Gospel on Palm Sunday doesn't reveal anything yet about the Resurrection, and we are left at the tomb. Fortunately, our Christian beliefs don't leave us there, and we have hope because of God's greatest gift. ◆ Read about others who have taken difficult journeys, such as Mahatma Ghandi, St. Teresa of Calcutta, or another saint. ◆ Make a step-by-step plan of a difficult task or life goal that you need to accomplish. Ask for God's help along the way. Try to provide yourself small rewards for reaching certain milestones as you move toward its completion. ◆ Affirm friends and family members who are inching toward a new beginning, and congratulate them in a special way for reaching their goal with grace and perseverance.

Download more questions and activities for families, Christian initiation groups, and other adult groups at http://www.ltp.org/ahw.

Scripture Insights

We recall in our liturgy Jesus' entry into the holy city, Jerusalem. The excitement of the crowd is evident in the Gospel at the procession as Jesus is welcomed as the Messiah: "Hosanna to the Son of David; / blessed is he who comes in the name the Lord."

The servant in the First Reading foreshadows Jesus. He speaks God's Word to his people who reject him. Though innocent, he endures sufferings, beatings, and insults. The Lord God sustains him through these persecutions.

Paul's letter to the Philippians quotes an ancient Christian hymn used in worship. It captures beautifully the person of Jesus Christ: Although fully divine, he emptied himself and became fully human to the extent of embracing a disgraceful death on the cross. The Father accepted his obedience by raising him for all to see that "Jesus Christ is Lord, to the glory of God the Father."

Today's Gospel reading is the passion narrative according to Matthew's account of the Gospel. We hear in graphic detail how Jesus is betrayed, derided, judged, sentenced, and finally crucified. His body is taken down and placed in a tomb. Everyone in the story displays some level of fear. The joy of the entry into Jerusalem is replaced by fear. The disciples who celebrated a final meal with Jesus all desert him. Peter denies he ever knew Jesus. Pilate was afraid of losing his own power. The Jewish religious leaders, afraid of having their positions of authority undermined, secured Jesus' conviction before Pilate.

◆ In what way does the servant in the First Reading resemble Jesus?

◆ As you prayerfully reflect on the account of the Lord's passion and death, what aspects strike you the most as you begin Holy Week?

◆ How will you participate in the Sacred Paschal Triduum so that it deepens your spiritual life?

April 9 to 12, 2020

THE SACRED PASCHAL TRIDUUM

Holy Thursday brings to an end the forty days of Lent, which make up the season of anticipation of the great Three Days. Composed of prayer, almsgiving, fasting, and the preparation of the catechumens for Baptism, the season of Lent is now brought to a close, and the Three Days begin as we approach the liturgy of Holy Thursday evening. As those to be initiated into the Church have prepared themselves for their entrance into the fullness of life, so have we been awakening in our hearts, minds, and bodies our own entrances into the life of Christ, experienced in the life of the Church.

Easter Triduum (Latin for "three days") is the center, the core, of the entire year for Christians. These Three Days mark the mystery around which our entire lives are played out. Adults in the community are invited to plan ahead so that the whole time from Thursday night until Easter Sunday is free of social engagements, free of entertainment, and free of meals except for the most basic nourishment. We measure these days—indeed, our very salvation in the life of God—in step with the catechumens themselves; we are revitalized as we support them along the way and participate in their initiation rites.

We are asked to fast on Good Friday and to continue fasting, if possible, all through Holy Saturday as strictly as we can so that we come to the Easter Vigil hungry and full of excitement, parched and longing to feel the sacred water of the font on our skin. We pare down distractions on Good Friday and Holy Saturday so that we may be free for prayer and anticipation, for reflection, preparation, and silence. The Church is getting ready for the great night of the Easter Vigil.

As one who has been initiated into the Church, as one whose life has been wedded to this community gathered at the table, you should anticipate the Triduum with concentration and vigor. With you, the whole Church knows that our presence for the liturgies of the Triduum is not just an invitation. Everyone is needed. We pull out all the stops for these days. As humans, wedded to humanity by the joys and travails of life and grafted onto the body of the Church by the sanctifying waters of Baptism, we lead the new members into new life in this community of faith.

To this end, the Three Days are seen not as three distinct liturgies, but as one movement. These days have been connected liturgically from the early days of the Christian Church. As members of this community, we should be personally committed to preparing for and attending the Triduum and its culmination in the Easter Vigil of Holy Saturday.

The Church proclaims the direction of the Triduum with the opening antiphon of Holy Thursday, which comes from Paul's Letter to the Galatians (6:14). With this verse the Church sets a spiritual environment into which we as committed Christians enter the Triduum:

We should glory in the cross of our Lord Jesus Christ, for he is our salvation, our life and resurrection; through him we are saved and made free.

HOLY THURSDAY

On Thursday evening we enter into this Triduum together. Whether presider, lector, preacher, greeter, altar server, minister of the Eucharist, decorator, or person in the remote corner in the last pew of the church, we begin, as always, by hearkening to the Word of God. These are the Scriptures for the liturgy of Holy Thursday:

Exodus 12:1–8, 11–14
Ancient instructions for the meal of the Passover.

1 Corinthians 11:23–26
Eat the bread and drink the cup until the return of the Lord.

John 13:1–15
Jesus washes the feet of the disciples.

Then the priest, like Jesus, does something strange: he washes feet. Jesus gave us this image of what the Church is supposed to look like, feel like, act like. Our position—whether as observer, washer or washed, servant or served—may be difficult. Yet we learn from the discomfort, from the awkwardness.

Then we celebrate the Eucharist. Because it is connected to the other liturgies of the Triduum on Good Friday and Holy Saturday night, the evening liturgy of Holy Thursday has no ending. Whether we stay to pray awhile or leave, we are now in the quiet, peace, and glory of the Triduum.

GOOD FRIDAY

We gather quietly in community on Friday and again listen to the Word of God:

Isaiah 52:13—53:12
The servant of the Lord was crushed for our sins.

Hebrews 4:14–16; 5:7–9
The Son of God learned obedience through his suffering.

John 18:1—19:42
The Passion of Jesus Christ.

After the sermon, we pray at length for all the world's needs: for the Church; for the pope, the clergy and all the baptized; for those preparing for initiation; for the unity of Christians; for Jews; for non-Christians; for atheists; for all in public office; and for those in special need.

Then there is another once-a-year event: the holy cross is held up in our midst, and we come forward one by one to do reverence with a kiss, bow, or genuflection. This communal reverence of an instrument of torture recalls the painful price, in the past and today, of salvation, the way in which our redemption is wrought, the scourging and humiliation of Jesus Christ that bring direction and life back to a humanity that is lost and dead. During the adoration of the cross, we sing not only of the sorrow, but of the glory of the Cross by which we have been saved.

Again, we bring to mind the words of Paul (Galatians 6:14), on which last night's entrance antiphon is loosely based: "May I never boast except in the cross of our Lord Jesus Christ, through which the world has been crucified to me, and I to the world."

We continue in fasting and prayer and vigil, in rest and quiet, through Saturday. This Saturday for us is God's rest at the end of creation. It is Christ's repose in the tomb. It is Christ's visit with the dead.

EASTER VIGIL

Hungry now, pared down to basics, lightheaded from vigilance and full of excitement, we, the already baptized, gather in darkness and light a new fire. From this blaze we light a great candle that will make this night bright for us and will burn throughout Easter Time.

We hearken again to the Word of God with some of the most powerful narratives and proclamations of our tradition:

Genesis 1:1—2:2
The creation of the world.

Genesis 22:1–18
The sacrifice of Isaac.

Exodus 14:15—15:1
The crossing of the Red Sea.

Isaiah 54:5–14
You will not be afraid.

Isaiah 55:1–11
Come, come to the water.

Baruch 3:9–15, 32—4:4
Walk by the light of wisdom.

Ezekiel 36:16–17a, 18–28
The Lord says: I will sprinkle water.

Romans 6:3–11
United with him in death.

Year A: Matthew 28:1–10, Year B: Mark 16:1–7, Year C: Luke 24:1–12
Jesus has been raised.

After the readings, we call on our saints to stand with us as we go to the font and the priest celebrant blesses the waters. The chosen of all times and all places attend to what is about to take place. The elect renounce evil, profess the faith of the Church, and are baptized and anointed.

All of us renew our Baptism. These are the moments when death and life meet, when we reject evil and make our promises to God. All of this is in the communion of the Church. So together we go to the table and celebrate the Easter Eucharist.

Easter Time

Prayer before Reading the Word

God of all creation,
whose mighty power raised Jesus
    from the dead,
be present to this community
    of disciples
whom you have called to the hope
of a glorious inheritance among
    the saints.

As we hear the word that
    brings salvation,
make our hearts burn within us,
that we may recognize Christ
    crucified and risen,
who opens our hearts to
    understand the Scriptures,
who is made known to us in the
    breaking of the bread,
and who lives and reigns with you
in the unity of the Holy Spirit,
one God for ever and ever. Amen.

Prayer after Reading the Word

O God of Easter glory,
gather your baptized people
around the teaching of the Apostles,
devoted to the life we share in
    the Church,
devoted to the breaking of
    the bread.

Make us so embrace the name
    of Christ,
that we glorify you in the world
and bear witness to your Word
made known to us by Jesus,
our Passover and our peace,
who lives and reigns with you
in the unity of the Holy Spirit,
one God for ever and ever. Amen.

Weekday Readings

April 13: Monday within the Octave of Easter
Acts 2:14, 22–33;
Matthew 28:8–15

April 14: Tuesday within the Octave of Easter
Acts 2:36–41; John 20:11–18

April 15: Wednesday within the Octave of Easter
Acts 3:1–10; Luke 24:13–35

April 16: Thursday within the Octave of Easter
Acts 3:11–26; Luke 24:35–48

April 17: Friday within the Octave of Easter
Acts 4:1–12; John 21:1–14

April 18: Saturday within the Octave of Easter
Acts 4:13–21; Mark 16:9–15

April 20: Acts 4:23–31; John 3:1–8
April 21: Acts 4:32–37;
John 3:7b–15
April 22: Acts 5:17–26;
John 3:16–21
April 23: Acts 5:27–33;
John 3:31–36
April 24: Acts 5:34–42;
John 6:1–15

April 25: Feast of St. Mark, Evangelist
1 Peter 5:5b–14;
Mark 16:15–20

April 27: Acts 6:8–15;
John 6:22–29
April 28: Acts 7:51—8:1a;
John 6:30–35
April 29: Acts 8:1b–8;
John 6:35–40
April 30: Acts 8:26–40;
John 6:44–51
May 1: Acts 9:1–20; John 6:52–59
May 2: Acts 9:31–42; John 6:60–69

May 4: Acts 11:1–18; John 10:11–18
May 5: Acts 11:19–26;
    John 10:22–30
May 6: Acts 12:24—13:5a;
    John 12:44–50
May 7: Acts 13:13–25;
    John 13:16–20
May 8: Acts 13:26–33; John 14:1–6
May 9: Acts 13:44–52;
    John 14:7–14

May 11: Acts 14:5–18;
    John 14:21–26
May 12: Acts 14:19–28;
    John 14:27–31a
May 13: Acts 15:1–6; John 15:1–8
**May 14: Feast of St. Matthias,
Apostle
Acts 1:15–17, 20–26;
John 15:9–17**
May 15: Acts 15:22–31;
    John 15:12–17
May 16: Acts 16:1–10;
    John 15:18–21

May 18: Acts 16:11–15;
    John 15:26—16:4a
May 19: Acts 16:22–34;
    John 16:5–11
May 20: Acts 17:15, 22—18:1;
    John 16:12–15
**May 21: Solemnity of the
Ascension of the Lord
[Ecclesiastical provinces of
Boston, Hartford, New York,
Newark, Omaha, and
Philadelphia]
Acts 1:1–11; Ephesians
1:17–23; Matthew 28:16–20**
May 21: Acts 18:1–8; John 16:16–20
May 22: Acts 18:9–18;
    John 16:20–23
May 23: Acts 18:23–28;
    John 16:23b–28

May 25: Acts 19:1–8;
    John 16:29–33
May 26: Acts 20:17–27;
    John 17:1–11a
May 27: Acts 20:28–38;
    John 17:11b–19
May 28: Acts 22:30; 23:6–11;
    John 17:20–26
May 29: Acts 25:13b–21;
    John 21:15–19
May 30: Acts 28:16–20, 30–31;
    John 21:20–25

April 12, 2020

EASTER SUNDAY: THE RESURRECTION OF THE LORD

READING I
Acts 10:34a, 37–43

Peter proceeded to speak and said: "You know what has happened all over Judea, beginning in Galilee after the baptism that John preached, how God anointed Jesus of Nazareth with the Holy Spirit and power. He went about doing good and healing all those oppressed by the devil, for God was with him. We are witnesses of all that he did both in the country of the Jews and in Jerusalem. They put him to death by hanging him on a tree. This man God raised on the third day and granted that he be visible, not to all the people, but to us, the witnesses chosen by God in advance, who ate and drank with him after he rose from the dead. He commissioned us to preach to the people and testify that he is the one appointed by God as judge of the living and the dead. To him all the prophets bear witness, that everyone who believes in him will receive forgiveness of sins through his name."

RESPONSORIAL PSALM
Psalm 118:1–2, 16–17, 22–23 (24)

R. This is the day the Lord
      has made; let us rejoice and
      be glad.
or: Alleluia.

Give thanks to the LORD,
      for he is good,
  for his mercy endures forever.
Let the house of Israel say,
  "His mercy endures forever."   R.

"The right hand of the LORD
      has struck with power;
  the right hand of the LORD
      is exalted."
I shall not die, but live,
  and declare the works
      of the LORD.   R.

The stone which the
      builders rejected
  has become the cornerstone.
By the LORD has this been done;
  it is wonderful in our eyes.   R.

READING II Colossians 3:1–4

Alternate: 1 Corinthians 5:6b–8

Brothers and sisters: If then you were raised with Christ, seek what is above, where Christ is seated at the right hand of God. Think of what is above, not of what is on earth. For you have died, and your life is hidden with Christ in God. When Christ your life appears, then you too will appear with him in glory.

GOSPEL John 20:1–9

Alternate: Matthew 28:1–10 and (afternoon or evening Mass) Luke 24:13–35

On the first day of the week, Mary of Magdala came to the tomb early in the morning, while it was still dark, and saw the stone removed from the tomb. So she ran and went to Simon Peter and to the other disciple whom Jesus loved, and told them, "They have taken the Lord from the tomb, and we don't know where they put him." So Peter and the other disciple went out and came to the tomb. They both ran, but the other disciple ran faster than Peter and arrived at the tomb first; he bent down and saw the burial cloths there, but did not go in. When Simon Peter arrived after him, he went into the tomb and saw the burial cloths there, and the cloth that had covered his head, not with the burial cloths but rolled up in a separate place. Then the other disciple also went in, the one who had arrived at the tomb first, and he saw and believed. For they did not yet understand the Scripture that he had to rise from the dead.

Practice of Charity

New life is all around us, but we often fail to see it. The cycle of life is awe-inspiring, yet overwhelming at times. Sometimes it is joyful and demanding, such as when caring for a baby through sleepless nights. At other times, it can be eye-opening, as when starting a new job or learning a new hobby or skill. ◆ Consider doing something new to revitalize yourself. Take steps, even small ones, toward new life. ◆ Nurture new life through plants, indoors or out. For some, this could be growing a few herbs in pots indoors, and for others, it could be starting a vegetable or flower garden. ◆ Offer to babysit for young parents so that they can have an evening out to help them revive their relationship. ◆ Call, email, or text a friend or relative whom you have not contacted in a while to reignite the relationship.

Download more questions and activities for families, Christian initiation groups, and other adult groups at http://www.ltp.org/ahw.

Scripture Insights

"The Lord is truly risen, alleluia," proclaims today's Entrance Antiphon. All three readings speak to this foundational confession. In the Acts of the Apostles, Peter witnesses to the life, death, and Resurrection of Christ Jesus and draws out its significance for us: "Everyone who believes in him will receive forgiveness of sins through his name."

Paul, in his letter to the Colossians, also expresses the meaning of Christ's death and Resurrection for us. Since we have been raised with Christ, our focus should not be on things of this world, but we "must seek what is above where Christ is seated at the right hand of God."

One figure central to all of the Gospel accounts of Jesus' Resurrection is Mary Magdalene. The early Christians called her "the apostle to the apostles." She was the first to break the news to the disciples of the empty tomb and the first to witness the Risen Lord.

In today's reading from John's Gospel, Mary, on discovering the tomb to be empty, tells this news to "Simon Peter and the other disciple whom Jesus loved." The two ran to the tomb. The Beloved Disciple arrives first but, out of deference, allows Peter to enter the tomb before him. Peter sees the burial cloths lying there. When the Beloved Disciple enters, the narrator deliberately comments that "he saw and believed." Until this time, they had failed to understand Jesus' teaching that "he had to rise from the dead." The Beloved Disciple was the first to believe. Only through love does one come to grasp the mystery of Jesus' Resurrection and God's love for us.

◆ The Beloved Disciple "saw and believed." How does that witness impact your life?

◆ How do your words or actions witness to the Risen Lord?

◆ How can you live out Paul's challenge to "think of what is above, not of what is on earth"?

April 19, 2020

SECOND SUNDAY OF EASTER / DIVINE MERCY SUNDAY

READING I Acts 2:42–47

They devoted themselves to the teaching of the apostles and to the communal life, to the breaking of bread and to the prayers. Awe came upon everyone, and many wonders and signs were done through the apostles. All who believed were together and had all things in common; they would sell their property and possessions and divide them among all according to each one's need. Every day they devoted themselves to meeting together in the temple area and to breaking bread in their homes. They ate their meals with exultation and sincerity of heart, praising God and enjoying favor with all the people. And every day the Lord added to their number those who were being saved.

RESPONSORIAL PSALM
Psalm 118:2–4, 13–15, 22–24 (1)

R. Give thanks to the Lord,
    for he is good, his love is
    everlasting.
or: Alleluia.

Let the house of Israel say,
  "His mercy endures forever."
Let the house of Aaron say,
  "His mercy endures forever."
Let those who fear the LORD say,
  "His mercy endures forever." R.

I was hard pressed and was falling,
  but the LORD helped me.
My strength and my courage
    is the LORD,
  and he has been my savior.
The joyful shout of victory
  in the tents of the just. R.

The stone which the
    builders rejected
  has become the cornerstone.
By the LORD has this been done;
  it is wonderful in our eyes.
This is the day the LORD has made;
  let us be glad and rejoice in it. R.

READING II 1 Peter 1:3–9

Blessed be the God and Father of our Lord Jesus Christ, who in his great mercy gave us a new birth to a living hope through the resurrection of Jesus Christ from the dead, to an inheritance that is imperishable, undefiled, and unfading, kept in heaven for you who by the power of God are safeguarded through faith, to a salvation that is ready to be revealed in the final time. In this you rejoice, although now for a little while you may have to suffer through various trials, so that the genuineness of your faith, more precious than gold that is perishable even though tested by fire, may prove to be for praise, glory, and honor at the revelation of Jesus Christ. Although you have not seen him you love him; even though you do not see him now yet believe in him, you rejoice with an indescribable and glorious joy, as you attain the goal of your faith, the salvation of your souls.

GOSPEL John 20:19–31

On the evening of that first day of the week, when the doors were locked, where the disciples were, for fear of the Jews, Jesus came and stood in their midst and said to them, "Peace be with you." When he had said this, he showed them his hands and his side. The disciples rejoiced when they saw the Lord. Jesus said to them again, "Peace be with you. As the Father has sent me, so I send you." And when he had said this, he breathed on them and said to them, "Receive the Holy Spirit. Whose sins you forgive are forgiven them, and whose sins you retain are retained."

Thomas, called Didymus, one of the Twelve, was not with them when Jesus came. So the other disciples said to him, "We have seen the Lord." But he said to them, "Unless I see the mark of the nails in his hands and put my finger into the nailmarks and put my hand into his side, I will not believe."

Now a week later his disciples were again inside and Thomas was with them. Jesus came, although the doors were locked, and stood in their midst and said, "Peace be with you." Then he said to Thomas, "Put your finger here and see my hands, and bring your hand and put it into my side, and do not be unbelieving, but believe." Thomas answered and said to him, "My Lord and my God!" Jesus said to him, "Have you come to believe because you have seen me? Blessed are those who have not seen and have believed."

Now, Jesus did many other signs in the presence of his disciples that are not written in this book. But these are written that you may come to believe that Jesus is the Christ, the Son of God, and that through this belief you may have life in his name.

Practice of Hope

On the Second Sunday of Easter, during the Jubilee of Mercy, Pope Francis said in his homily that the Gospels are filled with God's mercy. He noted that "everything that Jesus said and did is an expression of the Father's mercy." He continued, "[T]he Gospel of mercy remains an open book in which the signs of Christ's disciples— concrete acts of love and the best witness to mercy—continue to be written. We are all called to become living writers of the Gospel, heralds of the Good News to all men and women of today." ◆ Reread today's Gospel and savor the account of Jesus wishing peace to the frightened Apostles as he appears to them (through locked doors) and shows them his wounds, sign of his radical love. ◆ Prayerfully reflect on this statement from Pope Francis' homily on the Sunday of Divine Mercy in 2016: "The path that the Risen Master shows us is a one way street, it goes in only one direction: this means that we must move beyond ourselves to witness to the healing power of love that has conquered us." ◆ Consider how you can become a living example of mercy.

Download more questions and activities for families, Christian initiation groups, and other adult groups at http://www.ltp.org/ahw.

Scripture Insights

The Resurrection's transforming power is apparent in today's readings. In the Gospel, the frightened disciples are changed as Jesus enters the room in which they are hiding. With the greeting Shalom, Jesus offers them blessings on every dimension of their being. This blessing, translated as "Peace be to you," communicates God's mercy. Jesus goes further by extending the gift of the Holy Spirit to his disciples, saying, "Receive the Holy Spirit. Whose sins you forgive are forgiven them." The Spirit's power transforms their lives, enabling them to extend God's mercy and forgiveness to those who seek it.

The Risen Lord still bears the marks of his crucifixion. He is always the wounded Christ, as the Book of Revelation relates (5:6). The Apostle Thomas is not present on this occasion and refuses to believe the witness of the other disciples. A week later Thomas is present when the Risen Lord appears again. There, Thomas makes a confession of faith as he says, "My Lord and my God!"

Jesus responds by blessing those who have not seen and yet believed.

The reading from the Acts of the Apostles offers an insight into the life of that first Christian community transformed by the Risen Christ and the power of the Holy Spirit. United in Spirit, they shared their possessions, and no one was in need. They present the ideal Christian community open to God's grace.

Peter, in the Second Reading, uses the form of a Jewish blessing to praise God. These words remind people today of the Risen Christ's new life received in Baptism. "Although you have not seen him you love him" are the most reassuring words addressed to us today.

◆ What characteristics define that first Christian community?

◆ The Second Sunday of Easter is also called the "Sunday of Divine Mercy." What insights do each of the readings reveal about God's mercy?

◆ Have you, like Thomas, ever struggled to believe? How were your doubts resolved?

April 26, 2020

THIRD SUNDAY OF EASTER

READING I Acts 2:14, 22–33

Then Peter stood up with the Eleven, raised his voice, and proclaimed: "You who are Jews, indeed all of you staying in Jerusalem. Let this be known to you, and listen to my words. You who are Israelites, hear these words. Jesus the Nazorean was a man commended to you by God with mighty deeds, wonders, and signs, which God worked through him in your midst, as you yourselves know. This man, delivered up by the set plan and foreknowledge of God, you killed, using lawless men to crucify him. But God raised him up, releasing him from the throes of death, because it was impossible for him to be held by it. For David says of him:

«I saw the Lord ever before me,
    with him at my right hand
        I shall not be disturbed.
Therefore my heart has been glad
    and my tongue has exulted;
my flesh, too, will dwell in hope,
because you will not abandon
    my soul to the netherworld,
nor will you suffer your holy
        one to see corruption.
You have made known to me
    the paths of life;
you will fill me with joy in
        your presence.»

"My brothers, one can confidently say to you about the patriarch David that he died and was buried, and his tomb is in our midst to this day. But since he was a prophet and knew that God had sworn an oath to him that he would set one of his descendants upon his throne, he foresaw and spoke of the resurrection of the Christ, that neither was he abandoned to the netherworld nor did his flesh see corruption. God raised this Jesus; of this we are all witnesses. Exalted at the right hand of God, he received the promise of the Holy Spirit from the Father and poured him forth, as you see and hear."

READING II 1 Peter 1:17–21

Beloved: If you invoke as Father him who judges impartially according to each one's works, conduct yourselves with reverence during the time of your sojourning, realizing that you were ransomed from your futile conduct, handed on by your ancestors, not with perishable things like silver or gold but with the precious blood of Christ as of a spotless unblemished lamb.

He was known before the foundation of the world but revealed in the final time for you, who through him believe in God who raised him from the dead and gave him glory, so that your faith and hope are in God.

Gospel Luke 24:13–35

That very day, the first day of the week, two of Jesus' disciples were going to a village seven miles from Jerusalem called Emmaus, and they were conversing about all the things that had occurred. And it happened that while they were conversing and debating, Jesus himself drew near and walked with them, but their eyes were prevented from recognizing him. He asked them, "What are you discussing as you walk along?" They stopped, looking downcast. One of them, named Cleopas, said to him in reply, "Are you the only visitor to Jerusalem who does not know of the things that have taken place there in these days?" And he replied to them, "What sort of things?" They said to him, "The things that happened to Jesus the Nazarene, who was a prophet mighty in deed and word before God and all the people, how our chief priests and rulers both handed him over to a sentence of death and crucified him. But we were hoping that he would be the one to redeem Israel; and besides all this, it is now the third day since this took place. Some women from our group, however, have astounded us: they were at the tomb early in the morning and did not find his body; they came back and reported that they had indeed seen a vision of angels who announced that he was alive. Then some of those with us went to the tomb and found things just as the women had described, but him they did not see." And he said to them, "Oh, how foolish you are! How slow of heart to believe all that the prophets spoke! Was it not necessary that the Christ should suffer these things and enter into his glory?" Then beginning with Moses and all the prophets, he interpreted to them what referred to him in all the Scriptures. As they approached the village to which they were going, he gave the impression that he was going on farther. But they urged him, "Stay with us, for it is nearly evening and the day is almost over." So he went in to stay with them. And it happened that, while he was with them at table, he took bread, said the blessing, broke it, and gave it to them. With that their eyes were opened and they recognized him, but he vanished from their sight. Then they said to each other, "Were not our hearts burning within us while he spoke to us on the way and opened the Scriptures to us?" So they set out at once and returned to Jerusalem where they found gathered together the eleven and those with them who were saying, "The Lord has truly been raised and has appeared to Simon!" Then the two recounted what had taken place on the way and how he was made known to them in the breaking of bread.

Practice of Faith

Doing what is called the examen on a daily basis can help people discover how God is working in their lives. The examen also helps with recognizing the many positive, loving people who are in our midst. Just as the two disciples walking on the road toward Emmaus did not recognize Jesus, we often don't realize how Christ walks with us during our daily routine as well as through our struggles. ◆ Consider making the examen part of your prayer. Some examples of this prayer can be found on websites such as https://pray-as-you-go.org/prayer%20tools/ or apps such as https://www.ignatianspirituality.com/23542 /reimagining-examen-app. ◆ Read more about St. Ignatius from the chapter on him in My Life with the Saints, by James Martin, SJ, or a biography at the library. ◆ During a walk, reflect on how a common mode of transportation at the time of Jesus was by foot.

Download more questions and activities for families, Christian initiation groups, and other adult groups at http://www.ltp.org/ahw.

Scripture Insights

Today's Gospel reading vividly reveals the transforming power of an encounter with the Risen Lord. Two bitterly disappointed disciples are leaving Jerusalem, where their hopes have been destroyed. Jesus, "the Nazarene, who was a prophet mighty in deed and word" and whom they believed had promised a new kingdom, had been crucified, died, and was buried. All their hopes and expectations have come to nothing. Along the road to Emmaus, a stranger joins them, and they share with him their frustrations.

The stranger's words helps the disciples realize that the Scriptures did indeed teach that the Messiah had to suffer before he entered "into his glory." Their invitation to this stranger to spend the evening brings them a deeper awareness. Jesus takes bread, "said the blessing, broke it, and gave it to them." In these actions, the disciples recognize the Risen Lord with the eyes of faith, and their encounter sets their hearts on fire: "Were not our hearts burning within us while he spoke to us on the way and opened the Scriptures to us?"

This Gospel reading contains a remarkable message for us and every generation. Like those disciples on the road to Emmaus, we encounter the presence of the Risen Lord every time we gather to hear the Scriptures proclaimed and witness the bread of the Eucharist broken. "The Church has always venerated the divine Scriptures just as she venerates the body of the Lord, since, especially in the sacred liturgy, she unceasingly receives and offers to the faithful the bread of life from the table both of God's word and of Christ's body" (Dogmatic Constitution on Divine Revelation, 21).

◆ What events helped the disciples recognize the presence of the Risen Lord on their journey to Emmaus?

◆ What is the central message that Peter proclaims to the Jews in our First Reading?

◆ How does the Gospel reading help you understand the Eucharist more deeply?

May 3, 2020

FOURTH SUNDAY OF EASTER

READING I
Acts 2:14a, 36–41

Then Peter stood up with the Eleven, raised his voice, and proclaimed: "Let the whole house of Israel know for certain that God has made both Lord and Christ, this Jesus whom you crucified."

Now when they heard this, they were cut to the heart, and they asked Peter and the other apostles, "What are we to do, my brothers?" Peter said to them, "Repent and be baptized, every one of you, in the name of Jesus Christ for the forgiveness of your sins; and you will receive the gift of the Holy Spirit. For the promise is made to you and to your children and to all those far off, whomever the Lord our God will call." He testified with many other arguments, and was exhorting them, "Save yourselves from this corrupt generation." Those who accepted his message were baptized, and about three thousand persons were added that day.

RESPONSORIAL PSALM
Psalm 23:1–3a, 3b–4, 5, 6 (1)

R. The Lord is my shepherd; there
        is nothing I shall want.
or: Alleluia.

The LORD is my shepherd;
        I shall not want.
    In verdant pastures
        he gives me repose;
beside restful waters he leads me;
    he refreshes my soul.   R.

He guides me in right paths
        for his name's sake.
Even though I walk
        in the dark valley
    I fear no evil; for you are at
        my side,
with your rod and your staff
    that give me courage.   R.

You spread the table before me
    in the sight of my foes;
you anoint my head with oil;
    my cup overflows.   R.

Only goodness and kindness
        follow me
    all the days of my life;

and I shall dwell in the house
of the LORD
for years to come.   R.

READING II
1 Peter 2:20b–25

Beloved: If you are patient when you suffer for doing what is good, this is a grace before God. For to this you have been called, because Christ also suffered for you, leaving you an example that you should follow in his footsteps. «He committed no sin, and no deceit was found in his mouth.»

When he was insulted, he returned no insult; when he suffered, he did not threaten; instead, he handed himself over to the one who judges justly. He himself bore our sins in his body upon the cross, so that, free from sin, we might live for righteousness. By his wounds you have been healed. For you had gone astray like sheep, but you have now returned to the shepherd and guardian of your souls.

GOSPEL John 10:1–10

Jesus said: "Amen, amen, I say to you, whoever does not enter a sheepfold through the gate but climbs over elsewhere is a thief and a robber. But whoever enters through the gate is the shepherd of the sheep. The gatekeeper opens it for him, and the sheep hear his voice, as the shepherd calls his own sheep by name and leads them out. When he has driven out all his own, he walks ahead of them, and the sheep follow him, because they recognize his voice. But they will not follow a stranger; they will run away from him, because they do not recognize the voice of strangers." Although Jesus used this figure of speech, the Pharisees did not realize what he was trying to tell them.

So Jesus said again, "Amen, amen, I say to you, I am the gate for the sheep. All who came before me are thieves and robbers, but the sheep did not listen to them. I am the gate. Whoever enters through me will be saved, and will come in and go out and find pasture. A thief comes only to steal and slaughter and destroy; I came so that they might have life and have it more abundantly."

Practice of Charity

Whom do you usually see when you first walk into church on the weekends? Ushers and greeters comprise a ministry that is often underappreciated, yet they are vital for being an extension of Jesus as our "gate," based on today's Gospel. Effective ushers are nonjudgmental and welcoming to everyone who comes through the parish doors. They fill an even more vital role at Christmas and Easter Masses when parishes are filled with Catholics (and visitors of other faiths) who participate only at those times. In this era of declining Mass attendance, we need to foster all hospitable efforts that encourage people to return. After Mass, many parishes offer doughnuts, cookies, and coffee in an extended gathering space or nearby room. Some churches have ministries of welcome. ◆ If you are not already involved in a greeting or hospitality ministry, consider looking into it by talking with someone serving in that capacity.

◆ For more insight on parish hospitality, read <u>Guide for Ushers and Greeters</u>, by Karie Ferrell and Paul Turner, published by Liturgy Training Publications.

<u>Download more questions and activities for families, Christian initiation groups, and other adult groups at http://www.ltp.org/ahw.</u>

Scripture Insights

In the First Reading, Peter addresses the crowd by professing, "God has made both Lord and Christ this Jesus whom you crucified." His hearers respond to Peter's challenge to acknowledge the Risen Lord by accepting his message and being baptized.

Our Second Reading from the First Letter of Peter is a true gem. By encountering the Risen Christ, we experience the true meaning of the mystery of suffering. Though innocent, Jesus suffered willingly for us. In like manner, we should embrace suffering: "If you are patient, when you suffer for doing what is good, this is a grace before God. For to this you have been called."

We are most familiar with images referring to Jesus as the Resurrection and the Life or the Good Shepherd, but in today's Gospel, Jesus uses the image of "gatekeeping." Jesus begins with a parable about a gatekeeper who knows Jesus and opens the gate for the sheep to enter the sheepfold. Since the sheep are familiar with Jesus' voice, they trust him and follow wherever he leads.

Jesus tells this parable explicitly for the Pharisees to identify his role as leader of God's people. When the Pharisees fail to understand Jesus' message, he becomes more direct: "I am the gate for the sheep." As the gate, Jesus offers safety as well as freedom on the path to salvation. This image opens a richness for reflection. As the gate, Jesus offers access to what nourishes and protects from harm. The Risen Lord sustains us in our journey, accompanying us as we move toward the Father. Jesus ends with words expressing his mission: "I came so that they might have life and have it more abundantly."

◆ What does Peter mean, as he addresses the Jews, saying, "God has made both Lord and Christ this Jesus whom you crucified?"

◆ What meaning do you draw for yourself from the image of gatekeeping?

◆ Do Peter's words change your view of human suffering?

May 10, 2020

FIFTH SUNDAY OF EASTER

READING I Acts 6:1–7

As the number of disciples continued to grow, the Hellenists complained against the Hebrews because their widows were being neglected in the daily distribution. So the Twelve called together the community of the disciples and said, "It is not right for us to neglect the word of God to serve at table. Brothers, select from among you seven reputable men, filled with the Spirit and wisdom, whom we shall appoint to this task, whereas we shall devote ourselves to prayer and to the ministry of the word." The proposal was acceptable to the whole community, so they chose Stephen, a man filled with faith and the Holy Spirit, also Philip, Prochorus, Nicanor, Timon, Parmenas, and Nicholas of Antioch, a convert to Judaism. They presented these men to the apostles who prayed and laid hands on them. The word of God continued to spread, and the number of the disciples in Jerusalem increased greatly; even a large group of priests were becoming obedient to the faith.

RESPONSORIAL PSALM
Psalm 33:1–2, 4–5, 18–19 (22)

R. Lord, let your mercy be on us,
       as we place our trust in you.
or: Alleluia.

Exult, you just, in the LORD;
  praise from the upright is fitting.
Give thanks to the LORD on
      the harp;
  with the ten-stringed lyre
      chant his praises.   R.

Upright is the word of the LORD,
  and all his works are trustworthy.
He loves justice and right;
  of the kindness of the LORD
      the earth is full.   R.

See, the eyes of the LORD are upon
      those who fear him,
  upon those who hope
      for his kindness,
to deliver them from death
  and preserve them in spite
      of famine.   R.

Reading II 1 Peter 2:4–9

Beloved: Come to him, a living stone, rejected by human beings but chosen and precious in the sight of God, and, like living stones, let yourselves be built into a spiritual house to be a holy priesthood to offer spiritual sacrifices acceptable to God through Jesus Christ.

For it says in Scripture:

«Behold, I am laying a stone
    in Zion,
a cornerstone,
    chosen and precious,
and whoever believes in it shall
    not be put to shame.»

Therefore, its value is for you who have faith, but for those without faith:

«The stone that the builders
    rejected
has become the cornerstone,»

and

«A stone that will make
    people stumble,
and a rock that will make
    them fall.»

They stumble by disobeying the word, as is their destiny.

You are "a chosen race, a royal priesthood, a holy nation, a people of his own, so that you may announce the praises" of him who called you out of darkness into his wonderful light.

Gospel John 14:1–12

Jesus said to his disciples: "Do not let your hearts be troubled. You have faith in God; have faith also in me. In my Father's house there are many dwelling places. If there were not, would I have told you that I am going to prepare a place for you? And if I go and prepare a place for you, I will come back again and take you to myself, so that where I am you also may be. Where I am going you know the way." Thomas said to him, "Master, we do not know where you are going; how can we know the way?" Jesus said to him, "I am the way and the truth and the life. No one comes to the Father except through me. If you know me, then you will also know my Father. From now on you do know him and have seen him." Philip said to him,

"Master, show us the Father, and that will be enough for us." Jesus said to him, "Have I been with you for so long a time and you still do not know me, Philip? Whoever has seen me has seen the Father. How can you say, 'Show us the Father'? Do you not believe that I am in the Father and the Father is in me? The words that I speak to you I do not speak on my own. The Father who dwells in me is doing his works. Believe me that I am in the Father and the Father is in me, or else, believe because of the works themselves. Amen, amen, I say to you, whoever believes in me will do the works that I do, and will do greater ones than these, because I am going to the Father."

Practice of Faith

In this often-quoted passage from John's Gospel, we are reassured by Jesus, "I am the way and the truth and the life." The way of this faith is sacramental, connected with Christ himself, for example, in the Eucharistic meal that we share at each Mass. In his encyclical The Light of Faith, Pope Francis talks about the Church and our relationships where our faith is expressed and transmitted from generation to generation (38–45). As we say the Creed together, we remember intuitively that "all the truths in which we believe point to the mystery of the new life of faith as a journey of communion with the living God" (45). ◆ Relish the beauty of this encyclical, which celebrates the purpose of Jesus and our expression of faith (http://w2.vatican.va/content/francesco/en/encyclicals/documents/papa-francesco_20130629_enciclica-lumen-fidei.html). ◆ If you aren't familiar with lectio divina, consider learning about this practice and using this Gospel for sacred reading. ◆ As you pray with Scripture, imagine yourself in the role of Thomas in the Gospel.

Download more questions and activities for families, Christian initiation groups, and other adult groups at http://www.ltp.org/ahw.

Scripture Insights

The nature of the Church's ministry emerges in the First Reading from Acts. In response to the continued growth of the early Church, the Apostles choose seven men, filled with the Holy Spirit, to share their ministry of service. The role of deacon (from the Greek word <u>diakonein</u>, "to serve") emerges. Preaching (leading people in worship of God) and service (caring for the poor) are the two foundational pillars of ministry.

In his first letter, Peter identifies the Risen Lord as "a living stone," chosen by God the Father, as the cornerstone of a spiritual house where we, his followers, become "living stones." In spiritual unity with the Risen Christ, we are "a chosen race, a royal priesthood, a holy nation, a people of his own."

The context for the Gospel reading is Jesus' discourse with his followers at the Last Supper. Jesus refers to himself as "the way and the truth and the life." We are followers of the Way (Jesus) that leads us to the Father. Jesus reveals his intimate relationship with the Father: he is in the Father, as the Father is in him. Jesus' words are the Father's words, and Jesus' works are the Father's works. United with him, Jesus promises his followers that they too will do great works.

From these readings emerge a deeper understanding of Jesus and of our identity. Jesus is the human face of God, as Pope Benedict XVI described him in his encyclicals <u>Saved in Hope</u> and <u>Charity in Truth</u>. As God's "chosen race," we follow Jesus, the Way, to our eternal home.

◆ How are the tasks of the seven men in Acts related to our deacons today?

◆ What meaning does Jesus' identification as "the way and the truth and the life" have for you?

◆ "You are a chosen race, a royal priesthood, a holy nation, a people of his own." How do these words help you to appreciate yourself as a member of the Body of Christ?

May 17, 2020

SIXTH SUNDAY OF EASTER

READING I Acts 8:5-8, 14-17

Philip went down to the city of Samaria and proclaimed the Christ to them. With one accord, the crowds paid attention to what was said by Philip when they heard it and saw the signs he was doing. For unclean spirits, crying out in a loud voice, came out of many possessed people, and many paralyzed or crippled people were cured. There was great joy in that city.

Now when the apostles in Jerusalem heard that Samaria had accepted the word of God, they sent them Peter and John, who went down and prayed for them, that they might receive the Holy Spirit, for it had not yet fallen upon any of them; they had only been baptized in the name of the Lord Jesus. Then they laid hands on them and they received the Holy Spirit.

RESPONSORIAL PSALM
Psalm 66:1-3, 4-5, 6-7, 16, 20 (1)

R. Let all the earth cry out
         to God with joy.
or: Alleluia.

Shout joyfully to God, all the earth,
   sing praise to the glory
         of his name;
   proclaim his glorious praise.
Say to God, "How tremendous
         are your deeds!" R.

"Let all on earth worship and
         sing praise to you,
   sing praise to your name!"
Come and see the works of God,
   his tremendous deeds among
         the children of Adam. R.

He has changed the sea into
         dry land;
   through the river they passed
         on foot;
   therefore let us rejoice in him.
He rules by his might forever. R.

Hear now, all you who fear God,
    while I declare
what he has done for me.
Blessed be God who refused me not
    my prayer or his kindness!   R.

READING II 1 Peter 3:15-18

Beloved: Sanctify Christ as Lord in your hearts. Always be ready to give an explanation to anyone who asks you for a reason for your hope, but do it with gentleness and reverence, keeping your conscience clear, so that, when you are maligned, those who defame your good conduct in Christ may themselves be put to shame. For it is better to suffer for doing good, if that be the will of God, than for doing evil. For Christ also suffered for sins once, the righteous for the sake of the unrighteous, that he might lead you to God. Put to death in the flesh, he was brought to life in the Spirit.

GOSPEL John 14:15-21

Jesus said to his disciples: "If you love me, you will keep my commandments. And I will ask the Father, and he will give you another Advocate to be with you always, the Spirit of truth, whom the world cannot accept, because it neither sees nor knows him. But you know him, because he remains with you, and will be in you. I will not leave you orphans; I will come to you. In a little while the world will no longer see me, but you will see me, because I live and you will live. On that day you will realize that I am in my Father and you are in me and I in you. Whoever has my commandments and observes them is the one who loves me. And whoever loves me will be loved by my Father, and I will love him and reveal myself to him."

Practice of Hope

The Holy Spirit can be seen alive in the world in the ministry of the pope. The message of love that Jesus instilled in all of us is being amplified through the pope's travels around the world, his communications on the Internet, and his outreach to people in many ways. His humble examples of integrity are inspirational on a global scale, not just to Catholics.
◆ Take a step back from your current news sources and purposely search for positive news about how God's Spirit is at work. Tap into sources such as America magazine, news from the United States Conference of Catholic Bishops (www.usccb.org), Franciscan Media (www.franciscan media.org), or Dynamic Catholic (https://dynamiccatholic.com), for starters. ◆ As a way to grow your faith, consider becoming part of a parish Bible study or starting one of your own.

Download more questions and activities for families, Christian initiation groups, and other adult groups at http://www.ltp.org/ahw.

Scripture Insights

Our Gospel reading last week offered insight into the relationship between Jesus and the Father. Today's reading, also from Jesus' farewell discourse, develops this relationship further to include their relationship with the Holy Spirt. Here, Jesus is concerned that the disciples not feel alone when he leaves them. He tells them that they will not be "orphans" and that the Father will send another Advocate. In Greek, the word Paraclete means someone whose task is to speak on their behalf. Jesus promises the disciples the Holy Spirit as the Paraclete, to take his place to be with them and act on their behalf. This Spirit will live intimately within the disciples.

Jesus reminds his follows of his call to follow his commandment of love: "If you love me, you will keep my commandments." Love is at the heart of every relationship, especially our relationship with God and with our neighbor. We share in the very life of God, a life of love: "Whoever loves me will be loved by my Father."

In the reading from Acts, the life of the early Church flourishes through the power of the Holy Spirit. Hearing that the Word of God had been preached to the Samaritans, the Apostles send Peter and John to empower them with the gift of the Holy Spirit as "they had only been baptized in the name of the Lord Jesus." As Jesus came "to baptize with the holy Spirit" (John 1:33), the Apostles confer the gift of the Holy Spirit by "laying hands on them." Here the foundation for the Sacraments of Baptism and Confirmation is expressed clearly.

◆ What does Peter mean when he says, "it is better to suffer for doing good, if that be the will of God, than for doing evil"?

◆ How do we show love for Jesus by keeping the commandments?

◆ How have you experienced the presence of the Holy Spirit?

THE ASCENSION OF THE LORD

READING I Acts 1:1-11

In the first book, Theophilus, I dealt with all that Jesus did and taught until the day he was taken up, after giving instructions through the Holy Spirit to the apostles whom he had chosen. He presented himself alive to them by many proofs after he had suffered, appearing to them during forty days and speaking about the kingdom of God. While meeting with them, he enjoined them not to depart from Jerusalem, but to wait for "the promise of the Father about which you have heard me speak; for John baptized with water, but in a few days you will be baptized with the Holy Spirit."

When they had gathered together they asked him, "Lord, are you at this time going to restore the kingdom to Israel?" He answered them, "It is not for you to know the times or seasons that the Father has established by his own authority. But you will receive power when the Holy Spirit comes upon you, and you will be my witnesses in Jerusalem, throughout Judea and Samaria, and to the ends of the earth." When he had said this, as they were looking on, he was lifted up, and a cloud took him from their sight. While they were looking intently at the sky as he was going, suddenly two men dressed in white garments stood beside them. They said, "Men of Galilee, why are you standing there looking at the sky? This Jesus who has been taken up from you into heaven will return in the same way as you have seen him going into heaven."

RESPONSORIAL PSALM
Psalm 47:2-3, 6-7, 8-9 (6)

R. God mounts his throne to
     shouts of joy: a blare
     of trumpets for the Lord.
or: Alleluia.

All you peoples, clap your hands,
  shout to God with cries
     of gladness.
For the LORD, the Most High,
     the awesome,
  is the great king over all
     the earth.   R.

God mounts his throne amid
    shouts of joy;
  the LORD, amid trumpet blasts.
Sing praise to God, sing praise;
  sing praise to our king,
    sing praise. R.

For king of all the earth is God;
  sing hymns of praise.
God reigns over the nations,
  God sits upon his
    holy throne. R.

READING II
Ephesians 1:17–23

Brothers and sisters: May the
God of our Lord Jesus Christ, the
Father of glory, give you a Spirit of
wisdom and revelation resulting in
knowledge of him. May the eyes of
your hearts be enlightened, that
you may know what is the hope that
belongs to his call, what are the
riches of glory in his inheritance
among the holy ones, and what is
the surpassing greatness of his
power for us who believe, in accord
with the exercise of his great might,
which he worked in Christ, raising
him from the dead and seating
him at his right hand in the heavens,
far above every principality,
authority, power, and dominion,
and every name that is named not
only in this age but also in the one
to come. And he put all things
beneath his feet and gave him as
head over all things to the church,
which is his body, the fullness
of the one who fills all things in
every way.

GOSPEL Matthew 28:16–20

The eleven disciples went to Galilee,
to the mountain to which Jesus
had ordered them. When they saw
him, they worshiped, but they
doubted. Then Jesus approached
and said to them, "All power in
heaven and on earth has been given
to me. Go, therefore, and make
disciples of all nations, baptizing
them in the name of the Father,
and of the Son, and of the Holy
Spirit, teaching them to observe
all that I have commanded you.
And behold, I am with you always,
until the end of the age."

Practice of Faith

"I am with you always, until the end of the age." Jesus promises that the new life he brings will always be present. We may not understand this fully, but we know from our faith that God's Spirit lives within each of us. We are challenged by Jesus' words to "Go, therefore, and make disciples of all nations, baptizing them . . . teaching them to observe all that I have commanded you." By our actions of patience and mercy with each other, we can become God's healing presence. ◆ Speak gently with family members or friends who may have strayed from the practice of the Christian faith to explore how you could be a reconciling presence. ◆ The next time you drive to a destination with friends or family, consider talking with them without the radio on (as well as other devices) in the hope that more meaningful conversation ensues. ◆ Think about how you can get involved in the parish Christian initiation process as a companion for someone considering Catholicism. Be the Spirit's presence to a candidate or catechumen as they journey through the process.

Download more questions and activities for families, Christian initiation groups, and other adult groups at http://www.ltp.org/ahw.

Scripture Insights

The Solemnity of the Ascension marks a move from the Risen Lord at Easter to the coming of the Holy Spirit at Pentecost. In the reading from the Letter to the Ephesians, Paul reflects on God the Father's power that raised Jesus from the dead and seated him "at his right hand." This biblical image symbolizes Jesus' share in the Father's power by placing all things in the universe subject to him.

Jesus promises to communicate this power to his disciples in the reading from Acts: "But you will receive power when the Holy Spirit comes upon you." The Risen Lord makes this final promise on leaving his disciples at the Ascension, as Luke records in the opening of his second volume. The Holy Spirit will empower his disciples to "be my witnesses in Jerusalem, throughout Judea and Samaria, and to the ends of earth."

The Gospel reading contains the Risen Lord's final commission to his disciples before his Ascension. Jesus communicates his power to them for their mission to evangelize the world: "All power in heaven and on earth has been given to me. Go, therefore, and make disciples of all nations." This mission continues Jesus' mission to bring people into relationship with the Father, Son, and Holy Spirit through Baptism and to teach them "to observe all that I have commanded you." Jesus' final words that he will be with his followers "until the end of the age" are a reminder of his eternal relationship with us as proclaimed at his birth (Matthew 1:23): "and they shall name him Emmanuel, which means 'God is with us.'"

◆ What are the effects of the "power of the Holy Spirit" on the lives of the disciples?

◆ In the Gospel, what is the final commission the Risen Lord gives to his disciples?

◆ How have you experienced the presence of Jesus Christ in your daily life as he promised?

May 24, 2020

SEVENTH SUNDAY OF EASTER

READING I Acts 1:12–14

After Jesus had been taken up to heaven the apostles returned to Jerusalem from the mount called Olivet, which is near Jerusalem, a sabbath day's journey away.

When they entered the city they went to the upper room where they were staying, Peter and John and James and Andrew, Philip and Thomas, Bartholomew and Matthew, James son of Alphaeus, Simon the Zealot, and Judas son of James. All these devoted themselves with one accord to prayer, together with some women, and Mary the mother of Jesus, and his brothers.

RESPONSORIAL PSALM
Psalm 27:1, 4, 7–8 (13)

R. I believe that I shall see
        the good things of the Lord
        in the land of the living.
or: Alleluia.

The LORD is my light and
        my salvation;
    whom should I fear?
The LORD is my life's refuge;
    of whom should I be afraid?   R.

One thing I ask of the LORD;
    this I seek:
to dwell in the house of the LORD
    all the days of my life,
that I may gaze on the loveliness
        of the LORD
    and contemplate his temple.   R.

Hear, O LORD, the sound of my call;
    have pity on me, and answer me.
Of you my heart speaks;
        you my glance seeks.   R.

Reading II 1 Peter 4:13–16

Beloved: Rejoice to the extent that you share in the sufferings of Christ, so that when his glory is revealed you may also rejoice exultantly. If you are insulted for the name of Christ, blessed are you, for the Spirit of glory and of God rests upon you. But let no one among you be made to suffer as a murderer, a thief, an evildoer, or as an intriguer. But whoever is made to suffer as a Christian should not be ashamed but glorify God because of the name.

Gospel John 17:1–11a

Jesus raised his eyes to heaven and said, "Father, the hour has come. Give glory to your son, so that your son may glorify you, just as you gave him authority over all people, so that your son may give eternal life to all you gave him. Now this is eternal life, that they should know you, the only true God, and the one whom you sent, Jesus Christ. I glorified you on earth by accomplishing the work that you gave me to do. Now glorify me, Father, with you, with the glory that I had with you before the world began.

"I revealed your name to those whom you gave me out of the world. They belonged to you, and you gave them to me, and they have kept your word. Now they know that everything you gave me is from you, because the words you gave to me I have given to them, and they accepted them and truly understood that I came from you, and they have believed that you sent me. I pray for them. I do not pray for the world but for the ones you have given me, because they are yours, and everything of mine is yours and everything of yours is mine, and I have been glorified in them. And now I will no longer be in the world, but they are in the world, while I am coming to you."

Practice of Faith

As we approach the end of the Easter season, today's readings recall Christ's suffering and address the feelings of abandonment that the disciples would experience between the crucifixion and Resurrection. Even as Christ prepared for his passion and death, he also prepared his disciples for his departure and, in his prayer, promised to sustain them. Our Easter faith assures us that we never face trials alone. Christ has promised to be with us always and surrounds us with a faith-filled community to support and journey with us. Reach out through a phone call, letter, or visit to someone who might be feeling isolated or alone. ◆ Reflect on your experiences of loneliness and the gift of community as you read this passage from Dorothy Day's autobiography, The Long Loneliness: "We cannot love God unless we love each other, and to love we must know each other. We know him in the breaking of bread, and we are not alone any more." ◆ Pray in thanksgiving for the blessing of being part of the community of faith, the Church.

Download more questions and activities for families, Christian initiation groups, and other adult groups at http://www.ltp.org/ahw.

Scripture Insights

John 17 is known among Johannine scholars as Jesus' farewell prayer before his arrest and trial. In this prayer, Jesus prays for the protection and the unity of those who follow him during or after his life on earth.

The rest of Jesus's prayer in John 17 gives reasons for the need for God's protection and for Christian unity. The former is needed because Christ's followers may face hostility in "the world" (17:14–16), and the latter because it functions as an essential Christian witness (17:23). There also is a close connection between God's protection and the Christian unity that John emphasizes. Christian unity is itself a form of divine protection (see John 13). This is, in a sense, what the disciples are doing in Acts 1 when they huddle together in prayer in the upper room. After Jesus' Ascension, they may be feeling a sense of loss again; however, they are able to take up the mission of the Church through unity and mutual support.

First Peter gives a similar message. Written metaphorically to "aliens" and "sojourners" (1:1, 17; 2:11) who have left the lawless ways of their gentile ancestors and neighbors (1:18; 4:1–4), they have become vulnerable, troubled, and unsettled, as the verses we read today show. The letter begins and closes, however, by affirming that they, as strangers in their land and oppressed by kings and governors (2:13–14, 17), have found a new family with each other and anyone who has chosen to follow Jesus (1:1, 3–5; 5:9, 12–13). With the love and support of each other, they too can express confidence in God's protection in the midst of trials and fear.

◆ Who are the people who have become strangers in their own land today?

◆ How can your parish become a network of love and support for those who live in fear and under oppression?

◆ Do you think the Church is seen as a Church of comfort or one that comforts the afflicted?

May 31, 2020

PENTECOST

READING I Acts 2:1–11

When the time for Pentecost was fulfilled, they were all in one place together. And suddenly there came from the sky a noise like a strong driving wind, and it filled the entire house in which they were. Then there appeared to them tongues as of fire, which parted and came to rest on each one of them. And they were all filled with the Holy Spirit and began to speak in different tongues, as the Spirit enabled them to proclaim.

Now there were devout Jews from every nation under heaven staying in Jerusalem. At this sound, they gathered in a large crowd, but they were confused because each one heard them speaking in his own language. They were astounded, and in amazement they asked, "Are not all these people who are speaking Galileans? Then how does each of us hear them in his native language? We are Parthians, Medes, and Elamites, inhabitants of Mesopotamia, Judea and Cappadocia, Pontus and Asia, Phrygia and Pamphylia, Egypt and the districts of Libya near Cyrene, as well as travelers from Rome, both Jews and converts to Judaism, Cretans and Arabs, yet we hear them speaking in our own tongues of the mighty acts of God."

RESPONSORIAL PSALM
Psalm 104:1, 24, 29–30, 29, 31, 34 (see 30)

R. Lord, send out your Spirit,
    and renew the face of
    the earth.
or: Alleluia.

Bless the LORD, O my soul!
  O LORD, my God,
    you are great indeed!
How manifold are your works,
    O LORD!
  the earth is full of
    your creatures. R.

If you take away their breath,
    they perish
  and return to their dust.
When you send forth your spirit,
    they are created,
  and you renew the face
    of the earth. R.

May the glory of the LORD
    endure forever;
may the LORD be glad in
    his works!
Pleasing to him be my theme;
    I will be glad in the LORD. R.

READING II
1 Corinthians 12:3b–7, 12–13

Brothers and sisters: No one can say, "Jesus is Lord," except by the Holy Spirit.

There are different kinds of spiritual gifts but the same Spirit; there are different forms of service but the same Lord; there are different workings but the same God who produces all of them in everyone. To each individual the manifestation of the Spirit is given for some benefit.

As a body is one though it has many parts, and all the parts of the body, though many, are one body, so also Christ. For in one Spirit we were all baptized into one body, whether Jews or Greeks, slaves or free persons, and we were all given to drink of one Spirit.

GOSPEL John 20:19–23

On the evening of that first day of the week, when the doors were locked, where the disciples were, for fear of the Jews, Jesus came and stood in their midst and said to them, "Peace be with you." When he had said this, he showed them his hands and his side. The disciples rejoiced when they saw the Lord. Jesus said to them again, "Peace be with you. As the Father has sent me, so I send you." And when he had said this, he breathed on them and said to them, "Receive the Holy Spirit. Whose sins you forgive are forgiven them, and whose sins you retain are retained."

Practice of Hope

As the Church celebrates Pentecost, she remembers how the Holy Spirit emboldened those gathered in the upper room to proclaim the Gospel to the diverse populations gathered in Jerusalem, extending Jesus' message of peace to all. We look back so that we can recognize the Spirit's continuing work in the Church, uniting us as we celebrate our diversity of gifts and bringing the peace of Christ through forgiveness of sins. May our celebration of Pentecost inspire us to be people of hope and peace.
◆ With whom do you need to find peace? Ask for the Holy Spirit's guidance and take steps toward forgiveness and reconciliation.
◆ Reflect on Pope Francis' Pentecost message in 2017 to a general audience: "The expression 'God of hope' does not mean only that God is the object of our hope . . . ; it also means that God is the One who already makes us hope, rather, makes us 'rejoice in hope'" (Romans 12:12). ◆ Through this week, meditate on these words from today's Gospel: "Peace be with you. As the Father has sent me, so I send you."

Download more questions and activities for families, Christian initiation groups, and other adult groups at http://www.ltp.org/ahw.

Scripture Insights

A miracle of language takes place when the Holy Spirit descends on the Church. Only verse four in Acts 2 notes the speaking of various languages, but seven verses emphasize the ability of people to <u>hear</u> and <u>understand</u> (2:5–11). Despite the presence of people from "every nation under heaven" and hence of multiple languages, people are able to hear and understand each other.

If Acts 2 associates the Holy Spirit's coming with hearing and understanding, the verses in John 20 link it with peace and forgiveness. Forgiveness can help bring peace, but forgiveness seldom occurs without hearing and understanding, which enable one to put oneself in another's shoes.

Perhaps one of the reasons for our difficulties in hearing, understanding, forgiving, and being at peace with others is our failure to learn that difference is a gift of the Holy Spirit, as today's Second Reading makes clear. The same Holy Spirit does not bring about uniformity; instead, we are gifted with different abilities, roles, and functions. The reading further emphasizes that we are given gifts by the Holy Spirit "for some benefit."

In Acts 2, what people hear and understand are "the mighty acts of God" (2:11). Likewise, the giving of the Holy Spirit in John 20 has to do with the disciples being sent out to mission. That Jesus needs to give his peace pronouncement twice may indicate that the disciples' rejoicing is premature (20:20). They did not understand yet that they too will be sent out, and, in doing so, they may experience what Jesus experienced in his hands and side.

We find this larger purpose of Pentecost again in Psalm 104. The Holy Spirit works to renew all creation and the face of the earth. Pentecostal peace involves more than peace among human beings.

◆ How may we think of Pentecost as marking a challenging beginning rather than a happy ending?

◆ What keeps us from hearing and understanding difference?

◆ What may it mean to "renew the face of the earth" today?

Ordinary Time, Summer

Prayer before Reading the Word

God, sower of the seed,
we marvel at how your
  Word accomplishes
the purpose for which you sent
  it forth:
how few of the seeds you sow
  take root,
yet how spectacular their
  abundant yield.

Make us good soil, ready to receive
  what you sow,
that we may hear the Word and
  understand it,
bear fruit and yield a hundredfold.

We ask this through our Lord
  Jesus Christ, your Son,
who lives and reigns with you
in the unity of the Holy Spirit,
one God for ever and ever. Amen.

Prayer after Reading the Word

To us, sinners and yet disciples,
O Lord of the harvest,
you entrust a share in the mission
  of Jesus,
who sent the Twelve to proclaim
  the Good News
and to bear witness without fear.

With your love forever sheltering
  and surrounding us,
may we proclaim from
  the housetops
the Gospel we have heard
and acknowledge openly before all
the one whom we confess as Lord,
Jesus Christ, your Son, who lives
  and reigns with you
in the unity of the Holy Spirit,
one God for ever and ever. Amen.

Weekday Readings

June 1: Genesis 3:9–15, 20 or
    Acts 1:12–14; John 19:25–34

June 2: 2 Peter 3:12–15a, 17–18;
    Mark 12:13–17

June 3: 2 Timothy 1:1–3, 6–12;
    Mark 12:18–27

June 4: 2 Timothy 2:8–15;
    Mark 12:28–34

June 5: 2 Timothy 3:10–17;
    Mark 12:35–37

June 6: 2 Timothy 4:1–8;
    Mark 12:38–44

June 8: 1 Kings 17:1–6;
    Matthew 5:1–12

June 9: 1 Kings 17:7–16;
    Matthew 5:13–16

June 10: 1 Kings 18:20–39;
    Matthew 5:17–19

June 11: Acts 11:21b–26; 13:1–3;
    Matthew 5:20–26

June 12: 1 Kings 19:9a, 11–16;
    Matthew 5:27–32

June 13: 1 Kings 19:19–21;
    Matthew 5:33–37

June 15: 1 Kings 21:1–16;
    Matthew 5:38–42

June 16: 1 Kings 21:17–29;
    Matthew 5:43–48

June 17: 2 Kings 2:1, 6–14;
    Matthew 6:1–6, 16–18

June 18: Sirach 48:1–14;
    Matthew 6:7–15

**June 19: Solemnity of the Most
Sacred Heart of Jesus
Deuteronomy 7:6–11; 1 John
4:7–16; Matthew 11:25–30**

June 20: 2 Chronicles 24:17–25
    (370); Luke 2:41–51

June 22: 2 Kings 17:5–8, 13–15a,
    18; Matthew 7:1–5

June 23: 2 Kings 19:9b–11, 14–21,
    31–35a, 36;
    Matthew 7:6, 12–14

**June 24: Solemnity of the Nativity
of St. John the Baptist
Isaiah 49:1–6; Acts 13:22–26;
Luke 1:57–66, 80**

June 25: 2 Kings 24:8–17;
    Matthew 7:21–29

June 26: 2 Kings 25:1–12;
    Matthew 8:1–4

June 27: Lam 2:2, 10–14, 18–19;
    Matthew 8:5–17

**June 29: Solemnity of Sts. Peter
    and Paul, Apostles
    Acts 12:1–11;
    2 Timothy 4:6–8, 17–18;
    Matthew 16:13–19**

June 30: Amos 3:1–8; 4:11–12;
    Matthew 8:23–27

July 1: Amos 5:14–15, 21–24;
    Matthew 8:28–34

July 2: Amos 7:10–17;
    Matthew 9:1–8

**July 3: Feast of
    St. Thomas, Apostle
    Ephesians 2:19–22;
    John 20:24–29**

July 4: Amos 9:11–15;
    Matthew 9:14–17

July 6: Hosea 2:16, 17b–18, 21–22;
    Matthew 9:18–26

July 7: Hosea 8:4–7, 11–13;
    Matthew 9:32–38

July 8: Hosea 10:1–3, 7–8, 12;
    Matthew 10:1–7

July 9: Hosea 11:1–4, 8e–9;
    Matthew 10:7–15

July 10: Hosea 14:2–10;
    Matthew 10:16–23

July 11: Isaiah 6:1–8;
    Matthew 10:24–33

July 13: Isaiah 1:10–17;
    Matthew 10:34—11:1

July 14: Isaiah 7:1–9;
    Matthew 11:20–24

July 15: Isaiah 10:5–7, 13b–16;
    Matthew 11:25–27

July 16: Isaiah 26:7–9, 12, 16–19;
    Matthew 11:28–30

July 17: Isaiah 38:1–6, 21–22, 7–8;
    Matthew 12:1–8

July 18: Micah 2:1–5;
    Matthew 12:14–21

July 20: Micah 6:1–4, 6–8;
    Matthew 12:38–42

July 21: Micah 7:14–15, 18–20;
    Matthew 12:46–50

**July 22: Feast of
    St. Mary Magdalene
    Song of Songs 3:1–4b or
    2 Corinthians 5:14–17;
    John 20:1–2, 11–18**

July 23: Jeremiah 2:1–3, 7–8,
    12–13; Matthew 13:10–17

July 24: Jeremiah 3:14–17;
    Matthew 13:18–23

**July 25: Feast of St. James,
    Apostle; 2 Corinthians
    4:7–15; Matthew 20:20–28**

July 27: Jeremiah 13:1–11;
　　　　Matthew 13:31–35

July 28: Jeremiah 14:17–22;
　　　　Matthew 13:36–43

July 29: Jeremiah 15:10, 16–21
　　　　(403); John 11:19–27
　　　　or Luke 10:38–42

July 30: Jeremiah 18:1–6;
　　　　Matthew 13:47–53

July 31: Jeremiah 26:1–9;
　　　　Matthew 13:54–58

August 1: Jeremiah 26:11–16, 24;
　　　　Matthew 14:1–12

August 3: Jeremiah 28:1–17 (407);
　　　　Matthew 14:22–36

August 4: Jeremiah 30:1–2, 12–15,
　　　　18–22; Matthew 14:22–36 or
　　　　Matthew 15:1–2, 10–14

August 5: Jeremiah 30:1–2, 12–15,
　　　　18–22; Matthew 14:22–36 or
　　　　Matthew 15:1–2, 10–14

August 6: Feast of the
　　　　Transfiguration of the Lord
　　　　Daniel 7:9–10, 13–14; 2 Peter
　　　　1:16–19; Matthew 17:1–9

August 7: Nahum 2:1, 3; 3:1–3,
　　　　6–7; Matthew 16:24–28

August 8: Hebrews 1:12—2:4;
　　　　Matthew 17:14–20

August 10: Feast of St. Lawrence,
　　　　Deacon and Martyr
　　　　2 Corinthians 9:6–10;
　　　　John 12:24–26

August 11: Ezekiel 2:8—3:4;
　　　　Matthew 18:1–5, 10, 12–14

August 12: Ezekiel 9:1–7; 10:18–22;
　　　　Matthew 18:15–20

August 13: Ezekiel 12:1–12;
　　　　Matthew 18:21—19:1

August 14: Ezekiel 16:1–15, 60, 63
　　　　or 16:59–63;
　　　　Matthew 19:3–12

August 15: Solemnity of
　　　　the Assumption
　　　　of the Blessed Virgin Mary
　　　　Revelation 11:19a;
　　　　12:1–6a, 10ab;
　　　　1 Corinthians 15:20–27;
　　　　Luke 1:39–56

August 17: Ezekiel 24:15–24;
　　　　Matthew 19:16–22

August 18: Ezekiel 28:1–10;
　　　　Matthew 19:23–30

August 19: Ezekiel 34:1–11;
　　　　Matthew 20:1–16

August 20: Ezekiel 36:23–28;
　　　　Matthew 22:1–14

August 21: Ezekiel 37:1–14;
　　　　Matthew 22:34–40

August 22: Ezekiel 43:1–7ab;
　　　　Matthew 23:1–12

August 24: Feast of
St. Bartholomew, Apostle
Revelation 21:9b–14;
John 1:45–51

August 25: 2 Thessalonians 2:1–3a,
14–17;
Matthew 23:23–26

August 26: 2 Thessalonians 3:6–10,
16–18;
Matthew 23:27–32

August 27: 1 Corinthians 1:1–9;
Matthew 24:42–51

August 28: 1 Corinthians 1:17–25;
Matthew 25:1–13

August 29: 1 Corinthians 1:26–31
(430); Mark 6:17–29

June 7, 2020

THE MOST HOLY TRINITY

READING I
Exodus 34:4b–6, 8–9

Early in the morning Moses went up Mount Sinai as the LORD had commanded him, taking along the two stone tablets.

Having come down in a cloud, the LORD stood with Moses there and proclaimed his name, "LORD." Thus the LORD passed before him and cried out, "The LORD, the LORD, a merciful and gracious God, slow to anger and rich in kindness and fidelity." Moses at once bowed down to the ground in worship. Then he said, "If I find favor with you, O LORD, do come along in our company. This is indeed a stiff-necked people; yet pardon our wickedness and sins, and receive us as your own."

RESPONSORIAL PSALM
Daniel 3:52, 53, 54, 55, (52b)

R. Glory and praise for ever!

Blessed are you, O Lord,
     the God of our fathers,
  praiseworthy and exalted
     above all forever;
And blessed is your holy and
     glorious name,
  praiseworthy and exalted
     above all for all ages.   R.

Blessed are you in the temple
     of your holy glory,
  praiseworthy and glorious
     above all forever.   R.

Blessed are you on the throne
     of your kingdom,
  praiseworthy and exalted
     above all forever.   R.

Blessed are you who look
     into the depths
from your throne upon
     the cherubim,
  praiseworthy and exalted
     above all forever.   R.

Reading II
2 Corinthians 13:11–13

Brothers and sisters, rejoice. Mend your ways, encourage one another, agree with one another, live in peace, and the God of love and peace will be with you. Greet one another with a holy kiss. All the holy ones greet you.

The grace of the Lord Jesus Christ and the love of God and the fellowship of the Holy Spirit be with all of you.

Gospel John 3:16–18

God so loved the world that he gave his only Son, so that everyone who believes in him might not perish but might have eternal life. For God did not send his Son into the world to condemn the world, but that the world might be saved through him. Whoever believes in him will not be condemned, but whoever does not believe has already been condemned, because he has not believed in the name of the only Son of God.

Practice of Charity

The words that conclude today's Second Reading are also heard as a greeting at Mass. As we gather at the liturgy, we acknowledge that God is known in the ways that he pours out his love so that we may share in the divine life of the Trinity. Like Moses, we have the audacity to invite God who is love to dwell among us. ◆ Take extra care to reflect God's love and peace when greeting others this week. ◆ Consider this from the US bishops' 1998 statement, Sharing Catholic Social Teaching: Challenges and Directions: "We believe in the triune God whose very nature is communal and social. . . . God reveals himself to us as one who is not alone, but rather as one who is relational, one who is Trinity. Therefore, we who are made in God's image share this communal, social nature. We are called to reach out and to build relationships of love and justice." ◆ Pray to the Blessed Trinity to grow in communion with others.

Download more questions and activities for families, Christian initiation groups, and other adult groups at http://www.ltp.org/ahw.

Scripture Insights

Today's Responsorial Psalm from Daniel 3 comes from a hymn of praise sung by three Jews who were exiled to Babylon and put into a fiery furnace for refusing to worship a golden statue but were not burnt.

God's people have not always been so resolute against idolatry, however. In Exodus 34, Moses is instructed to make two new tablets of the covenant because he angrily broke the former tablets when he saw the people worshiping a golden calf. Like the people who want a more concrete and visible image for God in the absence of Moses, Moses seems to have trouble following a God whom he cannot see (Exodus 33), so he asks to see God's face (cf. Exodus 33:12–13). Despite all of this, God makes a point to repeat the covenant and ask Moses to remake the tablets to affirm that God is "merciful and gracious, slow to anger, and rich in kindness and fidelity."

We see God's love emphasized also in John 3. Note here that oft-articulated but utterly mistaken idea that there is a God of wrath in the Old Testament but a God of love in the New. In fact, it is difficult if not impossible to capture the God of the Bible in a single sentence. After all, today's Gospel mentions God's decisive condemnation of unbelievers. Likewise, the "merciful and gracious" God of Exodus 34 is also a "jealous God" who tells Moses that he must drive out people who are already populating the Promised Land (Exodus 34:11, 14). This, like the pronouncement of condemnation in John 3, is very different from the call to "live in peace" in 2 Corinthians 13.

◆ What may idolatry mean or involve besides the casting of idols?

◆ The word Israel means wrestling with God. How might that describe God's people today?

◆ How might steadfast love for others bring about peace?

June 14, 2020

THE MOST HOLY BODY AND BLOOD OF CHRIST

READING I Deuteronomy 8:2–3, 14b–16a

Moses said to the people: "Remember how for forty years now the LORD, your God, has directed all your journeying in the desert, so as to test you by affliction and find out whether or not it was your intention to keep his commandments. He therefore let you be afflicted with hunger, and then fed you with manna, a food unknown to you and your fathers, in order to show you that not by bread alone does one live, but by every word that comes forth from the mouth of the LORD.

"Do not forget the LORD, your God, who brought you out of the land of Egypt, that place of slavery; who guided you through the vast and terrible desert with its saraph serpents and scorpions, its parched and waterless ground; who brought forth water for you from the flinty rock and fed you in the desert with manna, a food unknown to your fathers."

RESPONSORIAL PSALM Psalm 147:12–13, 14–15, 19–20 (12)

R. Praise the Lord, Jerusalem.
or: Alleluia.

Glorify the LORD, O Jerusalem;
   praise your God, O Zion.
For he has strengthened
         the bars of your gates;
   he has blessed your children
         within you.   R.

He has granted peace in
         your borders;
   with the best of wheat
         he fills you.
He sends forth his command
         to the earth;
   swiftly runs his word!   R.

He has proclaimed his word
         to Jacob,
   his statutes and his ordinances
         to Israel.
He has not done thus for
         any other nation;
   his ordinances he has not made
         known to them.
         Alleluia.   R.

READING II
1 Corinthians 10:16–17

Brothers and sisters: The cup of blessing that we bless, is it not a participation in the blood of Christ? The bread that we break, is it not a participation in the body of Christ? Because the loaf of bread is one, we, though many, are one body, for we all partake of the one loaf.

GOSPEL John 6:51–58

Jesus said to the Jewish crowds: "I am the living bread that came down from heaven; whoever eats this bread will live forever; and the bread that I will give is my flesh for the life of the world."

The Jews quarreled among themselves, saying, "How can this man give us his flesh to eat?" Jesus said to them, "Amen, amen, I say to you, unless you eat the flesh of the Son of Man and drink his blood, you do not have life within you. Whoever eats my flesh and drinks my blood has eternal life, and I will raise him on the last day. For my flesh is true food, and my blood is true drink. Whoever eats my flesh and drinks my blood remains in me and I in him. Just as the living Father sent me and I have life because of the Father, so also the one who feeds on me will have life because of me. This is the bread that came down from heaven. Unlike your ancestors who ate and still died, whoever eats this bread will live forever."

Practice of Faith

We are a people hungry for connection with others, and this hunger is more than satisfied as we share in the Body and Blood of Christ. The Eucharist gives us life by uniting us with Christ, with Christ's Body, the Church, and with all whom the Eucharist calls us to serve. To share this communion now is already a taste of the fullness of life that is promised in the Eucharist.
◆ Allow your faith in the Eucharist to lead you to action that all may be fed by contributing to a local food pantry, or sharing an action recommended by organizations such as Catholic Relief Services.
◆ Reflect on the integral connection between the Eucharist and life-giving acts in these sentences from paragraph 14 of Deus caritas est: "Union with Christ is also union with all those to whom he gives himself. I cannot possess Christ just for myself; I can belong to him only in union with all those who have become, or who will become, his own." ◆ Spend some time in prayer before the Blessed Sacrament reflecting on the life-giving effects of the Eucharist in your life.

Download more questions and activities for families, Christian initiation groups, and other adult groups at http://www.ltp.org/ahw.

Scripture Insights

Paul's First Letter to the Corinthians addresses a problem of division, since the Church is made up of people of different social status, educational level, and economic standing. This root problem leads to many of the issues that Paul addresses in the letter, including that of meat consumption, idols, the Eucharist, and spiritual gifts (1 Corinthians 8—12). In the verses for our reading today, Paul is trying to tell the Corinthians that, despite their status and economic difference, they are partners in Christ through the sharing of the same cup and the same bread.

Recounting God's provision of manna during the Israelites' wandering in the desert, Deuteronomy 8 proceeds to remind the Israelites that they need to humbly realize that their lives are dependent on God and God's word. When the Israelites experienced hunger and thirst during their wandering in the wilderness, it was God's daily provision of manna that sustained them for the journey.

Experiencing God's blessings and miracles, however, can become a source of pride and exclusion. We see this not only in the well-to-do Corinthians but in the psalmist of Psalm 147. While praising God for protecting Jerusalem and for God's mighty word, the psalmist ends by pronouncing Israel's monopoly on God's statute and ordinance.

Perhaps that is why we find Jesus in John 6 downplaying the significance of manna. Not only is Jesus' proclamation of himself as the living bread from heaven set against manna in the context of the Passover (6:4), but Jesus further declares in the passage today that there is no life without him.

◆ What are the keys to humility?

◆ How can we focus on sharing, partnership, and inclusion rather than on comparison, competition, and exclusion?

◆ What can a parish do to better integrate people of different status and class?

June 21, 2020

TWELFTH SUNDAY IN ORDINARY TIME

READING I
Jeremiah 20:10–13

Jeremiah said:
"I hear the whisperings of many:
  'Terror on every side!
  Denounce! let us
    denounce him!'
All those who were my friends
  are on the watch for any
    misstep of mine.
  'Perhaps he will be trapped;
    then we can prevail,
  and take our vengeance on him.'
But the LORD is with me,
  like a mighty champion:
my persecutors will stumble,
  they will not triumph.
In their failure they will be put to
    utter shame,
  to lasting, unforgettable
  confusion.
O LORD of hosts,
  you who test the just,
  who probe mind and heart,
let me witness the vengeance you
    take on them,
  for to you I have entrusted
    my cause.

Sing to the LORD,
  praise the LORD,
for he has rescued the life of
    the poor
  from the power of the wicked!"

RESPONSORIAL PSALM
Psalm 69:8–10, 14, 17, 33–35 (14c)

R. Lord, in your great love,
    answer me.

For your sake I bear insult,
  and shame covers my face.
I have become an outcast to
    my brothers,
  a stranger to my children,
because zeal for your house
    consumes me,
  and the insults of those who
    blaspheme you fall upon
    me. R.

I pray to you, O LORD,
  for the time of your favor,
    O God!
In your great kindness answer me
  with your constant help.
Answer me, O LORD, for bounteous
    is your kindness;
  in your great mercy turn toward
    me. R.

"See, you lowly ones, and be glad;
  you who seek God, may your
     hearts revive!
For the LORD hears the poor,
  and his own who are in bonds he
     spurns not.
Let the heavens and the earth
     praise him,
  the seas and whatever moves in
     them!" R.

READING II Romans 5:12–15

Brothers and sisters: Through one man sin entered the world, and through sin, death, and thus death came to all men, inasmuch as all sinned—for up to the time of the law, sin was in the world, though sin is not accounted when there is no law. But death reigned from Adam to Moses, even over those who did not sin after the pattern of the trespass of Adam, who is the type of the one who was to come.

But the gift is not like the transgression. For if by the transgression of the one the many died, how much more did the grace of God and the gracious gift of the one man Jesus Christ overflow for the many.

GOSPEL Matthew 10:26–33

Jesus said to the Twelve: "Fear no one. Nothing is concealed that will not be revealed, nor secret that will not be known. What I say to you in the darkness, speak in the light; what you hear whispered, proclaim on the housetops. And do not be afraid of those who kill the body but cannot kill the soul; rather, be afraid of the one who can destroy both soul and body in Gehenna. Are not two sparrows sold for a small coin? Yet not one of them falls to the ground without your Father's knowledge. Even all the hairs of your head are counted. So do not be afraid; you are worth more than many sparrows. Everyone who acknowledges me before others I will acknowledge before my heavenly Father. But whoever denies me before others, I will deny before my heavenly Father."

Practice of Hope

At some point in life, we may face difficult circumstances, such as serious illness, sudden loss, natural disaster, and violence. Even ordinary challenges can seem overwhelming at times. God does not promise anyone a life untouched by difficulties or even tragedy. Instead, God offers abundant and providential care in all circumstances. Faith in this promise that we are not left to face our challenges and fears alone is a building block of resilience.
◆ How can you be an agent of God's care for those who are facing overwhelming challenges? Offer support, even if just by your presence, to someone facing difficulties. ◆ Look for examples of resilience and faith in the lives of the saints, such as St. Mother Theodore Guerin, the foundress of the Sisters of Providence (https://spsmw.org/about/saint-mother-theodore-guerin/her-story/).
◆ Lift up in prayer those who are feeling overwhelmed and afraid, and turn your struggles over to God. Consider concluding this time of prayer with a favorite hymn.

Download more questions and activities for families, Christian initiation groups, and other adult groups at http://www.ltp.org/ahw.

Scripture Insights

Our reading from Romans provides a twofold contrast of the impact that Adam's and Jesus' respective acts have on humanity. First, Adam's sin leads to death and condemnation (consider the Book of Genesis, starting with Cain's murder of Abel, to all the violence and deaths that follow, including Noah and the flood). Jesus' gift, however, brings about justification. Second, Paul uses the phrase "how much more" twice in quick succession (cf. 5:15, 17) to imply that Jesus' gift has a potentially greater scale of impact, even or especially when Paul has already stated that Adam's sin impacted "all." This is understandable given Paul's emphatic description of Jesus' act as "grace" and a "gift." Each of those terms signifies a sense of extravagant generosity (cf. Romans 5:6–11).

A gift, no matter how generous, cannot be received until it is recognized. We see Jesus sending out the Twelve in Matthew 10 and, in the process, warning them of inevitable sufferings but also assuring them of God's salvation.

Paul's Letter to the Romans will help us make sense of this juxtaposition of persecution and deliverance, which is also found in today's Old Testament readings. In his contrast of Adam and Jesus, Paul presents a conflict of two powers: the old power of violence and death against the new power of justice and life. Receiving Jesus' free gift of grace is to enter into this conflict, as Paul makes clear in Romans 5:1–5. These resistances, persecutions, and sufferings, however, point to and even prove the coming of the messianic age. That is why Paul suggests that current experiences of suffering can lead to endurance, character, and hope.

◆ Cain's killing of Abel is a fratricide. How may we think of the violence and deaths around us in similar terms?

◆ What are the violent, death-dealing, and unjust forces in our society today?

◆ How may we, as followers of Jesus, practice a generous and extravagant welcome today?

June 28, 2020

THIRTEENTH SUNDAY IN ORDINARY TIME

READING I
2 Kings 4:8–11, 14–16a

One day Elisha came to Shunem, where there was a woman of influence, who urged him to dine with her. Afterward, whenever he passed by, he used to stop there to dine. So she said to her husband, "I know that Elisha is a holy man of God. Since he visits us often, let us arrange a little room on the roof and furnish it for him with a bed, table, chair, and lamp, so that when he comes to us he can stay there." Sometime later Elisha arrived and stayed in the room overnight.

Later Elisha asked, "Can something be done for her?" His servant Gehazi answered, "Yes! She has no son, and her husband is getting on in years." Elisha said, "Call her." When the woman had been called and stood at the door, Elisha promised, "This time next year you will be fondling a baby son."

RESPONSORIAL PSALM Psalm 89:2–3, 16–17, 18–19 (2a)

R. Forever I will sing the goodness of the Lord.

The promises of the LORD I will sing forever,
through all generations my mouth shall proclaim your faithfulness.
For you have said, "My kindness is established forever";
in heaven you have confirmed your faithfulness. R.

Blessed the people who know the joyful shout;
in the light of your countenance, O LORD, they walk.
At your name they rejoice all the day,
and through your justice they are exalted. R.

You are the splendor of their strength,
and by your favor our horn is exalted.
For to the LORD belongs our shield,
and to the Holy One of Israel, our king. R.

READING II
Romans 6:3–4, 8–11

Brothers and sisters: Are you unaware that we who were baptized into Christ Jesus were baptized into his death? We were indeed buried with him through baptism into death, so that, just as Christ was raised from the dead by the glory of the Father, we too might live in newness of life.

If, then, we have died with Christ, we believe that we shall also live with him. We know that Christ, raised from the dead, dies no more; death no longer has power over him. As to his death, he died to sin once and for all; as to his life, he lives for God. Consequently, you too must think of yourselves as dead to sin and living for God in Christ Jesus.

GOSPEL Matthew 10:37–42

Jesus said to his apostles: "Whoever loves father or mother more than me is not worthy of me, and whoever loves son or daughter more than me is not worthy of me; and whoever does not take up his cross and follow after me is not worthy of me. Whoever finds his life will lose it, and whoever loses his life for my sake will find it.

"Whoever receives you receives me, and whoever receives me receives the one who sent me. Whoever receives a prophet because he is a prophet will receive a prophet's reward, and whoever receives a righteous man because he is a righteous man will receive a righteous man's reward. And whoever gives only a cup of cold water to one of these little ones to drink because the little one is a disciple—amen, I say to you, he will surely not lose his reward."

Practice of Charity

The practice of hospitality is affirmed throughout Scripture. In today's First Reading, extraordinary blessing is promised for the hospitality extended to Elisha. Jesus' words in the Gospel continue this theme, promising eternal reward to those who extend even the smallest act of hospitality to even the least ones. Through hospitality, we express our baptismal call and put faith into action. ◆ Our practice of hospitality ought not to be limited to strangers and guests but should also be extended to family, friends, neighbors, and coworkers. Take care to extend hospitality to those you encounter each day. ◆ Learn more about the Rule of St. Benedict and the practice of hospitality in the Benedictine tradition at this site: http://www .e-benedictine.com/abouttherule/. ◆ Take time to write in a journal, reflecting on acts of hospitality you've extended and received throughout this week. Give thanks to God for the opportunity to serve Christ in others.

Download more questions and activities for families, Christian initiation groups, and other adult groups at http://www.ltp.org/ahw.

Scripture Insights

Today's Second Reading elaborates what Paul has been developing in Romans 5: the contrast between two humanities because of Adam's sin and Jesus' death and Resurrection. While the former brings about human violence and death, the latter brings about the capacity to become just. To emphasize this fundamental change, Paul uses the language of death and life after death. Those who have accepted Jesus' free gift must live differently; they must not continue in sin but must live as if they have died, because sin is connected with death.

Paul illustrates this further with Baptism and with Jesus's death and Resurrection. We are baptized into Jesus' death, and the resurrected Jesus will no longer die. Put differently, sin and death are now behind us, and the life we have through Jesus has its end not in (another) death but in God.

What does it mean to live in God and in justice? Such living involves what we do for the vulnerable and those in need—for those whom Matthew calls "the little ones" (Matthew 10:42). That may be expressed in providing food and shelter for a stranger, such as what the Shunammite woman did for Elisha (2 Kings 4:8–17), or by giving aid to a destitute person to enable the individual to survive, as Elisha did earlier for a widow (2 Kings 4:1–7). Instead of condemning and killing each other, we welcome and help, especially those who cannot repay us.

This should not be surprising. Paul has reminded us that God's love for us becomes evident through Christ's death for us while we still were sinners (Romans 5:8). We did not deserve what God has done for us through Jesus; it is actually unreasonable. We need to praise God as the psalmist does in Psalm 89; better yet, we need to give extravagantly as God has given to us.

◆ Who are the "little ones" among and around us today?

◆ How would you live if death is behind and not before you?

◆ What does living in justice or justice making bring to your mind?

July 5, 2020

FOURTEENTH SUNDAY IN ORDINARY TIME

READING I Zechariah 9:9–10

Thus says the LORD:
Rejoice heartily, O daughter Zion,
　shout for joy,
　　O daughter Jerusalem!
See, your king shall come to you;
　a just savior is he,
meek, and riding on an ass,
　on a colt, the foal of an ass.
He shall banish the chariot
　　from Ephraim,
　and the horse from Jerusalem;
the warrior's bow shall
　　be banished,
and he shall proclaim peace
　　to the nations.
His dominion shall be
　　from sea to sea,
　and from the River to the ends
　　of the earth.

RESPONSORIAL PSALM
Psalm 145:1-2, 8-9, 10-11, 13-14 (see 1)

R. I will praise your name for ever,
　　my king and my God.
or: Alleluia.

I will extol you, O my God
　　and King,
　and I will bless your name
　　forever and ever.
Every day will I bless you,
　and I will praise your name
　　forever and ever. R.

The LORD is gracious and merciful,
　slow to anger and
　　of great kindness.
The LORD is good to all
　and compassionate toward
　　all his works. R.

Let all your works give you thanks,
　　O LORD,
　and let your faithful ones
　　bless you.
Let them discourse of the glory
　　of your kingdom
　and speak of your might. R.

The LORD is faithful in all his words
 and holy in all his works.
The LORD lifts up all who are falling
 and raises up all who are
 bowed down. R.

READING II
Romans 8:9, 11-13

Brothers and sisters: You are not
in the flesh; on the contrary, you
are in the spirit, if only the Spirit of
God dwells in you. Whoever does
not have the Spirit of Christ does
not belong to him. If the Spirit of
the one who raised Jesus from the
dead dwells in you, the one who
raised Christ from the dead will
give life to your mortal bodies also,
through his Spirit that dwells in
you. Consequently, brothers and
sisters, we are not debtors to the
flesh, to live according to the flesh.
For if you live according to the
flesh, you will die, but if by the
Spirit you put to death the deeds
of the body, you will live.

GOSPEL Matthew 11:25-30

At that time Jesus exclaimed:
"I give praise to you, Father, Lord
of heaven and earth, for although
you have hidden these things from
the wise and the learned you have
revealed them to little ones. Yes,
Father, such has been your gracious
will. All things have been handed
over to me by my Father. No one
knows the Son except the Father,
and no one knows the Father except
the Son and anyone to whom the
Son wishes to reveal him.

"Come to me, all you who labor
and are burdened, and I will give
you rest. Take my yoke upon you
and learn from me, for I am meek
and humble of heart; and you will
find rest for yourselves. For my
yoke is easy, and my burden light."

Practice of Faith

In today's Gospel, Jesus speaks of the intimate knowledge of the Father and the Son and the desire that this communion be shared with others. Indeed, this is what is given to us in Baptism, a share in the divine life of the Trinity. By the grace of the sacrament, we are made more like Christ so that he can work in us and through us to bring forth God's Kingdom.

◆ Pray for those recently baptized in your parish. If you know someone personally, consider writing a letter of welcome and encouragement to live always in the grace of the Spirit. ◆ Read and reflect on the implications of the divine life given to you at Baptism: www.usccb.org/about/justice -peace-and-human-develop ment /upload/baptism-handout.pdf.

◆ Spend time in prayer meditating on Christ's words in today's Gospel: "Take my yoke upon you and learn from me." Listen attentively to what Christ wants you to learn from him today.

Download more questions and activities for families, Christian initiation groups, and other adult groups at http://www.ltp.org/ahw.

Scripture Insights

Paul continues to develop his thoughts about the contrast between an Adamic humanity and a messianic humanity in Romans 8. Here, Paul expresses the contrast in terms of flesh and spirit. While flesh has incapacitated us with violence and death, spirit empowers us for life and justice.

Interestingly, Paul begins this chapter referring to a law of the spirit of life in Christ and a law of sin and of death (Romans 8:1–8). He connects the law of sin and death with the flesh. Going back to Adam and the first death in the Bible, the law of flesh may be one of measure and competition. It is seen in Cain's jealousy of Abel that leads to the first murder. That same law brings about condemnations and more deaths through punishment or revenge.

The law of the spirit gives up this jealous competition and hostile calculation. It enables a ruler to arrive unassumingly on a donkey (Zechariah 9:9–10) instead of showing up haughtily with a mighty military. With this law of the spirit, God not only is gracious, merciful, slow to anger, holding up the falling, and raising those who are bowed down (Psalm 145:8–9, 14) but also takes on vulnerable and sinful flesh (Romans 8:3). The law of the spirit leads to divine revelations to dependent infants instead of to self-assured elites, and to Jesus offering peace and rest to the weary and the humble (Matthew 11:25–30). The law of the spirit is a different value system and way of life.

◆ Paul links human inability under the law of flesh to follow God with our hostility to God— as opposed to God being hostile to or mad at us (Romans 8:7). How may this different emphasis change our theology?

◆ Spirit is the breath that animates and makes alive. As such, it is also creative. How can people of the spirit be creative to bring about life?

◆ What qualities do infants possess that allow them to see and receive revelations in ways that adults cannot?

July 12, 2020

FIFTEENTH SUNDAY IN ORDINARY TIME

READING I Isaiah 55:10–11

Thus says the LORD:
Just as from the heavens
   the rain and snow come down
and do not return there
   till they have watered the earth,
   making it fertile and fruitful,
giving seed to the one who sows
   and bread to the one who eats,
so shall my word be
   that goes forth from my mouth;
my word shall not return to
     me void,
   but shall do my will,
   achieving the end for which
     I sent it.

RESPONSORIAL PSALM
Psalm 65:10, 11, 12–13,
14 (Luke 8:8)

R. The seed that falls on good
     ground will yield
     a fruitful harvest.

You have visited the land and
     watered it;
  greatly have you enriched it.
God's watercourses are filled;
  you have prepared the grain. R.

Thus have you prepared the land:
     drenching its furrows,
  breaking up its clods,
Softening it with showers,
  blessing its yield. R.

You have crowned the year
     with your bounty,
and your paths overflow
     with a rich harvest;
the untilled meadows overflow
     with it,
and rejoicing clothes the hills. R.

The fields are garmented
     with flocks
and the valleys blanketed
     with grain.
They shout and sing for joy. R.

READING II Romans 8:18–23

Brothers and sisters: I consider
that the sufferings of this present
time are as nothing compared
with the glory to be revealed for
us. For creation awaits with eager
expectation the revelation of the
children of God; for creation was
made subject to futility, not of its
own accord but because of the one
who subjected it, in hope that
creation itself would be set free

from slavery to corruption and share in the glorious freedom of the children of God. We know that all creation is groaning in labor pains even until now; and not only that, but we ourselves, who have the firstfruits of the Spirit, we also groan within ourselves as we wait for adoption, the redemption of our bodies.

GOSPEL Matthew 13:1–23

Shorter: Matthew 13:1–9

On that day, Jesus went out of the house and sat down by the sea. Such large crowds gathered around him that he got into a boat and sat down, and the whole crowd stood along the shore. And he spoke to them at length in parables, saying: "A sower went out to sow. And as he sowed, some seed fell on the path, and birds came and ate it up. Some fell on rocky ground, where it had little soil. It sprang up at once because the soil was not deep, and when the sun rose it was scorched, and it withered for lack of roots. Some seed fell among thorns, and the thorns grew up and choked it. But some seed fell on rich soil, and produced fruit, a hundred or sixty or thirtyfold. Whoever has ears ought to hear."

The disciples approached him and said, "Why do you speak to them in parables?" He said to them in reply, "Because knowledge of the mysteries of the kingdom of heaven has been granted to you, but to them it has not been granted. To anyone who has, more will be given and he will grow rich; from anyone who has not, even what he has will be taken away. This is why I speak to them in parables, because «they look but do not see, and hear but do not listen or understand.» Isaiah's prophecy is fulfilled in them, which says:

«You shall indeed hear but
      not understand,
   you shall indeed look but
      never see.
Gross is the heart of this people,
   they will hardly hear with
      their ears,
   they have closed their eyes,
   lest they see with their eyes
   and hear with their ears
and understand with their hearts
      and be converted,
   and I heal them.»

"But blessed are your eyes, because they see, and your ears, because they hear. Amen, I say to you, many prophets and righteous people longed to see what you see but did not see it, and to hear what you hear but did not hear it.

"Hear then the parable of the sower. The seed sown on the path is the one who hears the word of the kingdom without understanding it, and the evil one comes and steals away what was sown in his heart. The seed sown on rocky ground is the one who hears the word and receives it at once with joy. But he has no root and lasts only for a time. When some tribulation or persecution comes because of the word, he immediately falls away. The seed sown among thorns is the one who hears the word, but then worldly anxiety and the lure of riches choke the word and it bears no fruit. But the seed sown on rich soil is the one who hears the word and understands it, who indeed bears fruit and yields a hundred or sixty or thirtyfold."

Practice of Hope

St. Paul uses nature metaphors, describing the longing of creation for the fulfillment of God's promise, even as the "firstfruits of the Spirit" are evident in the lives of the children of God. When we are open to God's Word, signs of the Kingdom of God are observed in us and point to its promised fulfillment. ◆ In whom do you see evidence of "seed that has fallen on rich soil"? Offer words of encouragement or write a note of thanks to this person. ◆ Learn more about opportunities to support sustainable agriculture and the dignity of work at http://ethicaltrade.crs.org/why-shop -ethically/faith-connection/. ◆ Spend time outdoors this week, observing signs of the fruitfulness of nature. Pray in thanksgiving for the gifts of God's creation.

Download more questions and activities for families, Christian initiation groups, and other adult groups at http://www.ltp.org/ahw.

Scripture Insights

Biblical texts often link the fate and well-being of humanity with the created world. Promising the exiled Israelites an exodus from Babylon, our passage from Isaiah 55 illustrates the reliability of God's Word and the certainty of God's purposes with an example that echoes that of Psalm 65: God's watering of the earth will result in food to feed people. The two last verses of that chapter, though left out of our Lectionary reading, portray the people exiting Babylon not only in joy and peace but also being accompanied by the singing and clapping of mountains and hills.

Similarly, Matthew's parable of the sower makes the connection by presenting humans as soil. After all, in Genesis, the first human is created out of soil, and the word Adam can be translated as (an) "earthling." Like Isaiah 55, Matthew hints at the blessing of a not yet fully visible revelation (verses 16–17).

Hope for humanity and the whole creation in the midst of, and in spite of, a difficult situation is also found in today's reading from Romans. Beginning with present suffering, Paul refers to a revelation and a first tasting of a coming glory to assert that humanity and the whole creation share in suffering and in longing for redemption. Since Paul has said earlier that humanity has been incapacitated by sin and death through Adam (Romans 5:12–14), he may be alluding to Adam's vocation to do something with the created world (Genesis 1:26). If so, Adam's subjection to sin and death might also end up subjecting creation to futility (Romans 8:20). If the subjugation and the redemption of humanity and the created world are not only shared but also related, humanity and the created order should be in solidarity instead of in enmity or competition with each other.

◆ In what specific ways do humanity and creation share a destiny?

◆ What causes people to think that humankind is more important than the rest of the universe?

◆ How is humanity causing the earth to groan today?

July 19, 2020

SIXTEENTH SUNDAY IN ORDINARY TIME

READING I
Wisdom 12:13, 16–19

There is no god besides you
> who have the care of all,
> that you need show you have
> not unjustly condemned.
For your might is the source
> of justice;
> your mastery over all things
> makes you lenient to all.
For you show your might when
> the perfection of your
> power is disbelieved;
> and in those who know you,
> you rebuke temerity.
But though you are master
> of might,
> you judge with clemency,
> and with much lenience you
> govern us;
> for power, whenever you will,
> attends you.
And you taught your people,
> by these deeds,
> that those who are just
> must be kind;
and you gave your children
> good ground for hope
> that you would permit
> repentance for their sins.

RESPONSORIAL PSALM
Psalm 86:5–6, 9–10, 15–16 (5a)

R. Lord, you are good and
> forgiving.

You, O LORD, are good
> and forgiving,
abounding in kindness
> to all who call upon you.
Hearken, O LORD, to my prayer
and attend to the sound of
> my pleading.   R.

All the nations you have made
> shall come
and worship you, O LORD,
and glorify your name.
For you are great, and you do
> wondrous deeds;
you alone are God.   R.

You, O LORD, are a God merciful
> and gracious,
slow to anger, abounding in
> kindness and fidelity.
Turn toward me,
> and have pity on me;
give your strength
> to your servant.   R.

READING II
Romans 8:26–27

Brothers and sisters: The Spirit comes to the aid of our weakness; for we do not know how to pray as we ought, but the Spirit himself intercedes with inexpressible groanings. And the one who searches hearts knows what is the intention of the Spirit, because he intercedes for the holy ones according to God's will.

GOSPEL Matthew 13:24–43

Shorter: Matthew 13:24–30

Jesus proposed another parable to the crowds, saying: "The kingdom of heaven may be likened to a man who sowed good seed in his field. While everyone was asleep his enemy came and sowed weeds all through the wheat, and then went off. When the crop grew and bore fruit, the weeds appeared as well. The slaves of the householder came to him and said, 'Master, did you not sow good seed in your field? Where have the weeds come from?' He answered, 'An enemy has done this.' His slaves said to him, 'Do you want us to go and pull them up?' He replied, 'No, if you pull up the weeds you might uproot the wheat along with them. Let them grow together until harvest; then at harvest time I will say to the harvesters, "First collect the weeds and tie them in bundles for burning; but gather the wheat into my barn."'"

He proposed another parable to them. "The kingdom of heaven is like a mustard seed that a person took and sowed in a field. It is the smallest of all the seeds, yet when full-grown it is the largest of plants. It becomes a large bush, and the 'birds of the sky come and dwell in its branches.'"

He spoke to them another parable. "The kingdom of heaven is like yeast that a woman took and mixed with three measures of wheat flour until the whole batch was leavened."

All these things Jesus spoke to the crowds in parables. He spoke to them only in parables, to fulfill what had been said through the prophet:

《I will open my mouth
       in parables,
I will announce what has lain
       hidden from the foundation
              of the world.》

Then, dismissing the crowds, he went into the house. His disciples approached him and said, "Explain to us the parable of the weeds in the field." He said in reply, "He who sows good seed is the Son of Man, the field is the world, the good seed the children of the kingdom. The weeds are the children of the evil one, and the enemy who sows them is the devil. The harvest is the end of the age, and the harvesters are angels. Just as weeds are collected and burned up with fire, so will it be at the end of the age. The Son of Man will send his angels, and they will collect out of his kingdom all who cause others to sin and all evildoers. They will throw them into the fiery furnace, where there will be wailing and grinding of teeth. Then the righteous will shine like the sun in the kingdom of their Father. Whoever has ears ought to hear."

Practice of Faith

In the parables of today's Gospel, Jesus prepares us for those times when we may lose patience with the slow progress of the Kingdom.

In this Gospel, and throughout Scripture, we find assurance that God is always working among us with mercy and kindness and we are encouraged to trust in God's purpose and plan. God knows what we need and promises to be with us always. ◆ As you receive this week's news, look beyond the headlines for signs that God is in charge, showing mercy, kindness, and fidelity. ◆ Spend time reflecting on divine providence as it is described in paragraph 302 of the Catechism of the Catholic Church: "By his providence God protects and governs all things which he has made, 'reaching mightily from one end of the earth to the other, and ordering all things well.' For 'all are open and laid bare to his eyes,' even those things which are yet to come into existence through the free action of creatures." ◆ Take to heart this quote from Julian of Norwich: "He did not say, 'You shall not be tempest-tossed, you shall not be work-weary, you shall not be discomforted,' But he said, 'You shall not be overcome.'"

Download more questions and activities for families, Christian initiation groups, and other adult groups at http://www.ltp.org/ahw.

Scripture Insights

In the verses just prior to those for today's reading, Paul speaks of humanity and creation yearning and groaning for redemption in the midst of suffering. "Groaning" is an interesting word, as it represents a longing that cannot yet be expressed. We are all in pain and long for deliverance, but we do not know what deliverance will look like. We don't have the right words for our prayers, so we groan to express our longing. Paul tells us that despite our ignorance and our inability to express ourselves, God's Spirit accompanies us by groaning in us and with us. Moreover, this groaning of the Spirit is somehow praying for us according to God's will, so this groaning is nothing less than the longing of the divine for us and in us. Paul describes a knowing and understanding God.

Wisdom 12 portrays a similar picture of a caring God, but it also gives two twists. First, this caring God is lenient and is likely to grant repentance. Second, secure in sovereignty and power, this God is slow to anger.

The fact that Psalm 86 also emphasizes the coming of all nations to this merciful and forgiving God reminds us of how Paul will suggest in Romans 11 that God will eventually save all of Israel. In light of this, we may consider how we interpret Matthew's parable of the weeds and the wheat, particularly the master's willingness to let both grow together until harvest time. Note also, in this regard, how the next two parables in the reading feature, respectively, the incredible growth of even a tiny seed and the ability of yeast to leaven all.

◆ What is causing you and creation to groan and long for God's redemption?

◆ How may one compare the Wisdom writer's discussion of God's security and leniency with Paul's description of a humanity that is envious and murderous?

◆ What examples can you think of to illustrate God's surprises?

July 26, 2020

SEVENTEENTH SUNDAY IN ORDINARY TIME

READING I 1 Kings 3:5, 7–12

The LORD appeared to Solomon in a dream at night. God said, "Ask something of me and I will give it to you." Solomon answered: "O LORD, my God, you have made me, your servant, king to succeed my father David; but I am a mere youth, not knowing at all how to act. I serve you in the midst of the people whom you have chosen, a people so vast that it cannot be numbered or counted. Give your servant, therefore, an understanding heart to judge your people and to distinguish right from wrong. For who is able to govern this vast people of yours?"

The LORD was pleased that Solomon made this request. So God said to him: "Because you have asked for this—not for a long life for yourself, nor for riches, nor for the life of your enemies, but for understanding so that you may know what is right—I do as you requested. I give you a heart so wise and understanding that there has never been anyone like you up to now, and after you there will come no one to equal you."

RESPONSORIAL PSALM
Psalm 119:57, 72, 76–77, 127–128, 129–130 (97a)

R. Lord, I love your commands.

I have said, O LORD, that my part
   is to keep your words.
The law of your mouth is to me
    more precious
   than thousands of gold and
    silver pieces.   R.

Let your kindness comfort me
   according to your promise
    to your servants.
Let your compassion come to me
    that I may live,
   for your law is my delight.   R.

For I love your commands
   more than gold, however fine.
For in all your precepts
    I go forward;
   every false way I hate.   R.

Wonderful are your decrees;
 therefore I observe them.
The revelation of your words
 sheds light,
 giving understanding
 to the simple. R.

READING II Romans 8:28–30

Brothers and sisters: We know that all things work for good for those who love God, who are called according to his purpose. For those he foreknew he also predestined to be conformed to the image of his Son, so that he might be the firstborn among many brothers and sisters. And those he predestined he also called; and those he called he also justified; and those he justified he also glorified.

GOSPEL Matthew 13:44–52

Shorter: Matthew 13:44–46

Jesus said to his disciples: "The kingdom of heaven is like a treasure buried in a field, which a person finds and hides again, and out of joy goes and sells all that he has and buys that field. Again, the kingdom of heaven is like a merchant searching for fine pearls. When he finds a pearl of great price, he goes and sells all that he has and buys it. Again, the kingdom of heaven is like a net thrown into the sea, which collects fish of every kind. When it is full they haul it ashore and sit down to put what is good into buckets. What is bad they throw away. Thus it will be at the end of the age. The angels will go out and separate the wicked from the righteous and throw them into the fiery furnace, where there will be wailing and grinding of teeth.

"Do you understand all these things?" They answered, "Yes." And he replied, "Then every scribe who has been instructed in the kingdom of heaven is like the head of a household who brings from his storeroom both the new and the old."

Practice of Charity

Listening to today's First Reading, we may find ourselves humbled by Solomon's request. Given the chance to present his heart's desire to God, Solomon sought an "understanding heart" and his request was granted, distinguishing him among the kings of Israel. Those whose hearts are filled with understanding are able to discern the treasure that is the kingdom of heaven and know to pursue it.

◆ Notice how often you seek counsel or give advice to others. Take extra care that your advice comes from an understanding heart, one that points to the treasure that is the kingdom of heaven. ◆ Reflect on words from Pope Francis' homily on this Gospel: "God lets himself be found, because it is he who first wants to meet us, and first tries to meet us. He came to be 'God with us.'"

◆ Pray a daily examen, considering questions such as these: What is it that you treasure most? What efforts or price have you paid to obtain this treasure? You might wish to use a guide for prayer such as this one: https://godinallthings.com/prayer/evening-examen/.

Download more questions and activities for families, Christian initiation groups, and other adult groups at http://www.ltp.org/ahw.

Scripture Insights

Paul's words in Romans 8:28–30 are best understood when read within the context of the verses before and after them. The surrounding verses lead us to understand God's goodness and generosity.

After the gift of kingship, God further offers Solomon the freedom to ask for any gift he desires. The contrast that the text highlights in terms of what Solomon did not request (namely, longevity, wealth, or his enemies' demise) suggests that his choice of gift is impressive because of both its content and its objective. He wants a wise, discerning, and understanding mind to govern the people. He wants something for the public good and not something solely for himself. Because of Solomon's good choice, God ends up giving to him even other gifts that Solomon did not name.

Psalm 119, in a sense, affirms Solomon's choice by presenting God and God's teaching, not wealth, as the psalmist's choice. The psalmist further explains that God's Word is what gives understanding.

The parables in today's reading from Matthew are also about choices and whether we have the discernment to choose wisely. Such choices, according to these parables, may involve the giving up of other valuables and often incur sobering consequences.

◆ What examples would you give to illustrate God's goodness and generosity?

◆ What single gift would you request of God to bring about the greatest public good?

◆ Psalm 119:130 presents God's Word as giving understanding, but God's Word (for example, parables) are often difficult to understand. What do people need to do to better interpret, discern, and understand what they find in the Bible?

August 2, 2020

READING I Isaiah 55:1–3

Thus says the LORD:
All you who are thirsty,
  come to the water!
You who have no money,
  come, receive grain and eat;
come, without paying and
        without cost,
  drink wine and milk!

Why spend your money for what is
        not bread;
  your wages for what fails
        to satisfy?
Heed me, and you shall eat well,
  you shall delight in rich fare.
Come to me heedfully,
  listen, that you may have life.
I will renew with you the
        everlasting covenant,
  the benefits assured to David.

RESPONSORIAL PSALM
Psalm 145:8–9, 15–16, 17–18
(see 16)

R. The hand of the Lord feeds us;
        he answers all our needs.

The LORD is gracious and merciful,
  slow to anger and of great
        kindness.
The LORD is good to all
  and compassionate toward all
        his works. R.

The eyes of all look hopefully
        to you,
  and you give them their food
        in due season;
you open your hand
  and satisfy the desire of every
        living thing. R.

The LORD is just in all his ways
  and holy in all his works.
The LORD is near to all who call
        upon him,
  to all who call upon him
        in truth. R.

Reading II
Romans 8:35, 37–39

Brothers and sisters: What will separate us from the love of Christ? Will anguish, or distress, or persecution, or famine, or nakedness, or peril, or the sword? No, in all these things we conquer overwhelmingly through him who loved us. For I am convinced that neither death, nor life, nor angels, nor principalities, nor present things, nor future things, nor powers, nor height, nor depth, nor any other creature will be able to separate us from the love of God in Christ Jesus our Lord.

Gospel Matthew 14:13–21

When Jesus heard of the death of John the Baptist, he withdrew in a boat to a deserted place by himself. The crowds heard of this and followed him on foot from their towns. When he disembarked and saw the vast crowd, his heart was moved with pity for them, and he cured their sick. When it was evening, the disciples approached him and said, "This is a deserted place and it is already late; dismiss the crowds so that they can go to the villages and buy food for themselves." Jesus said to them, "There is no need for them to go away; give them some food yourselves." But they said to him, "Five loaves and two fish are all we have here." Then he said, "Bring them here to me," and he ordered the crowds to sit down on the grass. Taking the five loaves and the two fish, and looking up to heaven, he said the blessing, broke the loaves, and gave them to the disciples, who in turn gave them to the crowds. They all ate and were satisfied, and they picked up the fragments left over — twelve wicker baskets full. Those who ate were about five thousand men, not counting women and children.

Practice of Faith

Themes of hunger, satisfaction, and abundance pervade today's readings. As God provides food in abundance to satisfy physical hunger, so too does God provide abundant grace in Christ, grace that more than satisfies our spiritual hungers. God's grace is so abundant that it overflows, working in us and through us to provide for the needs of others. The Eucharist we receive is the source of this abundant grace and commits us to lives of service. ◆ Through the Corporal and Spiritual Works of Mercy, we share God's abundant grace with those in need. Let one or more of these Works of Mercy guide your response to the needs of those you encounter this week. ◆ During a homily on this Gospel, Pope Francis explained that those who receive the Eucharist need to be compassionate, just as Jesus is in sharing himself with us. "One who goes to the Eucharist without having compassion for the needy and without sharing is not at ease with Jesus," Pope Francis said.

Consider how Christ unites himself with us in the Eucharist and how the sacrament calls us to solidarity with the poor. ◆ In prayer, request an increase in compassion for the needs of others and the strength to respond in faith.

Download more questions and activities for families, Christian initiation groups, and other adult groups at http://www.ltp.org/ahw.

Scripture Insights

Remember that Paul's audience was a small and vulnerable group living in the imperial center of Rome, the very power that condemned and crucified Jesus. Paul states in our verses today that they should have no fear for any condemnation because (1) God, who is good and generous, loves in a way that surmounts all, and (2) Jesus, as one who has been condemned, is not going to turn around and condemn. What they worry may separate them from Christ's love—such as hardship, distress, persecution, nakedness, and peril—actually unites them to him, because Christ has also experienced these things.

These words also brought particular resonance. Paul's audience lived with a worldview that assumed the stationary earth was surrounded by seven moving spheres inhabited with malicious spirits and evil powers. Deity and safety could only be found by going beyond those spheres. Paul tells the Romans, instead, that nothing can separate them from their God. In fact, he says that they don't need to go anywhere, because God has come to them in Jesus Christ.

We see the love of God in action in today's Gospel. Matthew clearly tells us that Jesus has taken time to cure the sick out of compassion, despite his original plans for a retreat. When it becomes late and in response to the disciples' suggestion to disperse the crowd, Jesus replies that there is no need for the crowd to go anywhere or to buy food. Instead, he performs a miracle and, with his disciples' assistance, feeds five thousand people with five loaves and two fish. Just as our readings from the psalms and from Isaiah announce, God responds to our needs and provides free sustenance and nourishment.

◆ In what ways do we send needy people away or meet needy people where they are?

◆ How do needs and hurts bring people together or push people apart?

◆ What assumptions do you have about God's love that today's readings challenge?

August 9, 2020

NINETEENTH SUNDAY IN ORDINARY TIME

READING I
1 Kings 19:9a, 11–13a

At the mountain of God, Horeb, Elijah came to a cave where he took shelter. Then the LORD said to him, "Go outside and stand on the mountain before the LORD; the LORD will be passing by." A strong and heavy wind was rending the mountains and crushing rocks before the LORD—but the LORD was not in the wind. After the wind there was an earthquake—but the LORD was not in the earthquake. After the earthquake there was fire—but the LORD was not in the fire. After the fire there was a tiny whispering sound. When he heard this, Elijah hid his face in his cloak and went and stood at the entrance of the cave.

RESPONSORIAL PSALM
Psalm 85:9, 10, 11–12, 13–14 (8)

R. Lord, let us see your kindness,
  and grant us
  your salvation.

I will hear what God proclaims;
  the LORD—for he
   proclaims peace.
Near indeed is his salvation
  to those who fear him,
  glory dwelling in our land.   R.

Kindness and truth shall meet;
  justice and peace shall kiss.
Truth shall spring out of the earth,
  and justice shall look down
   from heaven.   R.

The LORD himself will give
   his benefits;
  our land shall yield its increase.
Justice shall walk before him,
  and prepare the way
   of his steps.   R.

Reading II Romans 9:1–5

Brothers and sisters: I speak the truth in Christ, I do not lie; my conscience joins with the Holy Spirit in bearing me witness that I have great sorrow and constant anguish in my heart. For I could wish that I myself were accursed and cut off from Christ for the sake of my own people, my kindred according to the flesh. They are Israelites; theirs the adoption, the glory, the covenants, the giving of the law, the worship, and the promises; theirs the patriarchs, and from them, according to the flesh, is the Christ, who is over all, God blessed forever. Amen.

Gospel Matthew 14:22–33

After he had fed the people, Jesus made the disciples get into a boat and precede him to the other side, while he dismissed the crowds. After doing so, he went up on the mountain by himself to pray. When it was evening he was there alone. Meanwhile the boat, already a few miles offshore, was being tossed about by the waves, for the wind was against it. During the fourth watch of the night, he came toward them walking on the sea. When the disciples saw him walking on the sea they were terrified. "It is a ghost," they said, and they cried out in fear. At once Jesus spoke to them, "Take courage, it is I; do not be afraid." Peter said to him in reply, "Lord, if it is you, command me to come to you on the water." He said, "Come." Peter got out of the boat and began to walk on the water toward Jesus. But when he saw how strong the wind was he became frightened; and, beginning to sink, he cried out, "Lord, save me!" Immediately Jesus stretched out his hand and caught Peter, and said to him, "O you of little faith, why did you doubt?" After they got into the boat, the wind died down. Those who were in the boat did him homage, saying, "Truly, you are the Son of God."

Practice of Hope

God meets us in the most unexpected places, sometimes in the tiny whisper as at the cave at Horeb, sometimes in the midst of the storm-tossed sea. When we find ourselves in deserted places, we seek to have the courage to meet the Lord in whatever way he appears and allow ourselves to be transformed. ◆ Seek inspiration in the witness of those whose lives have been transformed by their encounter with God. Who has been an example for you, showing courage to meet God wherever God chooses to be revealed? ◆ Consider the new perspective that emerged from Thomas Merton's openness to encountering God. In Conjectures of a Guilty Bystander, he wrote of standing on a corner in Louisville, Kentucky, and realizing that he is at one with each person there. He writes, "I have the immense joy of being man, a member of a race in which God Himself became incarnate." ◆ "Contemplative prayer . . . is nothing else than a close sharing between friends; it means taking time frequently to be alone with him who we know loves us" (Catechism of the Catholic Church, paragraph 2709, quoting St. Teresa of Avila). In your prayer, seek to encounter God as a friend and rest in the knowledge of God's love for you.

Download more questions and activities for families, Christian initiation groups, and other adult groups at http://www.ltp.org/ahw.

Scripture Insights

In Romans 9, Paul turns from discussing an Adamic humanity to the people who have descended from Abraham. Earlier Paul asserted the priority of Jews in God's salvation plans (Romans 1:16; 2:9–10). Paul has already asked in Romans 3:1–8 if the Jews' rejection of the messiah can revoke the entrusting of God's Word given to them. and hence whether God is faithful. This issue is important, especially given the long anti-Jewish history of the Christian church. Just as—and because—Paul has adamantly declared God's goodness and generosity in Romans 8, he will argue fiercely for Israel's salvation and God's faithfulness.

We see Jesus' faithful determination to save in our Gospel reading today. Although the disciples mistook him as a ghost and Peter doubted, Jesus walks on the stormy sea to join them and reaches out to save a sinking Peter.

Psalm 85 and Elijah's story in 1 Kings 19 affirm this divine and faithful determination to save. Because of Jezebel's death threat against him, Elijah becomes fearful, runs away, feels sorry for himself, and even asks God to take his life. But God's angel provides for him, and God assures him that he still has a mission to perform and that God will have a faithful following despite how things may look (1 Kings 19:15–18).

Paul also expresses a wish for self-destruction in Romans 9, not as a way to end one's disappointment, but so his fellow Jews would replace him in God's redemption. To be condemned and cast off himself so others would be saved is precisely what happened to Jesus. By alluding to this, Paul points to God's faithfulness while showing his own commitment to salvation through solidarity with Jesus' suffering.

◆ What can be done to remedy or rectify the Church's anti-Jewish legacies?

◆ What implications does this divine and faithful determination to redeem have for us today?

◆ How may we mistake setbacks or detours as (divine) failures?

219

August 16, 2020

TWENTIETH SUNDAY IN ORDINARY TIME

READING I   Isaiah 56:1, 6–7

Thus says the LORD:
Observe what is right, do what
 is just;
 for my salvation is about
  to come,
 my justice, about to be revealed.

The foreigners who join
  themselves to the LORD,
 ministering to him,
loving the name of the LORD,
 and becoming his servants—
all who keep the sabbath free
  from profanation
 and hold to my covenant,
them I will bring to my
  holy mountain
 and make joyful in my house
  of prayer;
their burnt offerings and sacrifices
 will be acceptable on my altar,
for my house shall be called
 a house of prayer for all peoples.

RESPONSORIAL PSALM
Psalm 67:2–3, 5, 6, 8 (4)

R. O God, let all the nations
   praise you!

May God have pity on us
   and bless us;
 may he let his face shine upon us.
So may your way be known
   upon earth;
 among all nations,
   your salvation.   R.

May the nations be glad and exult
 because you rule the peoples
   in equity;
 the nations on the earth
   you guide.   R.

May the peoples praise you, O God;
 may all the peoples praise you!
May God bless us,
 and may all the ends of the earth
   fear him!   R.

READING II
Romans 11:13–15, 29–32

Brothers and sisters: I am speaking to you Gentiles. Inasmuch as I am the apostle to the Gentiles, I glory in my ministry in order to make my race jealous and thus save some of them. For if their rejection is the reconciliation of the world, what will their acceptance be but life from the dead?

For the gifts and the call of God are irrevocable. Just as you once disobeyed God but have now received mercy because of their disobedience, so they have now disobeyed in order that, by virtue of the mercy shown to you, they too may now receive mercy. For God delivered all to disobedience, that he might have mercy upon all.

GOSPEL Matthew 15:21–28

At that time, Jesus withdrew to the region of Tyre and Sidon. And behold, a Canaanite woman of that district came and called out, "Have pity on me, Lord, Son of David! My daughter is tormented by a demon." But Jesus did not say a word in answer to her. Jesus' disciples came and asked him, "Send her away, for she keeps calling out after us." He said in reply, "I was sent only to the lost sheep of the house of Israel." But the woman came and did Jesus homage, saying, "Lord, help me." He said in reply, "It is not right to take the food of the children and throw it to the dogs." She said, "Please, Lord, for even the dogs eat the scraps that fall from the table of their masters." Then Jesus said to her in reply, "O woman, great is your faith! Let it be done for you as you wish." And the woman's daughter was healed from that hour.

Practice of Charity

In today's Gospel, we are offered an example of intercessory prayer as the Canaanite woman is persistent and undeterred by challenges as she presents her daughter's need for healing to Jesus. Our prayer for others is both an act of faith and an expression of Christian charity. ◆ Notice the variety of circumstances in which you find yourself called to pray for others: Who are the people you lift up to God in prayer? In what ways have you known your prayers to be answered? Tell people that you are praying for them. ◆ Reflect on the variety of needs expressed as we pray the Universal Prayer, or Prayer of the Faithful, at Mass. ◆ Write your intercessory prayers on slips of paper or in a prayer journal as a visible sign of your prayer for others. Consider utilizing a prayer box, a box in which you put slips of paper on which you have written concerns or issues for which to pray.

Download more questions and activities for families, Christian initiation groups, and other adult groups at http://www.ltp.org/ahw.

Scripture Insights

In Psalm 67, we see how the Bible has long emphasized every nation's coming to Israel's God. Isaiah 56 also speaks of God gathering one day both Israel's outcast and Gentiles.

For Paul, this universal emphasis has become a reality through Jesus. Paul's problem is no longer the inclusion of gentiles but of Jews who reject the messianic claim and call of Jesus. What will God do with these whom God has chosen and called first?

In chapters 9—11 in Romans, Paul references various Old Testament stories to argue for Israel's eventual salvation. First, judging from God's choice of Isaac and Jacob over the firstborn (Ishmael and Esau), God often works in surprising ways. Second, from the same examples (especially that of the deceitful and unreliable Jacob), the realization of God's purposes relies less on human reliability and more on God's faithful persistence. Third, from the stories involving foreign powers, we see that even those who oppose God can be used. Fourth and finally, from prophetic traditions such as Hosea and Isaiah, God's aim is always the salvation of all, even though there may be temporary punishment or an interim remnant.

These arguments, especially God's irrevocable call and emphasis to save all, are repeated in our verses today from Romans 11. God is faithful and generous and will not stop working toward the goal of saving all, including those thought to be rejected or dead.

We see these dynamics also in Matthew's story about the Canaanite woman. Jesus first turns down the woman because of her ethnicity and then insults her by calling her a dog. But then he responds to her faith and the story ends with salvation being extended beyond Israel without denying Israel's priority.

◆ Should we think of God's justice more in terms of God's mercy?

◆ How do we treat those who reject or disagree with us?

◆ Given God's irrevocable call, is there room to think of our faith and faithfulness as loyalty?

223

August 23, 2020

TWENTY-FIRST SUNDAY IN ORDINARY TIME

READING I Isaiah 22:19-23

Thus says the LORD to Shebna,
     master of the palace:
"I will thrust you from
     your office
     and pull you down
     from your station.
On that day I will summon
     my servant
     Eliakim, son of Hilkiah;
I will clothe him with your robe,
     and gird him with your sash,
     and give over to him
     your authority.
He shall be a father to
     the inhabitants of Jerusalem,
     and to the house of Judah.
I will place the key of the
     House of
     David on Eliakim's
     shoulder;
     when he opens, no one
     shall shut;
     when he shuts, no one
     shall open.
I will fix him like a peg in
     a sure spot,
     to be a place of honor
     for his family."

RESPONSORIAL PSALM
Psalm 138:1-2, 2-3, 6, 8 (8bc)

R. Lord, your love is eternal;
     do not forsake the work of
     your hands.

I will give thanks to you, O LORD,
     with all my heart,
     for you have heard the words
     of my mouth;
in the presence of the angels I will
     sing your praise;
     I will worship at your holy
     temple.   R.

I will give thanks to your name,
     because of your kindness and
     your truth:
when I called, you answered me;
     you built up strength
     within me.   R.

The LORD is exalted,
     yet the lowly he sees,
     and the proud he knows
     from afar.
Your kindness, O LORD,
     endures forever;
forsake not the work
     of your hands.   R.

READING II
Romans 11:33–36

Oh, the depth of the riches and wisdom and knowledge of God! How inscrutable are his judgments and how unsearchable his ways!

«For who has known the mind
    of the Lord
      or who has been his counselor?
Or who has given the
    Lord anything
      that he may be repaid?»

For from him and through him and for him are all things. To him be glory forever. Amen.

GOSPEL Matthew 16:13–20

Jesus went into the region of Caesarea Philippi and he asked his disciples, "Who do people say that the Son of Man is?" They replied, "Some say John the Baptist, others Elijah, still others Jeremiah or one of the prophets." He said to them, "But who do you say that I am?" Simon Peter said in reply, "You are the Christ, the Son of the living God." Jesus said to him in reply, "Blessed are you, Simon son of Jonah. For flesh and blood has not revealed this to you, but my heavenly Father. And so I say to you, you are Peter, and upon this rock I will build my church, and the gates of the netherworld shall not prevail against it. I will give you the keys to the kingdom of heaven. Whatever you bind on earth shall be bound in heaven; and whatever you loose on earth shall be loosed in heaven." Then he strictly ordered his disciples to tell no one that he was the Christ.

Practice of Faith

Authority is given as a gift from God for the good of all. After Simon Peter's confession of faith, Jesus announces that the Apostle is the "rock" on which the Church will be built and promises him the keys to the kingdom of heaven. With this authority comes the responsibility to follow Christ's example of service. God entrusts both Church and civic leaders with authority so that they may serve others in love. ◆ In what ways do you exercise authority in your home, in your community, in your workplace? What steps can you take to ensure that you are utilizing this gift for service? ◆ Consider how the common good is advanced when authority is used for service. Paragraphs 2234–2237 of the Catechism of the Catholic Church note that those in authority lead as servants and that political authorities are to "respect the fundamental rights of the human person." ◆ Offer prayers for those who exercise authority in public life.

Download more questions and activities for families, Christian initiation groups, and other adult groups at http://www.ltp.org/ahw.

Scripture Insights

Paul closes his discussion in Romans about salvation and the Jews by alluding to Isaiah 40:13 and Job 35:7, which tell of God's surprises and generosity. Psalm 138 praises God's steadfast love, but Paul has shown that God works in unpredictable ways. This unpredictability, however, is related to God's faithful commitment to humanity. Because human beings are unreliable and God's love does not coerce, God often improvises to achieve the purpose to save all. (We see this in Isaiah 22 with Shebna's replacement by Eliakim.) God will not give up on the first-chosen Jews, so God will likewise not give up on Gentiles if they fail again somehow.

We cannot presume to know God's ways, or assume that God works by our expectation or calculation. Doing so reduces the Christian life to one of predictable repetitions, when life with God is a mystery of astonishing discoveries. We cannot dictate how God works, but we can trust God's love and the ultimate achievement of God's purposes. The question is whether we can follow and accept God's new work and revelations as they happen.

Peter, unlike some religious leaders, is able to accept Jesus as God's new revelation. In response, Jesus gives him special authority and responsibility. Of course, Peter also fails later by denying Jesus but is fully restored, because God will and can always improvise to bring mercy and redemption.

Matthew plays with the Greek words for "Peter" and "rock," as they sound very similar. Paul, in discussing the rejection of Jesus by some Jews, conflates several verses from Isaiah (8:14–15; 28:16) to talk about a rock on which some will stumble and fall (Romans 9:33). That is what happens when someone misses God's new acts because of presumptions about God.

◆ What new things is God doing today?

◆ In what ways may we stumble over God's surprises?

◆ Do you see tension between God's steadfast love and unpredictable ways?

August 30, 2020

TWENTY-SECOND SUNDAY IN ORDINARY TIME

READING I Jeremiah 20:7–9

You duped me, O LORD,
    and I let myself be duped;
  you were too strong for me,
    and you triumphed.
All the day I am an object
    of laughter;
  everyone mocks me.

Whenever I speak, I must cry out,
  violence and outrage
    is my message;
the word of the Lord has
    brought me
  derision and reproach all
    the day.

I say to myself, I will not
    mention him,
  I will speak in his name
    no more.
But then it becomes like fire
    burning in my heart,
  imprisoned in my bones;
I grow weary holding it in,
    I cannot endure it.

RESPONSORIAL PSALM
Psalm 63:2, 3–4, 5–6, 8–9 (2b)

R. My soul is thirsting for you,
    O Lord my God.

O God, you are my God whom
    I seek;
  for you my flesh pines and
    my soul thirsts
  like the earth, parched, lifeless
    and without water.   R.

Thus have I gazed toward you
    in the sanctuary
  to see your power and
    your glory,
for your kindness is a greater good
    than life;
  my lips shall glorify you.   R.

Thus will I bless you while I live;
  lifting up my hands,
    I will call upon your name.
As with the riches of a banquet
    shall my soul be satisfied,
  and with exultant lips my mouth
    shall praise you.   R.

You are my help,
   and in the shadow of your wings
     I shout for joy.
My soul clings fast to you;
   your right hand upholds me. R.

READING II Romans 12:1–2

I urge you, brothers and sisters, by the mercies of God, to offer your bodies as a living sacrifice, holy and pleasing to God, your spiritual worship. Do not conform yourselves to this age but be transformed by the renewal of your mind, that you may discern what is the will of God, what is good and pleasing and perfect.

GOSPEL Matthew 16:21–27

Jesus began to show his disciples that he must go to Jerusalem and suffer greatly from the elders, the chief priests, and the scribes, and be killed and on the third day be raised. Then Peter took Jesus aside and began to rebuke him, "God forbid, Lord! No such thing shall ever happen to you." He turned and said to Peter, "Get behind me, Satan! You are an obstacle to me. You are thinking not as God does, but as human beings do."

Then Jesus said to his disciples, "Whoever wishes to come after me must deny himself, take up his cross, and follow me. For whoever wishes to save his life will lose it, but whoever loses his life for my sake will find it. What profit would there be for one to gain the whole world and forfeit his life? Or what can one give in exchange for his life? For the Son of Man will come with his angels in his Father's glory, and then he will repay all according to his conduct."

Practice of Hope

Like Jeremiah in today's First Reading, or Peter in today's Gospel, we sometimes resist God's call and turn away from the full realization of the path of discipleship. To deny oneself, take up the cross, and follow Christ is not an easy path. And yet, as the psalmist prays, our souls thirst for God, who has planted this call deep within us and in whose service we find fullness of life. ◆ We follow Christ by taking up the cross each day in lives of service. Offer to Christ the daily sacrifices you make for others. ◆ Consider Christ's call to take up the cross as you read Pope Francis' words in The Joy of the Gospel: "Jesus wants us to touch human misery, to touch the suffering flesh of others. He hopes that we will . . . enter into the reality of other people's lives and know the power of tenderness." ◆ Ask God to strengthen your resolve to follow Christ as his disciple. Consider joining your prayer with St. Francis of Assisi, who prayed: "Most High, glorious God, enlighten the darkness of my heart and give me true faith, certain hope, and perfect charity, sense and knowledge, Lord, that I may carry out your holy and true command. Amen."

Download more questions and activities for families, Christian initiation groups, and other adult groups at http://www.ltp.org/ahw.

Scripture Insights

Beginning with Romans 12, Paul outlines the implications of God's faithfulness and generosity, particularly God's commitment to save all. Speaking of both a bodily sacrifice and an intellectual transformation, Paul effectually suggests that grace and gift should impact the entire person. Our response to God must be embodied; it has to do with how we live, move, and interact with others and with the material world. John's Gospel also emphasizes Jesus's Incarnation, or the Word becoming flesh in the world to live among others (John 1:14). Since Christ's death for us while we were still sinners (Romans 5:8) has made evident God's groundless, unreasonable, and extravagant gift, the living sacrifice of one's body through solidarity with the vulnerable and needy, including especially the undeserving, becomes our "spiritual worship" or response.

Paul is clear that we must not conform to "this age." We must put aside the old ways of competitive calculation that belong to the Adamic humanity. Just as God is always improvising and doing something new and surprising to save all, we must also renew our minds to discern and follow God's creative, novel acts. Not conforming to the world but renewing the mind enables the psalmist and compel Jeremiah to follow God's will and share God's words despite opposition and ridicule.

This is precisely what Peter is unable to do in Matthew 16. Having just confessed Jesus as the Messiah, Peter fails to change his thinking further when Jesus talks about his suffering and sacrifice at the hands of the powerful. Unable to discern and follow God's will in ways that will please God, Peter risks becoming a stumbling block rather than a "rock" on which the Church is built.

◆ What may be Peter's presumptions or assumptions about the Messiah that prevent him from heeding Jesus' teaching?

◆ Can you think of some examples of disembodied discipleship?

◆ Where do you need to think differently about others and about the world today?

Ordinary Time, Autumn

Prayer before Reading the Word

In humility and service, O God,
your Son came among us
to form a community of disciples
who have one Father in heaven,
and one teacher, the Messiah.

Let your Spirit make our hearts
docile to the challenge of
        your Word,
and let the same mind be in us
that was in Christ Jesus.

We ask this through our Lord
        Jesus Christ, your Son,
who lives and reigns with you
in the unity of the Holy Spirit,
one God for ever and ever. Amen.

Prayer after Reading the Word

To the last as to the first, O God,
you are generous and more
        than just,
for as high as the heavens are
        above the earth,
so high are your ways above
        our ways
and your thoughts above
        our thoughts.

Open our hearts to the wisdom of
        your Son,
fix in our minds his sound
        teaching,
that, without concern for the cost
        of discipleship,
we may work without ceasing
for the coming of your Kingdom.

We ask this through our Lord
        Jesus Christ, your Son,
who lives and reigns with you
in the unity of the Holy Spirit,
one God for ever and ever. Amen.

Weekday Readings

August 31: 1 Corinthians 2:1–5;
   Luke 4:16–30

September 1: 1 Corinthians
   2:10b–16; Luke 4:31–37

September 2: 1 Corinthians 3:1–9;
   Luke 4:38–44

September 3: 1 Corinthians
   3:18–23; Luke 5:1–11

September 4: 1 Corinthians 4:1–5;
   Luke 5:33–39

September 5: 1 Corinthians
   4:6b–15; Luke 6:1–5

September 7: 1 Corinthians 5:1–8;
   Luke 6:6–11

**September 8: Feast of the Nativity
   ofthe Blessed Virgin Mary
   Micah 5:1–4a or
   Romans 8:28–30;
   Matthew 1:1–16, 18–23 or
   1:18–23**

September 9: 1 Corinthians
   7:25–31; Luke 6:20–26

September 10: 1 Corinthians
   8:1b–7, 11–13; Luke 6:27–38

September 11: 1 Corinthians
   9:16–19, 22b–27;
   Luke 6:39–42

September 12: 1 Corinthians
   10:14–22; Luke 6:43–49

**September 14: Feast of the
   Exaltation of the Holy Cross
   Numbers 21:4b–9; Phil
   2:6–11; John 3:13–17**

September 15: 1 Corinthians
   12:12–14, 27–31a (444);
   John 19:25–27 or Luke
   2:33–35

September 16: 1 Corinthians
   12:31—13:13; Luke 7:31–35

September 17: 1 Corinthians
   15:1–11; Luke 7:36–50

September 18: 1 Corinthians
   15:12–20; Luke 8:1–3

September 19: 1 Corinthians
   15:35–37, 42–49; Luke 8:4–15

**September 21: Feast of
   St. Matthew,
   Apostle and Evangelist
   Ephesians 4:1–7, 11–13;
   Matthew 9:9–13**

September 22: Proverbs 21:1–6,
   10–13; Luke 8:19–21

September 23: Proverbs 30:5–9;
   Luke 9:1–6

September 24: Ecclesiastes 1:2–11;
   Luke 9:7–9

September 25: Ecclesiastes 3:1–11;
   Luke 9:18–22

September 26: Ecclesiastes
   11:9—12:8; Luke 9:43b–45

September 28: Job 1:6–22;
Luke 9:46–50

September 29: Feast of Sts. Michael, Gabriel, and Raphael, Archangels Daniel 7:9–10, 13–14 or Revelation 12:7–12a; John 1:47–51

September 30: Job 9:1–12, 14–16;
Luke 9:57–62

October 1: Job 19:21–27;
Luke 10:1–12

October 2: Job 38:1, 12–21; 40:3–5 (459); Matthew 18:1–5, 10

October 3: Job 42:1–3, 5–6, 12–17;
Luke 10:17–24

October 5: Galatians 1:6–12;
Luke 10:25–37

October 6: Galatians 1:13–24;
Luke 10:38–42

October 7: Galatians 2:1–2, 7–14;
Luke 11:1–4

October 8: Galatians 3:1–5;
Luke 11:5–13

October 9: Galatians 3:7–14;
Luke 11:15–26

October 10: Galatians 3:22–29;
Luke 11:27–28

October 12: Galatians 4:22–24, 26–27, 31—5:1; Luke 11:29–32

October 13: Galatians 5:18–25;
Luke 11:42–46

October 14: Galatians 5:18–25;
Luke 11:42–46

October 15: Ephesians 1:1–10;
Luke 11:47–54

October 16: Ephesians 1:11–14;
Luke 12:1–7

October 17: Ephesians 1:15–23;
Luke 12:8–12

October 19: Ephesians 2:1–10;
Luke 12:13–21

October 20: Ephesians 2:12–22;
Luke 12:35–38

October 21: Ephesians 3:2–12;
Luke 12:39–48

October 22: Ephesians 3:14–21;
Luke 12:49–53

October 23: Ephesians 4:1–6;
Luke 12:54–59

October 24: Ephesians 4:7–16;
Luke 13:1–9

Weekday Readings (continued)

October 26: Ephesians 4:32—5:8; Luke 13:10–17

October 27: Ephesians 5:21–33; Luke 13:18–21

October 28: Feast of Sts. Simon and Jude, Apostles Ephesians 2:19–22; Luke 6:12–16

October 29: Ephesians 6:10–20; Luke 13:31–35

October 30: Philippians 1:1–11; Luke 14:1–6

October 31: Philippians 1:18b–26; Luke 14:1, 7–11

November 2: The Commemoration of All the Faithful Departed Wisdom 3:1–9; Romans 5:5–11 or Romans 6:3–9; John 6:37–40

November 3: Philippians 2:5–11; Luke 14:15–24

November 4: Philippians 2:12–18; Luke 14:25–33

November 5: Philippians 3:3–8a; Luke 15:1–10

November 6: Philippians 3:17—4:1; Luke 16:1–8

November 7: Philippians 4:10–19; Luke 16:9–15

November 9: Feast of the Dedication of the Lateran Basilica Ezekiel 47:1–2, 8–9, 12; 1 Corinthians 3:9c–11, 16–17; John 2:13–22

November 10: Titus 2:1–8, 11–14; Luke 17:7–10

November 11: Titus 3:1–7; Luke 17:11–19

November 12: Philemon 7–20; Luke 17:20–25

November 13: 2 John 4–9; Luke 17:26–37

November 14: 3 John 5–8; Luke 18:1–8

November 16: Revelation 1:1–4; 2:1–5; Luke 18:35–43

November 17: Revelation 3:1–6, 14–22; Luke 19:1–10

November 18: Revelation 4:1–11; Luke 19:11–28

November 19: Revelation 5:1–10; Luke 19:41–44

November 20: Revelation 10:8–11; Luke 19:45–48

November 21: Revelation 11:4–12; Luke 20:27–40

November 23: Revelation 14:1–3, 4b–5; Luke 21:1–4

November 24: Revelation 14:14–19; Luke 21:5–11

November 25: Revelation 15:1–4; Luke 21:12–19

November 26: Revelation 18:1–2, 21–23; 19:1–3, 9a; Luke 21:20–28

November 27: Revelation 20:1–4, 11—21:2; Luke 21:29–33

November 28: Revelation 22:1–7; Luke 21:34–36

September 6, 2020

TWENTY-THIRD SUNDAY IN ORDINARY TIME

READING I Ezekiel 33:7–9

Thus says the LORD: You, son of man, I have appointed watchman for the house of Israel; when you hear me say anything, you shall warn them for me. If I tell the wicked, "O wicked one, you shall surely die," and you do not speak out to dissuade the wicked from his way, the wicked shall die for his guilt, but I will hold you responsible for his death. But if you warn the wicked, trying to turn him from his way, and he refuses to turn from his way, he shall die for his guilt, but you shall save yourself.

RESPONSORIAL PSALM
Psalm 95:1–2, 6–7, 8–9 (8)

R. If today you hear his voice,
    harden not your hearts.

Come, let us sing joyfully to
    the LORD;
  let us acclaim the rock
    of our salvation.
Let us come into his presence
    with thanksgiving;
  let us joyfully sing psalms
    to him.   R.

Come, let us bow down in worship;
  let us kneel before the LORD
    who made us.
For he is our God,
  and we are the people
    he shepherds,
    the flock he guides.   R.

Oh, that today you would hear
    his voice:
  "Harden not your hearts
    as at Meribah,
  as in the day of Massah
    in the desert,
where your fathers tempted me;
  they tested me though they had
    seen my works."   R.

READING II Romans 13:8–10

Brothers and sisters: Owe nothing to anyone, except to love one another; for the one who loves another has fulfilled the law. The commandments, "You shall not commit adultery; you shall not kill; you shall not steal; you shall not covet," and whatever other commandment there may be, are summed up in this saying, namely, "You shall love your neighbor as yourself." Love does no evil to the neighbor; hence, love is the fulfillment of the law.

GOSPEL Matthew 18:15–20

Jesus said to his disciples: "If your brother sins against you, go and tell him his fault between you and him alone. If he listens to you, you have won over your brother. If he does not listen, take one or two others along with you, so that 'every fact may be established on the testimony of two or three witnesses.' If he refuses to listen to them, tell the church. If he refuses to listen even to the church, then treat him as you would a Gentile or a tax collector. Amen, I say to you, whatever you bind on earth shall be bound in heaven, and whatever you loose on earth shall be loosed in heaven. Again, amen, I say to you, if two of you agree on earth about anything for which they are to pray, it shall be granted to them by my heavenly Father. For where two or three are gathered together in my name, there am I in the midst of them."

Practice of Charity

This week's readings call us to confront a difficult, but important, reality: conflict is inevitable and is found even among like-minded believers. To prepare us for this, today's Gospel lays out a Christian response to discord and conflict within the community. In these rules for offering correction, we are shown that we are responsible for one another, and to one another, in all of our actions. The choices we make have social consequences and, through our personal actions, we have opportunities to be a reconciling presence in the world today. ◆ One thing is clear in today's Gospel: conflict should not be ignored. Take steps to address a situation of conflict and seek a path to reconciliation. ◆ Consider the social dimensions of sin as you read these sentences from paragraph 16 in John Paul II's Post-Synodal Apostolic Exhortation, Reconciliation and Penance: "With greater or lesser violence, with greater or lesser harm, every sin has repercussions on the entire ecclesial body and the whole human family. According to this first meaning of the term, every sin can undoubtedly be considered as social sin." ◆ Pray for a peaceful resolution to situations of conflict.

Download more questions and activities for families, Christian initiation groups, and other adult groups at http://www.ltp.org/ahw.

Scripture Insights

Ezekiel 33 presents God's people as sentinels: they have responsibilities to guard Israel's safety by sharing God's words so others will have a chance to make their own decisions. Psalm 95 pleads that God's people would not harden their hearts and repeat their ancestors' mistakes in Meribah and Massah (cf. Exodus 17 and Numbers 20), where they complained about not having water during their wilderness wandering and, as a result, missed their entry into Canaan.

Matthew 18 is known as Jesus' "community discourse," where Jesus teaches how his followers should treat each other. Matthew's Christianity is not individualistic; it requires patience and understanding toward those who have committed an offense or sin against a person. Matthew suggests multiple attempts be made to address grievances within the Church. He also expresses great faith in the Christ-following community, which is blessed with Christ's presence and spirit.

Paul's focus after Romans 12:1–2 is also relational. Note that when Paul cites the Old Testament commandments he does not cite those that concern our relationship with God but only those that concern our relationships with others.

What fulfills "the law" for Paul is an excessive love or generosity toward one's neighbor. "Love does no evil to the neighbor," Paul writes, but Paul has given a more positive and more demanding imperative in Romans 12:17–18: "Do not repay anyone evil for evil. . . . If it is possible, on your part, live at peace with all." Paul's "neighbor" is everyone, including those who have wronged the individual. His focus here is arguably broader than what is in Matthew 18. Love, as Jesus shows and as Paul argues, may make one vulnerable, but that is what we are called to be. The reasonable response to God's generosity is to love, share, and welcome others.

♦ Should Christian communities relate similarly or differently to those inside and outside their folds?

♦ In what ways does love "fulfill the law"?

♦ How does Jesus treat Gentiles and tax collectors in Matthew?

September 13, 2020

TWENTY-FOURTH SUNDAY IN ORDINARY TIME

READING Sirach 27:30—28:7

Wrath and anger are
    hateful things,
  yet the sinner hugs them tight.
The vengeful will suffer the
    LORD's vengeance,
  for he remembers their sins
    in detail.

Forgive your neighbor's injustice;
  then when you pray, your own
    sins will be forgiven.
Could anyone nourish anger
    against another
  and expect healing from
    the LORD?
Could anyone refuse mercy
    to another like himself,
  can he seek pardon for
    his own sins?
If one who is but flesh
    cherishes wrath,
  who will forgive his sins?
Remember your last days,
    set enmity aside;
  remember death and decay,
    and cease from sin!
Think of the commandments,
    hate not your neighbor;

remember the
    Most High's covenant,
  and overlook faults.

RESPONSORIAL PSALM Psalm 103:1–2, 3–4, 9–10, 11–12 (8)

R. The Lord is kind and merciful,
    slow to anger, and rich
    in compassion.

Bless the LORD, O my soul;
  and all my being, bless his
    holy name.
Bless the LORD, O my soul,
  and forget not all his
    benefits. R.

He pardons all your iniquities,
  heals all your ills,
redeems your life from destruction,
  he crowns you with kindness
    and compassion. R.

He will not always chide,
  nor does he keep his
    wrath forever.
Not according to our sins does he
    deal with us,
  nor does he requite us according
    to our crimes. R.

For as the heavens are high above
    the earth,
  so surpassing is his kindness
    toward those who fear him.
As far as the east is from the west,
  so far has he put our
    transgressions from us. R.

READING II Romans 14:7–9

Brothers and sisters: None of us lives for oneself, and no one dies for oneself. For if we live, we live for the Lord, and if we die, we die for the Lord; so then, whether we live or die, we are the Lord's. For this is why Christ died and came to life, that he might be Lord of both the dead and the living.

GOSPEL Matthew 18:21–35

Peter approached Jesus and asked him, "Lord, if my brother sins against me, how often must I forgive? As many as seven times?" Jesus answered, "I say to you, not seven times but seventy-seven times. That is why the kingdom of heaven may be likened to a king who decided to settle accounts with his servants. When he began the accounting, a debtor was brought before him who owed him a huge amount. Since he had no way of paying it back, his master ordered him to be sold, along with his wife, his children, and all his property, in payment of the debt. At that, the servant fell down, did him homage, and said, 'Be patient with me, and I will pay you back in full.' Moved with compassion the master of that servant let him go and forgave him the loan. When that servant had left, he found one of his fellow servants who owed him a much smaller amount. He seized him and started to choke him, demanding, 'Pay back what you owe.' Falling to his knees, his fellow servant begged him, 'Be patient with me, and I will pay you back.' But he refused. Instead, he had the fellow servant put in prison until he paid back the debt. Now when his fellow servants saw what had happened, they were deeply disturbed, and went to their master and reported the whole affair. His master summoned him and said to him, 'You wicked servant! I forgave you your entire debt because you begged me to. Should you not have had pity on your fellow servant, as I had pity on you?' Then in anger his master handed him over to the torturers until he should pay back the whole debt. So will my heavenly Father do to you, unless each of you forgives your brother from your heart."

Practice of Faith

Today's Scripture readings recall the centrality of mercy and forgiveness in the Christian life. This was the focus a few years ago of the Jubilee Year of Mercy called by Pope Francis that featured our call to be "Merciful like the Father." Those who have received mercy must, in turn, extend mercy to others through words and actions, as individuals and as a Church. As we dare to pray in the Lord's Prayer, "forgive us . . . as we forgive . . ." ◆ We demonstrate mercy in action in the Spiritual and Corporal Works of Mercy. Recognize and celebrate times when you have the opportunity to extend, and receive, mercy this week. ◆ Reflect on how essential forgiveness is to the Christian life as you reflect on these words from Pope Francis' message on

September 21, 2016: "The Christian must forgive! Why? Because he has been forgiven." ◆ Bring to prayer situations and relationships in which forgiveness is needed. Pray for the grace to be "merciful like the Father."

Download more questions and activities for families, Christian initiation groups, and other adult groups at http://www.ltp.org/ahw.

Scripture Insights

Starting in Romans 12, Paul has outlined our proper or "reasonable" response to God's generosity by emphasizing a new messianic community of love and welcome. At the end of Romans 13, Paul asks his recipients to "put on the Lord Jesus Christ, and make no provision for the flesh" (Romans 13:14). We should remember that Jesus is identifiable by his vulnerability, and that "flesh" for Paul refers to a humanity that is calculating and competitive.

In Romans 14, Paul explains that love and welcome are not judgmental but accepting of difference, so a messianic community will not choose between what Paul calls a "weak" (rigid vegetarianism) and a "strong" (indiscriminate) eating practice; instead, each person should practice as his or her conscience dictates. Why? Because God has welcomed all, each belongs to and is accountable to God. Instead of being judgmental of others, Paul recommends the attitude of gratitude to God, who has welcomed us despite our unworthiness.

In this context, Paul reinforces his point that we belong to God even with the ultimate difference and divider: life and death. Since Christ has demolished the dividing difference between the living and the dead, we should no longer let other differences divide us. The messianic community lives in solidarity with and in commitment to others. We put aside our privileges to serve and care for each other, especially those who are weak.

Offense can create division and enmity between persons. The parable of the unforgiving servant in Matthew 18 reminds us that we should do for one another what God has done for us. Today's readings from Sirach and from the Psalms also remind us that God is forgiving and does not judge or repay us with anger. We need to remember, be grateful, and be gracious to one another.

◆ Why is it so difficult for us to forgive?

◆ What does it mean to welcome, especially welcoming difference?

◆ How do we distinguish being judgmental and being indifferent?

September 20, 2020

TWENTY-FIFTH SUNDAY IN ORDINARY TIME

READING I Isaiah 55:6–9

Seek the LORD
    while he may be found,
    call him while he is near.
Let the scoundrel forsake his way,
    and the wicked his thoughts;
let him turn to the LORD for mercy;
    to our God, who is generous
      in forgiving.
For my thoughts are not
    your thoughts,
    nor are your ways my ways,
      says the LORD.
As high as the heavens are
    above the earth,
    so high are my ways
      above your ways
    and my thoughts
      above your thoughts.

RESPONSORIAL PSALM
Psalm 145:2–3, 8–9, 17–18 (18a)

R. The Lord is near to all
    who call upon him.

Every day will I bless you,
    and I will praise your name
      forever and ever.
Great is the LORD and highly
      to be praised;
    his greatness is unsearchable.   R.

The LORD is gracious and merciful,
    slow to anger and
      of great kindness.
The LORD is good to all
    and compassionate toward
      all his works.   R.

The LORD is just in all his ways
    and holy in all his works.
The LORD is near to all
    who call upon him,
    to all who call upon him
      in truth.   R.

Reading II
Philippians 1:20c–24, 27a

Brothers and sisters: Christ will be magnified in my body, whether by life or by death. For to me life is Christ, and death is gain. If I go on living in the flesh, that means fruitful labor for me. And I do not know which I shall choose. I am caught between the two. I long to depart this life and be with Christ, for that is far better. Yet that I remain in the flesh is more necessary for your benefit.

Only, conduct yourselves in a way worthy of the gospel of Christ.

Gospel Matthew 20:1–16a

Jesus told his disciples this parable: "The kingdom of heaven is like a landowner who went out at dawn to hire laborers for his vineyard. After agreeing with them for the usual daily wage, he sent them into his vineyard. Going out about nine o'clock, the landowner saw others standing idle in the marketplace, and he said to them, 'You too go into my vineyard, and I will give you what is just.' So they went off. And he went out again around noon, and around three o'clock, and did likewise. Going out about five o'clock, the landowner found others standing around, and said to them, 'Why do you stand here idle all day?' They answered, 'Because no one has hired us.' He said to them, 'You too go into my vineyard.' When it was evening the owner of the vineyard said to his foreman, 'Summon the laborers and give them their pay, beginning with the last and ending with the first.' When those who had started about five o'clock came, each received the usual daily wage. So when the first came, they thought that they would receive more, but each of them also got the usual wage. And on receiving it they grumbled against the landowner, saying, 'These last ones worked only one hour, and you have made them equal to us, who bore the day's burden and the heat.' He said to one of them in reply, 'My friend, I am not cheating you. Did you not agree with me for the usual daily wage? Take what is yours and go. What if I wish to give this last one the same as you? Or am I not free to do as I wish with my own money? Are you envious because I am generous?' Thus, the last will be first, and the first will be last."

Practice of Hope

Jealousy and envy are often based on "zero-sum" thinking, an understanding that if one has more, then another has less. These feelings emerge in us when facing a limit, whether real or perceived. These emotions make no sense, however, when that which we seek has no limit. The parable in today's Gospel points to an understanding and appreciation that God's generosity and mercy are infinite. ◆ Even within the limits of our humanity, we are given the opportunity to act as agents of God's mercy in the love, time, and care we give to others. Be generous in sharing these gifts that lead others to know the infinite love and mercy of God. ◆ In chapter 5 of <u>Revelations of Divine Love</u>, mystic Julian of Norwich tells of how, while holding a hazelnut, she understood that God's love for us is revealed in little things. This week consider which small things in your life portray God's love for you. ◆ Take time in prayer to rest in the assurance of God's infinite mercy. You may wish to pray with a hymn, such as "There's a Wideness in God's Mercy."

<u>Download more questions and activities for families, Christian initiation groups, and other adult groups at http://www.ltp.org/ahw.</u>

Scripture Insights

Today's parable from Matthew is notoriously difficult. Some have questioned the landowner's statement that he can do whatever he likes with his money, as it implies that he may be exploitative if he pleases. The parable seems to focus, however, on the landowner's generosity by juxtaposing two economies to make a statement about drastic change or complete reversal.

The economies on display are an exchange economy and a gift economy. An exchange economy is based on a tit-for-tat agreement; you know what you will get in exchange for what you give. This economy is generally to the advantage of the owner, centering on cost, price, and profit. Laborers, in exchange for their work, receive wages, but they will only receive what is rightfully earned and rarely more. An exchange economy can be described by the words <u>debt</u> and <u>obligation</u>: laborers owe owners service or toil, and owners are obligated to pay laborers money.

In contrast, a gift economy declines this tit-for-tat calculation to operate by another principle. It goes by unmerited favor or extravagant generosity. Instead of something negotiated or agreed on, it turns calculated exchange into ungrounded magnanimity, or, in Christian terminology, grace.

Psalm 145 praises God's goodness and declares that God is always just. Matthew's parable shifts the ground of how we think of justice or fairness: divine justice has to do with gift and generosity, not exchange of service for wages. God's way is beyond our ways because of God's mercy, so people can eat and drink without money (Isaiah 55:1, 7–9).

God's generosity with us should model our interaction with each other. We see this in Paul's willingness to stop calculating what would benefit him and forego his personal preference, so he can imitate Christ and give to the Philippians.

◆ What do you find disturbing about this parable from Matthew?

◆ How may an exchange economy be helpful and unjust?

◆ How may a gift economy be just and problematic?

September 27, 2020

TWENTY-SIXTH SUNDAY IN ORDINARY TIME

READING I Ezekiel 18:25–28

Thus says the LORD: You say, "The LORD's way is not fair!" Hear now, house of Israel: Is it my way that is unfair, or rather, are not your ways unfair? When someone virtuous turns away from virtue to commit iniquity, and dies, it is because of the iniquity he committed that he must die. But if he turns from the wickedness he has committed, and does what is right and just, he shall preserve his life; since he has turned away from all the sins that he has committed, he shall surely live, he shall not die.

RESPONSORIAL PSALM
Psalm 25:4-5, 6-7, 8-9 (6a)

R. Remember your mercies, O Lord.

Your ways, O LORD,
    make known to me;
  teach me your paths,
guide me in your truth and
    teach me,
  for you are God my savior. R.

Remember that your compassion,
    O LORD,
  and your love are from of old.
The sins of my youth and
    my frailties remember not;
  in your kindness remember me,
because of your goodness,
    O LORD. R.

Good and upright is the LORD;
  thus he shows sinners the way.
He guides the humble to justice,
  and teaches the humble
    his way. R.

READING II
Philippians 2:1–11

Shorter: Philippians 2:1–5

Brothers and sisters: If there is any encouragement in Christ, any solace in love, any participation in the Spirit, any compassion and mercy, complete my joy by being of the same mind, with the same love, united in heart, thinking one thing. Do nothing out of selfishness or out of vainglory; rather, humbly regard others as more important than yourselves, each looking out not for his own interests, but also for those of others.

Have in you the same attitude
that is also in Christ Jesus,
  Who, though he was
      in the form of God,
    did not regard equality
      with God
    something to be grasped.
Rather, he emptied himself,
    taking the form of a slave,
    coming in human likeness;
    and found human
      in appearance,
    he humbled himself,
    becoming obedient to the
      point of death,
    even death on a cross.
Because of this, God greatly
      exalted him
    and bestowed on him the name
    which is above every name,
    that at the name of Jesus
    every knee should bend,
    of those in heaven and on earth
      and under the earth,
    and every tongue confess that
Jesus Christ is Lord,
    to the glory of God the Father.

GOSPEL Matthew 21:28–32

Jesus said to the chief priests and elders of the people: "What is your opinion? A man had two sons. He came to the first and said, 'Son, go out and work in the vineyard today.' He said in reply, 'I will not,' but afterwards changed his mind and went. The man came to the other son and gave the same order. He said in reply, 'Yes, sir,' but did not go. Which of the two did his father's will?" They answered, "The first." Jesus said to them, "Amen, I say to you, tax collectors and prostitutes are entering the kingdom of God before you. When John came to you in the way of righteousness, you did not believe him; but tax collectors and prostitutes did. Yet even when you saw that, you did not later change your minds and believe him."

Practice of Charity

Our readings today offer an invitation to reflect on our call to conversion, which is seldom a once-and-for-all event but rather an ongoing work of the Holy Spirit in us. Metanoia is a change of mind as well as a change of heart made evident in our actions. Ultimately, conversion leads us to adopt Christ's attitude of humble service. ◆ As we put the interests of others before ours, we demonstrate the attitude of Christ, a work of grace in us. Be attentive to opportunities to serve others in humility this week and offer these daily actions as a prayer. ◆ Paragraph 1993 of the Catechism of the Catholic Church asserts that humankind can only move toward justice in God's sight through the grace that the Holy Spirit provides. Reflect on the grace of God at work leading you to conversion. ◆ Pray with an image of Christ's example of humble service, such as Fritz Eichenberg's Washing of the Feet (https://cjd.org/wp-content/uploads/2012/12/FE_IMG_0026.jpg).

Download more questions and activities for families, Christian initiation groups, and other adult groups at http://www.ltp.org/ahw.

Scripture Insights

Today's parable from Matthew is part of Jesus' response to the religious establishment's question about his authority. In many ways, the parable repeats a consistent emphasis throughout Matthew. The difference between the two sons in the parable is that one fails to do what he says, and the other ends up doing what he fails to say. What matters is not what you hear and say, but what you do (cf. Matthew 7:21, 24). Note also how Matthew's Jesus ends this parable with not only a mention of how prostitutes and tax collectors will enter the kingdom before the religious establishment but also multiple references to belief. Belief for Matthew is not something merely in one's head; a change of mind must involve a change in actions.

We find this emphasis on doing right not only in the mouth of Matthew's Jesus but also in the actions of Christ, as indicated in the well-known hymn in Philippians. Christ is praised for his coming in human form and dying on the cross, but the significance of these is set in the context of his deference to God and his generosity toward humanity—or what we do with and for others (cf. Matthew 25:31–46). This hymn's emphasis on humility is also seen in Psalm 25; to be able to take instructions to change, one has to be humble and teachable. This is also what the religious leaders lack; hence, they accept the authority of neither John nor Jesus.

Ezekiel 18 is an affirmation of God's justice and a call to responsibility, repentance, and right actions toward others. With a humble and teachable mind, one is not limited by the past but can change interactions with others and one's relationship with God.

◆ What does humble obedience to God look like in our context?

◆ How do our relationships with others impact our relationship to God?

◆ What does it take to become humble and teachable?

October 4, 2020

TWENTY-SEVENTH SUNDAY IN ORDINARY TIME

READING I Isaiah 5:1–7

Let me now sing of my friend,
   my friend's song concerning
      his vineyard.
My friend had a vineyard
   on a fertile hillside;
he spaded it, cleared it of stones,
   and planted the choicest vines;
within it he built a watchtower,
   and hewed out a wine press.
Then he looked for the crop
      of grapes,
   but what it yielded was
      wild grapes.

Now, inhabitants of Jerusalem
      and people of Judah,
   judge between me and
      my vineyard:
What more was there to do
      for my vineyard
   that I had not done?
Why, when I looked for the crop
      of grapes,
   did it bring forth wild grapes?
Now, I will let you know
   what I mean to do with
      my vineyard:

take away its hedge, give it
      to grazing,
   break through its wall,
      let it be trampled!
Yes, I will make it a ruin:
   it shall not be pruned or hoed,
      but overgrown with thorns
         and briers;
I will command the clouds
   not to send rain upon it.
The vineyard of the LORD of
      hosts is the house of Israel,
   and the people of Judah are his
      cherished plant;
he looked for judgment, but see,
      bloodshed!
   for justice, but hark,
      the outcry!

RESPONSORIAL PSALM
Psalm 80:9, 12, 13–14, 15–16, 19–20 (Isaiah 5:7a)

R. The vineyard of the Lord is the
      house of Israel.

A vine from Egypt
      you transplanted;
   you drove away the nations and
      planted it.
It put forth its foliage to the Sea,
   its shoots as far as the River.   R.

Why have you broken down
   its walls,
     so that every passer-by
      plucks its fruit,
the boar from the forest lays
     it waste,
   and the beasts of the field
      feed upon it? R.

Once again, O Lord of hosts,
   look down from heaven, and see;
take care of this vine,
   and protect what your
      right hand has planted,
the son of man whom you
      yourself made strong. R.

Then we will no more withdraw
   from you;
   give us new life, and we will call
   upon your name.
O Lord, God of hosts, restore us;
   if your face shine upon us,
      then we shall be saved. R.

READING II Philippians 4:6–9

Brothers and sisters: Have no
anxiety at all, but in everything,
by prayer and petition, with
thanksgiving, make your requests
known to God. Then the peace of
God that surpasses all
understanding will guard your
hearts and minds in Christ Jesus.

Finally, brothers and sisters,
whatever is true, whatever is
honorable, whatever is just,
whatever is pure, whatever is lovely,
whatever is gracious, if there is any
excellence and if there is anything
worthy of praise, think about
these things. Keep on doing what
you have learned and received and
heard and seen in me. Then the
God of peace will be with you.

GOSPEL Matthew 21:33–43

Jesus said to the chief priests and
the elders of the people: "Hear
another parable. There was a
landowner who planted a vineyard,
put a hedge around it, dug a wine
press in it, and built a tower. Then
he leased it to tenants and went
on a journey. When vintage time
drew near, he sent his servants to
the tenants to obtain his produce.
But the tenants seized the servants
and one they beat, another they
killed, and a third they stoned.
Again he sent other servants, more
numerous than the first ones, but
they treated them in the same way.
Finally, he sent his son to them,
thinking, 'They will respect my
son.' But when the tenants saw the
son, they said to one another, 'This

is the heir. Come, let us kill him and acquire his inheritance.' They seized him, threw him out of the vineyard, and killed him. What will the owner of the vineyard do to those tenants when he comes?" They answered him, "He will put those wretched men to a wretched death and lease his vineyard to other tenants who will give him the produce at the proper times." Jesus said to them, "Did you never read in the Scriptures:

« The stone that the
builders rejected
has become the cornerstone;
by the Lord has this been done,
and it is wonderful in
our eyes? »

Therefore, I say to you, the kingdom of God will be taken away from you and given to a people that will produce its fruit."

Practice of Hope

Today's readings speak to us of labor and harvests, pointing out that each of us is a laborer in God's vineyard and is expected to bear fruit for the Kingdom of God. This might be a source of anxiety for us if we thought that the work is ours alone. In faith, however, we know that this is not the case. Christ works in us and through us to bring forth God's Kingdom. ◆ Through our work and family life, we are given the privilege of tending a part of God's vineyard. What fruits of the Kingdom of God do you seek in your vocation? ◆ The US bishops wrote that work is a sacred task in their 2017 Labor Day Statement. Reflect on their words in this sentence: "Work, properly understood, can be a place of great sanctity, giving expression to the deep yearnings of the human person; where people are permitted to—and, indeed, do—embrace work as a cooperation with God's creative power." ◆ Offer your labors to God throughout the day. Consider using this prayer attributed to St. John Baptist de la Salle: "Lord, the work is yours."

Download more questions and activities for families, Christian initiation groups, and other adult groups at http://www.ltp.org/ahw.

Scripture Insights

Both of our Old Testament passages today refer to God's people as a vine that God has planted deliberately and carefully. Despite God's efforts, something goes wrong with the vine in both scenarios. While Isaiah 5 clearly faults Judah, the vine, for failing God's intention with its social injustice in the eighth century BC and threatens its destruction, Psalm 80 is a plea for God to restore this ravaged vine.

Matthew's parable extends this metaphor by referring to God as a landowner who planted a vineyard and rents it out to tenants, but these tenants end up trying to take over the vineyard with violence, including the killing of the landowner's slaves and heir. The parable ends with a similar declaration as Isaiah 5: God expects a harvest or produce of right(eous) fruits and will not tolerate injustice.

Paul writes to a Philippian community that is struggling with conflict and division (cf. 1:27; 2:1–15; 4:1–3). In our passage today, Paul offers what seems like indispensable ingredients to peace—even the peace of God that "surpasses all understanding" (4:7, 9). Note how Paul contrasts thanksgiving with worry (4:4–6). Conflict and chaos happen when gratitude gives way to anxiety. Anxiety makes people insecure, self-interested, competitive, and hungry for power; what inevitably results then is social discord. In contrast, if we can trust in God's limitless love for us and in God's provision, we can share with God in prayer for our needs, be gentle with each other, focus on what is good, and live in joy and peace, even if we do not know what life will bring or understand how everything will work out. Failing to be grateful to God is failing to trust in God and turning away from the peace of God.

◆ What makes you anxious today?

◆ How do we place limits on God's love?

◆ What fruit may God expect from us?

October 11, 2020

TWENTY-EIGHTH SUNDAY IN ORDINARY TIME

READING I Isaiah 25:6–10a

On this mountain the LORD
    of hosts
  will provide for all peoples
a feast of rich food and
    choice wines,
  juicy, rich food and pure,
    choice wines.
On this mountain he will destroy
  the veil that veils all peoples,
the web that is woven over
    all nations;
  he will destroy death forever.
The Lord GOD will wipe away
  the tears from every face;
the reproach of his people
    he will remove
  from the whole earth;
    for the LORD has spoken.
  On that day it will be said:
"Behold our God, to whom
    we looked to save us!
  This is the LORD for whom
    we looked;
  let us rejoice and be glad that
    he has saved us!"
For the hand of the LORD will
    rest on this mountain.

RESPONSORIAL PSALM Psalm 23:1–3a, 3b–4, 5, 6 (6cd)

R. I shall live in the house of the
      Lord all the days of my life.

The LORD is my shepherd;
    I shall not want.
  In verdant pastures he
    gives me repose;
beside restful waters he leads me;
  he refreshes my soul.   R.

He guides me in right paths
  for his name's sake.
Even though I walk in the
    dark valley
  I fear no evil; for you are
    at my side
with your rod and your staff
  that give me courage.   R.

You spread the table before me
  in the sight of my foes;
you anoint my head with oil;
  my cup overflows.   R.

Only goodness and kindness
    follow me
all the days of my life;
and I shall dwell in the house
    of the LORD
for years to come.   R.

READING II Philippians 4:12–14, 19–20

Brothers and sisters: I know how to live in humble circumstances; I know also how to live with abundance. In every circumstance and in all things I have learned the secret of being well fed and of going hungry, of living in abundance and of being in need. I can do all things in him who strengthens me. Still, it was kind of you to share in my distress.

My God will fully supply whatever you need, in accord with his glorious riches in Christ Jesus. To our God and Father, glory forever and ever. Amen.

GOSPEL Matthew 22:1–14

<u>Shorter: Matthew 22:1–10</u>

Jesus again in reply spoke to the chief priests and elders of the people in parables, saying, "The kingdom of heaven may be likened to a king who gave a wedding feast for his son. He dispatched his servants to summon the invited guests to the feast, but they refused to come. A second time he sent other servants, saying, 'Tell those invited: "Behold, I have prepared my banquet, my calves and fattened cattle are killed, and everything is ready; come to the feast." ' Some ignored the invitation and went away, one to his farm, another to his business. The rest laid hold of his servants, mistreated them, and killed them. The king was enraged and sent his troops, destroyed those murderers, and burned their city. Then he said to his servants, 'The feast is ready, but those who were invited were not worthy to come. Go out, therefore, into the main roads and invite to the feast whomever you find.' The servants went out into the streets and gathered all they found, bad and good alike, and the hall was filled with guests. But when the king came in to meet the guests, he saw a man there not dressed in a wedding garment. The king said to him, 'My friend, how is it that you came in here without a wedding garment?' But he was reduced to silence. Then the king said to his attendants, 'Bind his hands and feet, and cast him into the darkness outside, where there will be wailing and grinding of teeth.' Many are invited, but few are chosen."

Practice of Faith

In Scripture, images of abundance and feasting point to the gift of God's grace. Today's Gospel of the parable of the wedding feast offers images of the grace made present to us through the sacraments. In the abundant feast of the Eucharist, God provides food that strengthens life in us. In Baptism, God provides the garment as well, clothing us in holiness and enlivening the Holy Spirit's power in us so that we might accept the invitation to the feast. ◆ Make one of your meals this week a special occasion by inviting family members, friends, coworkers, or neighbors to join you as you give thanks for God's abundant grace. ◆ In her prayer on the grace of the Eucharist, St. Catherine of Siena reflected on how God's love gave us not only food but the whole divine essence. Reflect on how you allow the Eucharist to affect you. ◆ Spend time in prayer savoring the abundance of God's grace already given to you in the sacraments, a foretaste of the eternal banquet.

Download more questions and activities for families, Christian initiation groups, and other adult groups at http://www.ltp.org/ahw.

Scripture Insights

Today's parable from Matthew compares the kingdom of heaven to a king and his lavish feast for his son's wedding. This king's behaviors are rather disturbing. Since some of his original guests declined his invitation to attend to their farm or business, they are people with resources and the banquet is not meant to provide for the needy. The subsequent filling of the banquet hall with people off the street reads like a face-saving move, given how the king gets upset with a replacement guest who does not dress right. How could he expect all to have the proper attire when they were just gathered off the streets? His burning the cities harms more than those who arrested, attacked, or killed his slaves.

Note that the parable never indicates who is making this comparison and that it is part of Jesus' response to the religious leaders, who question his authority after his celebrated entry into Jerusalem and his cleansing of the Temple. The closing statement, "For many are called but few are chosen," may conclude Jesus' series of three parables instead of merely this parable. In fact, this statement hardly fits the parable since the king kicks out only one guest. Those chosen may refer to people who reject this parable's comparison.

Psalm 23 and Isaiah 25 also present God as one who provides abundant food and drink, but they present a different picture of God. In these passages, God is a provider and a protector rather than a temperamental tyrant.

We see a similar expression of faith by Paul in Philippians 4. Because Paul has experienced both prosperity and paucity, he has learned the secret that Christ is sufficient and can strengthen him to face any situation. God, for Paul, is one who will meet our every need.

◆ What is your image of God?

◆ What causes people to see God as vengeful and unreasonably demanding?

◆ How has God been a provider and protector in your life?

October 18, 2020

TWENTY-NINTH SUNDAY IN ORDINARY TIME

READING I Isaiah 45:1, 4–6

Thus says the LORD to his
 anointed, Cyrus,
  whose right hand I grasp,
subduing nations before him,
  and making kings run in
   his service,
opening doors before him
  and leaving the gates
   unbarred:
For the sake of Jacob, my servant,
  of Israel, my chosen one,
I have called you by your name,
  giving you a title, though you
   knew me not.
I am the LORD and there is
  no other,
  there is no God besides me.
It is I who arm you, though you
   know me not,
  so that toward the rising and
   the setting of the sun
  people may know that there
   is none besides me.
I am the LORD, there is no other.

RESPONSORIAL PSALM
Psalm 96:1, 3, 4–5, 7–8, 9–10 (7b)

R. Give the Lord glory and honor.

Sing to the LORD a new song;
  sing to the Lord, all you lands.
Tell his glory among the nations;
  among all peoples,
   his wondrous deeds.   R.

For great is the LORD and
   highly to be praised;
  awesome is he, beyond all gods.
For all the gods of the nations are
   things of nought,
  but the Lord
   made the heavens.   R.

Give to the LORD,
   you families of nations,
  give to the Lord glory and praise;
  give to the Lord the glory due
   his name!
Bring gifts, and enter his courts.   R.

Worship the LORD, in holy attire;
  tremble before him, all the earth;
say among the nations:
   The LORD is king,
  he governs the peoples
   with equity.   R.

READING II
1 Thessalonians 1:1–5b

Paul, Silvanus, and Timothy to the church of the Thessalonians in God the Father and the Lord Jesus Christ: grace to you and peace. We give thanks to God always for all of you, remembering you in our prayers, unceasingly calling to mind your work of faith and labor of love and endurance in hope of our Lord Jesus Christ, before our God and Father, knowing, brothers and sisters loved by God, how you were chosen. For our gospel did not come to you in word alone, but also in power and in the Holy Spirit and with much conviction.

GOSPEL Matthew 22:15–21

The Pharisees went off and plotted how they might entrap Jesus in speech. They sent their disciples to him, with the Herodians, saying, "Teacher, we know that you are a truthful man and that you teach the way of God in accordance with the truth. And you are not concerned with anyone's opinion, for you do not regard a person's status. Tell us, then, what is your opinion: Is it lawful to pay the census tax to Caesar or not?" Knowing their malice, Jesus said, "Why are you testing me, you hypocrites? Show me the coin that pays the census tax." Then they handed him the Roman coin. He said to them, "Whose image is this and whose inscription?" They replied, "Caesar's." At that he said to them, "Then repay to Caesar what belongs to Caesar and to God what belongs to God."

Practice of Hope

We respond to the love that God has planted in our hearts by offering our lives in service to God. When we fulfill our obligations to worship and serve God at all times, in our interactions with others, in our use of time and money, and in the choices we make each day, we show that God is first in our lives. In all that we do, we seek to repay to God, who loved us first, "what belongs to God." ◆ Mindful that our daily obligations are opportunities to serve God, recommit to offering each choice and action for God's glory. ◆ The Vatican II Decree on the Apostolate of the Laity points to the role of the laity in the mission of the Church of evangelizing and sanctifying the world. The document states, "Everywhere and in all things they must seek the justice of God's kingdom" (7). Consider the many ways in which you are called to work for the Kingdom. ◆ Take this verse from today's Responsorial Psalm to heart and pray it frequently this week: "Give the Lord glory and honor."

Download more questions and activities for families, Christian initiation groups, and other adult groups at http://www.ltp.org/ahw.

Scripture Insights

Today's passage in Matthew uses a Greek rhetorical technique that employs a deductive logic but has an unstated premise. Jesus wins the argument without being trapped because the text assumes that everyone agrees with a principle: namely, having your image on something signifies possession. From that principle, one has to agree that coins bearing Caesar's image belong to Caesar. The second deduction that leaves Jesus' opponents speechless is that humans, bearing the image of God, belong to God.

While these deductions are derived from the same premise, they represent a contrast. As Psalm 96 declares, "families of nations" should glorify and worship this God, who, according to Isaiah 45, is more powerful than earthly kings and emperors, including the Persian King Cyrus, whom God uses to defeat Babylon's empire and to deliver Israel.

There is also a contrast between coins that a person possesses as belonging to someone else and an individual belonging to someone else. What does it mean to belong to someone? One should be careful here given the reality of slavery in New Testament times, US history, and still today. Slaves, though, are accountable to and can be commanded or disciplined by their master. It also means that other people cannot interfere with someone who already belongs to someone else.

What does that mean for imperial claims being made on people who belong to God? What does it mean regarding Caesar's coins, which Jesus' imperative says to "give" or "give back"? Does it imply an abandonment of an imperial economic system? Or does it suggest something else? In any case, the first chapter of 1 Thessalonians shows not only the importance of God's choice but also the need for human work or response. How should we think about and respond to this passage?

◆ What does it mean to belong to God?

◆ How does one give back to Caesar what belongs to Caesar?

◆ What does it mean that God can use a foreign and imperialistic ruler such as Cyrus?

October 25, 2020

THIRTIETH SUNDAY IN ORDINARY TIME

READING I Exodus 22:20–26

Thus says the LORD: "You shall not molest or oppress an alien, for you were once aliens yourselves in the land of Egypt. You shall not wrong any widow or orphan. If ever you wrong them and they cry out to me, I will surely hear their cry. My wrath will flare up, and I will kill you with the sword; then your own wives will be widows, and your children orphans.

"If you lend money to one of your poor neighbors among my people, you shall not act like an extortioner toward him by demanding interest from him. If you take your neighbor's cloak as a pledge, you shall return it to him before sunset; for this cloak of his is the only covering he has for his body. What else has he to sleep in? If he cries out to me, I will hear him; for I am compassionate."

RESPONSORIAL PSALM
Psalm 18:2–3, 3–4, 47, 51 (2)

R. I love you, Lord, my strength.

I love you, O LORD, my strength,
  O LORD, my rock, my fortress,
    my deliverer. R.

My God, my rock of refuge,
  my shield, the horn of my
    salvation, my stronghold!
Praised be the LORD, I exclaim,
  and I am safe from
    my enemies. R.

The LORD lives and blessed be
    my rock!
  Extolled be God my savior.
You who gave great victories
    to your king
  and showed kindness to your
    anointed. R.

READING II
1 Thessalonians 1:5c–10

Brothers and sisters: You know what sort of people we were among you for your sake. And you became imitators of us and of the Lord, receiving the word in great affliction, with joy from the Holy Spirit, so that you became a model for all the believers in Macedonia and in Achaia. For from you the word of the Lord has sounded forth not only in Macedonia and in Achaia, but in every place your faith in God has gone forth, so that we have no need to say anything. For they themselves openly declare about us what sort of reception we had among you, and how you turned to God from idols to serve the living and true God and to await his Son from heaven, whom he raised from the dead, Jesus, who delivers us from the coming wrath.

GOSPEL Matthew 22:34–40

When the Pharisees heard that Jesus had silenced the Sadducees, they gathered together, and one of them, a scholar of the law, tested him by asking, "Teacher, which commandment in the law is the greatest?" He said to him, "You shall love the Lord, your God, with all your heart, with all your soul, and with all your mind. This is the greatest and the first commandment. The second is like it: You shall love your neighbor as yourself. The whole law and the prophets depend on these two commandments."

Practice of Charity

In the Judeo-Christian tradition, hospitality flows from the Ten Commandments, which show that love of God and love of neighbor are integrally connected. As Christians, we seek to welcome others into our lives as we would welcome Christ. This Christian hospitality extends to family, friends, and neighbors, as well as to those we do not yet know, especially to those most vulnerable. ◆ Hospitality is an attitude expressed in our daily encounters with others, especially shown in our care for the poor and vulnerable. Take steps to ensure that you are reflecting the fullness of Christian hospitality in your relationships. ◆ The shared response of Christians to migrants and refugees should be "to welcome, to protect, to promote and to integrate," the pontiff states in the "Message of His Holiness Pope Francis for the 104th World Day of Migrants and Refugees 2018." Reflect on how your parish community can enact the holy father's message. ◆ Consider making this question part of your daily examination of conscience: how did you respond as you met Christ in those you encountered this day?

Download more questions and activities for families, Christian initiation groups, and other adult groups at http://www.ltp.org/ahw.

Scripture Insights

When Jesus is asked about "the greatest commandment," he replies with a dual commandment: love of God and love of neighbor. There is neither opposition nor separation between these two loves, as if one must choose one over the other. One cannot have one without the other. Jesus has no problem, then, loving people by understanding their need for food or by healing them on the Sabbath, a day that some think should be reserved solely for loving God (cf. Matthew 12:1–14). The way Jesus juxtaposes these two loves as dual and the greatest commandment implies that the violation of neighbor violates God and the commandment.

In Matthew Jesus responds to those who want to honor God but bypass their needy neighbors with a statement that places mercy before sacrifice (Matthew 12:7). Today's passage from Exodus 22 seems to compare offering sacrifices to other gods with the reluctance to care for aliens, widows, orphans, and the poor, since both practices result in the wrath of and punishment from God. In addition, our passage concludes with a declaration that our compassionate God will always hear the cries of our neighbors. As Psalm 18 indicates, God will save those in distress and under oppression but will also exact vengeance on those who act unjustly and abusively.

Paul, in the beginning of his First Letter to the Thessalonians, emphasizes the welcoming of others as a marker of discipleship that deserves emulation from others. Just as consideration for the Thessalonians brought them to follow Jesus and imitate Paul and his fellow missionaries, the Thessalonians' reciprocal welcoming of Paul and his missionaries became a model for followers of Jesus all over the region. Relations among people, as we have seen in the other passages, define discipleship and human relationship with God.

◆ Who is your neighbor?

◆ What is the relationship between love and welcome?

◆ How does Jesus welcome?

November 1, 2020

SOLEMNITY OF ALL SAINTS

READING I
Revelation 7:2–4, 9–14

I, John, saw another angel come up from the East, holding the seal of the living God. He cried out in a loud voice to the four angels who were given power to damage the land and the sea, "Do not damage the land or the sea or the trees until we put the seal on the foreheads of the servants of our God." I heard the number of those who had been marked with the seal, one hundred and forty-four thousand marked from every tribe of the children of Israel.

After this I had a vision of a great multitude, which no one could count, from every nation, race, people, and tongue. They stood before the throne and before the Lamb, wearing white robes and holding palm branches in their hands. They cried out in a loud voice:

"Salvation comes from our God,
who is seated on the throne,
and from the Lamb."

All the angels stood around the throne and around the elders and the four living creatures. They prostrated themselves before the throne, worshiped God, and exclaimed:

"Amen. Blessing and glory,
wisdom and thanksgiving,
honor, power, and might
be to our God forever and ever.
Amen."

Then one of the elders spoke up and said to me, "Who are these wearing white robes, and where did they come from?" I said to him, "My lord, you are the one who knows." He said to me, "These are the ones who have survived the time of great distress; they have washed their robes and made them white in the Blood of the Lamb."

RESPONSORIAL PSALM
Psalm 24:1–2, 3–4, 5–6(see 6)

R. Lord, this is the people that
longs to see your face.

The LORD's are the earth and
its fullness;

the world and those who dwell
    in it.

For he founded it upon the seas
    and established it upon the
       rivers. R.

Who can ascend the mountain of
    the Lord?
or who may stand in his
    holy place?
One whose hands are sinless,
    whose heart is clean,
who desires not what is vain. R.

He shall receive a blessing from
    the Lord,
a reward from God his savior.
Such is the race that seeks for him,
    that seeks the face of the God
       of Jacob. R.

READING II 1 John 3:1–3

Beloved: See what love the Father has bestowed on us that we may be called the children of God. Yet so we are. The reason the world does not know us is that it did not know him. Beloved, we are God's children now; what we shall be has not yet been revealed. We do know that when it is revealed we shall be like him, for we shall see him as he is. Everyone who has this hope based

on him makes himself pure, as he is pure.

GOSPEL Matthew 5:1–12a

When Jesus saw the crowds, he went up the mountain, and after he had sat down, his disciples came to him. He began to teach them, saying:

"Blessed are the poor in spirit,
    for theirs is the Kingdom
       of heaven.
Blessed are they who mourn,
    for they will be comforted.
Blessed are the meek,
    for they will inherit the land.
Blessed are they who hunger and
       thirst for righteousness,
    for they will be satisfied.
Blessed are the merciful,
    for they will be shown mercy.
Blessed are the clean of heart,
    for they will see God.
Blessed are the peacemakers,
    for they will be called children
       of God.
Blessed are they who are
       persecuted for the sake
       of righteousness,
    for theirs is the Kingdom
       of heaven.

Blessed are you when they insult you and persecute you and utter every kind of evil against you falsely because of me. Rejoice and be glad, for your reward will be great in heaven."

Practice of Faith

All Saints' Day is an opportunity to reflect on what it means to live as children of God. As Jesus teaches in the Beatitudes, true happiness and the path to holiness are found in unexpected circumstances that call forth acts of self-giving. We find witnesses to this way of life in the saints who have taken to heart Jesus' words and example. The fruits of living the Beatitudes are found in the communion we share with the saints and the glory promised to us in eternity. ◆ The Beatitudes describe the mystery of holiness, that true happiness is found in acts of self-giving. In whom have you observed the lived reality described in the Beatitudes? ◆ Reflect on your call to holiness as you read chapter 1 of Pope Francis' apostolic exhortation

Rejoice and Be Glad! http://w2 .vatican.va/content/francesco/en /apost_exhortations/documents /papa-francesco_esortazione-ap _20180319_gaudete -et-exsultate .html. ◆ Pray a Litany of the Saints, and give thanks to God for the saints who are living in your midst.

Download more questions and activities for families, Christian initiation groups, and other adult groups at http://www.ltp.org/ahw.

Scripture Insights

John's vision of seven trumpets presents an escalating tension, with crises and calamities coming from the four horsemen, martyrdom, and cosmic challenges. Just before the seventh and last trumpet blows, John gives us an interlude between Revelation 6 and 8 that feels like a catharsis or a release of the building tension. It tells of 144,000 being sealed for God out of the twelve tribes as well as a great multitude, in white robes, from every nation worshiping and praising. In many cultures, white is the color of purity. John assumes the same in his vision of the faithful who have survived the ordeal. Like the Lamb and because of the Lamb, they have been washed in blood; the Lamb's blood also works ironically to wash and purify this great multitude.

Using the metaphor of clean hands and pure hearts, Psalm 24 declares that God will bless and vindicate those who stay away from falsehood. In the Beatitudes that begin the Sermon on the Mount, experiences often deemed to be undesirable (such as mourning, persecution, and being falsely accused) turn out to be marks of blessing. In addition to having a place in God's Kingdom, for example, these individuals will "see God" (Matthew 5:8).

We also find in 1 John 3 a promise of hope and vindication. Though unrecognized by the world as God's children, we are loved by God. Besides emphasizing this current and abiding love, 1 John continues with the metaphor of children and suggests that we will not only witness God's full self-revelation but also grow to be like God. If being like God is the goal, 1 John encourages taking an active role in pursuing purity since God is pure.

◆ What characteristics do the faithful or the blessed share in these passages?

◆ What is God like besides being pure?

◆ What is the relationship between persecution and vindication?

November 8, 2020

THIRTY-SECOND SUNDAY IN ORDINARY TIME

READING I Wisdom 6:12–16

Resplendent and unfading
    is wisdom,
    and she is readily perceived
        by those who love her,
    and found by those who
        seek her.
She hastens to make herself
        known in anticipation
        of their desire;
    whoever watches for her
        at dawn shall not
        be disappointed,
    for he shall find her sitting
        by his gate.
For taking thought of wisdom
        is the perfection
        of prudence,
    and whoever for her sake
        keeps vigil
    shall quickly be free from care;
because she makes her own
        rounds, seeking those
        worthy of her,
    and graciously appears to them
        in the ways,
    and meets them with all
        solicitude.

RESPONSORIAL PSALM
Psalm 63:2, 3–4, 5–6,
7–8 (2b)

R. My soul is thirsting for you,
        O Lord my God.

O God, you are my God whom
        I seek;
    for you my flesh pines and my
        soul thirsts
    like the earth, parched, lifeless
        and without water.   R.

Thus have I gazed toward you in
        the sanctuary
    to see your power and
        your glory,
for your kindness is a greater good
        than life;
    my lips shall glorify you.   R.

Thus will I bless you while I live;
    lifting up my hands,
        I will call upon your name.
As with the riches of a banquet
        shall my soul be satisfied,
    and with exultant lips my mouth
        shall praise you.   R.

I will remember you upon
      my couch,
   and through the night-watches
      I will meditate on you:
you are my help,
   and in the shadow of your wings
      I shout for joy. R.

READING II
1 Thessalonians 4:13–18

Shorter: 1 Thessalonians 4:13–14

We do not want you to be unaware, brothers and sisters, about those who have fallen asleep, so that you may not grieve like the rest, who have no hope. For if we believe that Jesus died and rose, so too will God, through Jesus, bring with him those who have fallen asleep. Indeed, we tell you this, on the word of the Lord, that we who are alive, who are left until the coming of the Lord, will surely not precede those who have fallen asleep. For the Lord himself, with a word of command, with the voice of an archangel and with the trumpet of God, will come down from heaven, and the dead in Christ will rise first. Then we who are alive, who are left, will be caught up together with them in the clouds to meet the Lord in the air.

Thus we shall always be with the Lord. Therefore, console one another with these words.

GOSPEL Matthew 25:1–13

Jesus told his disciples this parable: "The kingdom of heaven will be like ten virgins who took their lamps and went out to meet the bridegroom. Five of them were foolish and five were wise. The foolish ones, when taking their lamps, brought no oil with them, but the wise brought flasks of oil with their lamps. Since the bridegroom was long delayed, they all became drowsy and fell asleep. At midnight, there was a cry, 'Behold, the bridegroom! Come out to meet him!' Then all those virgins got up and trimmed their lamps. The foolish ones said to the wise, 'Give us some of your oil, for our lamps are going out.' But the wise ones replied, 'No, for there may not be enough for us and you. Go instead to the merchants and buy some for yourselves.' While they went off to buy it, the bridegroom came and those who were ready went into the wedding feast with him. Then the door was locked. Afterwards the other virgins came and said, 'Lord, Lord, open the door for us!' But he said in reply, 'Amen, I say to you, I do not know you.' Therefore, stay awake, for you know neither the day nor the hour."

Practice of Hope

It is tempting to avoid consideration of the mystery of death and dying, as this calls to mind losses we have experienced as well as the prospect of our mortality. And yet, our readings for today remind us that we are called to face the reality of death with hope, wisely recognizing the longing within us to be in God's holy presence and the necessity of making ourselves ready for this anticipated future. ◆ Take time with a loved one to reflect together on the mystery of death and the promise of eternal life. Name those you have known who have prepared well for their death and consider what you can learn from their example. ◆ Deepen your understanding of what our faith teaches us about life and death. ◆ Pray for those who have died, and pray also that you will be prepared to meet God at the time of your death.

Download more questions and activities for families, Christian initiation groups, and other adult groups at http://www.ltp.org/ahw.

Scripture Insights

According to Wisdom 6, those who seek wisdom will not be disappointed because wisdom desires to be accessible. Wisdom is indeed needed as we seek to understand the parable of the ten bridesmaids. That the wise, like the foolish, also fell asleep should alert us to think more carefully about the meaning of the parable. The wise in the parable are prepared, bringing both lamps and oil to await the bridegroom's arrival. When the bridegroom finally appears, the wise, instead of sharing their oil with the foolish, tell the foolish to go to the store to buy oil. Delayed by the refusal of the wise to share their resources, the foolish end up being shut out by the bridegroom, who refuses to share the joy of his wedding banquet with latecomers.

How different is the picture in 1 Thessalonians. While the living may be able to do things that the dead cannot, Paul is adamant that the dead will have priority over the living in the time of Christ's return: the dead will be raised first. Rather than grieving without hope,

worrying about preparations, or hoarding resources, we should, Paul says, "console one another." Unlike Matthew's bridegroom who shuts people out of his banquet, the Lord in Paul's letter will descend from heaven to meet and welcome those who are alive after the dead have been resurrected. While there are order and sequence, there is no rejection. This God welcomes both the dead and the living.

For the psalmist, God's love is steadfast, and God helps and upholds. God's kindness, power, and glory fill the psalmist, who sings, "as with the riches of a banquet shall my soul be satisfied." The psalmist and Paul relate that God provides abundantly and gives reasons for celebrations.

◆ If you were to describe God in each reading, what adjectives would you use?

◆ How is wisdom understood in these texts and generally defined in our world?

◆ What do hopeless people tend to do?

November 15, 2020

THIRTY-THIRD SUNDAY IN ORDINARY TIME

READING I Proverbs 31:10–13, 19–20, 30–31

When one finds a worthy wife,
    her value is far beyond pearls.
Her husband, entrusting his
      heart to her,
    has an unfailing prize.
She brings him good, and not evil,
    all the days of her life.
She obtains wool and flax
    and works with loving hands.
She puts her hands to the distaff,
    and her fingers ply the spindle.
She reaches out her hands
      to the poor,
    and extends her arms
      to the needy.
Charm is deceptive and
      beauty fleeting;
    the woman who fears the
      LORD is to be praised.
Give her a reward for her labors,
    and let her works praise her
      at the city gates.

RESPONSORIAL PSALM
Psalm 128:1–2, 3, 4–5
(see 1a)

R. Blessed are those who
      fear the Lord.

Blessed are you who fear the LORD,
    who walk in his ways!
For you shall eat the fruit of
      your handiwork;
    blessed shall you be,
      and favored. R.

Your wife shall be like a fruitful vine
    in the recesses of your home;
your children like olive plants
    around your table. R.

Behold, thus is the man blessed
    who fears the LORD.
The LORD bless you from Zion:
    may you see the prosperity
      of Jerusalem
    all the days of your life. R.

READING II
1 Thessalonians 5:1–6

Concerning times and seasons, brothers and sisters, you have no need for anything to be written to you. For you yourselves know very well that the day of the Lord will come like a thief at night. When people are saying, "Peace and security," then sudden disaster comes upon them, like labor pains upon a pregnant woman, and they will not escape.

But you, brothers and sisters, are not in darkness, for that day to overtake you like a thief. For all of you are children of the light and children of the day. We are not of the night or of darkness. Therefore, let us not sleep as the rest do, but let us stay alert and sober.

GOSPEL Matthew 25:14–30

Shorter: Matthew 25:14–15, 19–21

Jesus told his disciples this parable: "A man going on a journey called in his servants and entrusted his possessions to them. To one he gave five talents; to another, two; to a third, one—to each according to his ability. Then he went away.

Immediately the one who received five talents went and traded with them, and made another five. Likewise, the one who received two made another two. But the man who received one went off and dug a hole in the ground and buried his master's money.

"After a long time the master of those servants came back and settled accounts with them. The one who had received five talents came forward bringing the additional five. He said, 'Master, you gave me five talents. See, I have made five more.' His master said to him, 'Well done, my good and faithful servant. Since you were faithful in small matters, I will give you great responsibilities. Come, share your master's joy.' Then the one who had received two talents also came forward and said, 'Master, you gave me two talents. See, I have made two more.' His master said to him, 'Well done, my good and faithful servant. Since you were faithful in small matters, I will give you great responsibilities. Come, share your master's joy.' Then the one who had received the one talent came forward and said, 'Master, I knew

279

you were a demanding person, harvesting where you did not plant and gathering where you did not scatter; so out of fear I went off and buried your talent in the ground. Here it is back.' His master said to him in reply, 'You wicked, lazy servant! So you knew that I harvest where I did not plant and gather where I did not scatter? Should you not then have put my money in the bank so that I could have got it back with interest on my return? Now then! Take the talent from him and give it to the one with ten. For to everyone who has, more will be given and he will grow rich; but from the one who has not, even what he has will be taken away. And throw this useless servant into the darkness outside, where there will be wailing and grinding of teeth.' "

Practice of Charity

Today's readings challenge us to consider how we make use of the gifts that God has entrusted to us. Each of us is given the gift of time, as well as the particular strengths that we have and the skills that we

have learned. As children of the light, we do not hoard or hide away these gifts. Rather, we seek to practice good stewardship by utilizing these gifts in service to the Kingdom of God. ◆ God has given each person a wide variety of gifts so that we might participate in building up God's Kingdom. Which gifts are you being called to cultivate, strengthen, and share more generously? ◆ "To Be a Christian Steward: A Summary of the U.S. Bishops' Pastoral Letter on Stewardship" states: "As Christian stewards, we receive God's gifts gratefully, cultivate them responsibly, share them lovingly in justice with others, and return them with increase to the Lord." Reflect on that statement as you consider your stewardship. ◆ Ask God to receive the gift of your service each day as you pray a Morning Offering or other prayer.

Download more questions and activities for families, Christian initiation groups, and other adult groups at http://www.ltp.org/ahw.

Scripture Insights

Without denying the value of family, hard work, or financial stability, we must consider today's readings carefully in our context of global capitalism, the prosperity gospel, and ongoing patriarchy. We must, as Paul suggests, stay awake and alert. Like Psalm 128 and Proverbs 31, Matthew's parable of the talents is challenging to interpret. New Testament parables often create "aha" moments of dramatic discovery or even existential crisis that listeners or readers did not expect. Nor do they necessarily align with the teller's view. Instead, they present scenarios that ask one to take a side and, in the process, often reveal not only a reversal of conventional assumptions but also the self-understandings of a listener or reader.

A "talent" in those days was more than a daily wage a worker could make in fifteen years; eight talents would be more than 120 years of daily wages. The slave master must be rich indeed to have that kind of wealth to give to his slaves. Although capitalism did not exist at the time, wealth was generally in the hands of a few who did not hesitate to exploit the poor majority, including through the practice of usury. More insidiously, if the slaves received the money and lost it for whatever reasons (including investment losses), they could become liable for losing their owner's money.

In other words, a "harsh" slave master who harvests where he "did not plant" and gathers "where he did not scatter" seed would be a familiar figure for Matthew's first readers. Many of them, like the last slave, would be "afraid" of such an unjust rich person; they knew that the whole setup was a trap.

◆ What may the third slave's action or inaction signify besides fear?

◆ What role does work play in these passages? Who benefits from the work?

◆ What are the parallels between "the wife" in the Old Testament passages and the slaves in Matthew? What makes them good or bad?

November 22, 2020

OUR LORD JESUS CHRIST, KING OF THE UNIVERSE

READING I
Ezekiel 34:11–12, 15–17

Thus says the Lord GOD: I myself will look after and tend my sheep. As a shepherd tends his flock when he finds himself among his scattered sheep, so will I tend my sheep. I will rescue them from every place where they were scattered when it was cloudy and dark. I myself will pasture my sheep; I myself will give them rest, says the Lord GOD. The lost I will seek out, the strayed I will bring back, the injured I will bind up, the sick I will heal, but the sleek and the strong I will destroy, shepherding them rightly.

As for you, my sheep, says the Lord GOD, I will judge between one sheep and another, between rams and goats.

RESPONSORIAL PSALM
Psalm 23:1–2, 2–3, 5–6 (1)

R. The Lord is my shepherd;
there is nothing I shall want.

The LORD is my shepherd;
I shall not want.
In verdant pastures
he gives me repose.   R.

Beside restful waters he leads me;
he refreshes my soul.
He guides me in right paths
for his name's sake.   R.

You spread the table before me
in the sight of my foes;
you anoint my head with oil;
my cup overflows.   R.

Only goodness and
kindness follow me
all the days of my life;
and I shall dwell in
the house of the LORD
for years to come.   R.

READING II
1 Corinthians 15:20–26, 28

Brothers and sisters: Christ has been raised from the dead, the firstfruits of those who have fallen asleep. For since death came through man, the resurrection of the dead came also through man. For just as in Adam all die, so too in Christ shall all be brought to life, but each one in proper order: Christ the firstfruits; then, at his coming, those who belong to Christ; then comes the end, when he hands over the kingdom to his God and Father, when he has destroyed every sovereignty and every authority and power. For he must reign until he has put all his enemies under his feet. The last enemy to be destroyed is death. When everything is subjected to him, then the Son himself will also be subjected to the one who subjected everything to him, so that God may be all in all.

Gospel Matthew 25:31–46

Jesus said to his disciples: "When the Son of Man comes in his glory, and all the angels with him, he will sit upon his glorious throne, and all the nations will be assembled before him. And he will separate them one from another, as a shepherd separates the sheep from the goats. He will place the sheep on his right and the goats on his left. Then the king will say to those on his right, 'Come, you who are blessed by my Father. Inherit the kingdom prepared for you from the foundation of the world.

For I was hungry and you gave me food, I was thirsty and you gave me drink, a stranger and you welcomed me, naked and you clothed me, ill and you cared for me, in prison and you visited me.' Then the righteous will answer him and say, 'Lord, when did we see you hungry and feed you, or thirsty and give you drink? When did we see you a stranger and welcome you, or naked and clothe you? When did we see you ill or in prison, and visit you?' And the king will say to them in reply, 'Amen, I say to you, whatever you did for one of the least brothers of mine, you did for me.' Then he will say to those on his left, 'Depart from me, you accursed, into the eternal fire prepared for the devil and his angels. For I was hungry and you gave me no food, I was thirsty and you gave me no drink, a stranger and you gave me no welcome, naked and you gave me no clothing, ill and in prison, and you did not care for me.' Then they will answer and say, 'Lord, when did we see you hungry or thirsty or a stranger or naked or ill or in prison, and not minister to your needs?' He will answer them,

'Amen, I say to you, what you did not do for one of these least ones, you did not do for me.' And these will go off to eternal punishment, but the righteous to eternal life."

Practice of Faith

Today we praise Christ, King of the Universe, who has made us his own in Baptism. As we do so, we are reminded that belonging to Christ makes claims on us that cannot be ignored. Our Gospel today is quite clear: God's disposition toward us at the time of judgment will be based on our practice of the Works of Mercy. To belong to Christ means that we recognize and serve our Lord as he is found here and now in the faces of the poor. ◆ Take time this week to notice more fully the hungry, the thirsty, the strangers, the naked, the ill, and the imprisoned who walk in your midst. In what ways are you being called to practice the Works of Mercy? ◆ Deepen your understanding of the Corporal Works of Mercy as you view this slideshow from Catholic Relief Services: https://www.crs.org /resource-center/corporal-works -mercy-slideshow. ◆ During prayer, seek God's help to recognize and serve Christ in those most in need.

Download more questions and activities for families, Christian initiation groups, and other adult groups at http://www.ltp.org/ahw.

Scripture Insights

Today's Old Testament passages present God's people as sheep. Matthew's parable continues this metaphor but contrasts them with goats. The parable's setting is similar to the one in 1 Corinthians 15. There, Paul assures the Corinthians of the resurrection and that, just as God raised Jesus, God through Christ will raise us from the dead and give Christ a place of supremacy.

Although the sheep are accepted and the goats rejected before the supreme Christ in Matthew's parable, they share two things in common. First, both call Jesus "Lord." Matthew's Jesus has made it clear that "not everyone who says . . . 'Lord, Lord' will enter the kingdom of heaven but only the one who does the will of my Father in heaven" (Matthew 7:21). Our actions are more important than our words, and God desires that our actions are expressions of mercy for the weak and vulnerable. In fact, that is how today's Old Testament passages describe God's attitude and actions toward us as our shepherd: God cares for us with goodness and mercy, even or especially when we are lost, astray, or injured.

Second, both the sheep and the goats express that they have never seen Jesus in a needy condition. Neither group knows or understands the reasons or implications of their actions, but one chose to act with mercy while the other chose to ignore the needs of people they encountered. The point here is not that ignorance is bliss, as Matthew's Jesus spends a lot of time teaching (such as the Sermon on the Mount in chapters 5—7), and he tells people to learn and practice the teachings of the religious leaders (Matthew 23:2–3). Rather, the significance is that while our understandings can be limited, the most important thing is how we treat "these least ones" (Matthew 25:40, 45).

◆ What does the metaphor of God as shepherd communicate?

◆ Who would you identify as today's "least ones"?

◆ Is there a human or social need that you see but do not understand?

285